THE GOLD MISSUS

A Woman Prospector in Sierra Leone

KATHARINE FOWLER-LUNN · *A portrait study by Elizabeth Leland.*

THE
GOLD
MISSUS

A WOMAN PROSPECTOR IN SIERRA LEONE

BY KATHARINE FOWLER-LUNN

W · W · NORTON & COMPANY · INC ·
PUBLISHERS · NEW YORK

PRINTED IN THE UNITED STATES OF AMERICA
FOR THE PUBLISHERS BY THE VAIL-BALLOU PRESS

CONTENTS

v

Part III.   *Mapping Molybdenum*

Appendix

LIST OF ILLUSTRATIONS

MAPS.

ACKNOWLEDGMENTS

THE author wishes to take this opportunity to thank all her friends who have given assistance in the preparation of the book. Her especial gratitude is extended to Miss Helen Fairbanks who has given her time freely in helping prepare the manuscript. Her advice and ever ready suggestions have been invaluable to the author.

Miss Margaret Arnold has drawn the black and white illustrations. She has caught the spirit of the tropics in her sketches.

Mr. Erwin Raisz drafted the three maps of the routes traveled by the author.

INTRODUCTION

"THE GOLD MISSUS" is not the title of a novel or a romance. It is what I was called by my native boys. I hunted for gold. And I was a "missus." So I was explained to strange chiefs simply as, "Missus be Gold Missus." That placed me immediately. No more need of explanations.

If I had a native name, it was never revealed to me. That was their secret. My secret from them was the "juju" or magic of being able to find specks of that shiny yellow sand for which white men squandered fortunes, and before which native eyes became round and sparkling as they uttered ums and ahs of surprise and awe. They valued their few gold ornaments handed down from generation to generation. But they had been so untouched by the world around them that they could not understand white men, and much less an unaccompanied white woman, coming into their "bush" to hunt for these specks.

The hinterland of Sierra Leone, West Africa, is a true frontier. It is the kind of place an explorer dreams about when he opens a map of the world and searches for a place to roam. A place where he might have unusual experiences. But a place where he hesitates to go. Too near the equator.

Too low. Too much heat and humidity. A place reeking with malaria and tropical disease. Not a country to tempt game hunters, for there are too many forests and little open grazing land. A country of primitive natives who have never contributed a great art to the world. So he decides to go elsewhere.

Why should I have gone there? Surely not to write a book. That was the last thing I intended to do. Too many Americans who go to Africa write books—mostly about East Africa and game hunting. I saw very little game. I wasn't looking for animals. But my prospecting job in Sierra Leone was full of the unexpected, and because it happened to me, a woman, alone in West Africa, my friends wanted to hear about it. They wanted to share my feelings in this world, so different from their own, and to see through my eyes a little of what I had seen and felt. This is my only reason for writing this story.

Every writer has to be explained, especially when he writes for the public for the first time. Readers will naturally want to know who I am, and what kind of training I had—why I ever went to Africa.

I shall have to admit that I was not brought up to do dangerous things in Africa. In fact, my parents would turn in their graves if they could know of all the foolhardy things I have done in my short life, what chances fate has thrown across my path. The very fact that I was reared in Boston, with the typically Puritanical upbringing which the name "Boston" implies, shows how sheltered and uneventful my early days must have been. I was sent, rebelling, to dancing school—wearing frilly, Irish lace dresses, and two long pigtails with huge silk bows. I went through a select girls' school—then flatly refused to "come out." I had never set my foot out of New England, so I chose Bryn Mawr for my college because it was *out* of New England. This decision met with the approval of my parents, since Bryn Mawr was considered "select, high standing, and only nice girls went there."

I liked science best, among all my courses. I was curious about the things around me. Geology satisfied my craving to have everything explained. I have loved an outdoor life ever since my hay-fever vacations in the White Mountains, when I was sent away, entrusted to the hands of a dear old lady who encouraged my desire to explore brooks and climb mountains.

During the summer of my sophomore year in college, an aunt took me around Europe, as part of my education, on a tour of cathedrals and museums. I finally balked in Switzerland—I had to climb some Alps. I was sick of being educated. Persuading Auntie that she needed a rest, and that mountain climbing was as safe as walking up and down the Esplanade, I scaled the Jungfrau, the Breithorn, and the Eiger. The trip up the Eiger was unfortunately visible through the telescope at our hotel in Mürren. The strain of knowing our movements for thirteen hours, when we encountered difficult going and had to cut steps in the ice all the way up and down the Eiger's cone, was too much for Auntie. We took the next train to London.

Determined to be a geologist, I went to the University of Wisconsin for my first graduate work. I wanted to see if I was able to compete with men in a man's field. For I knew that women weren't usually geologists, or, at least, the kind of geologist I hoped to be. Here in Wisconsin I had my first practical training in field work. I learned how to make maps, and I visited my first mines.

I also discovered the West, and began my wanderings, hitchhiking through the Black Hills, and on to Butte, Montana, and a glimpse into more mines. To get into some of the mines I had to be smuggled along as a boy.

There were many exciting incidents, but the one that stands uppermost in my memory was the time when I got caught in a bad forest fire just west of Lake McDonald, while doing geological mapping in Glacier Park. Luckily, fate was with me, and I managed to reach the lake shore, where I was finally rescued by means of a motorboat.

My thesis work for a Ph.D. at Columbia University was in the Laramie Mountains, Wyoming. I made a geological map, and collected material to work on in the laboratory in the winters. I worked alone in the field, partly because there was no other woman who could and would go along and watch me do the drudgery of geology, and partly because I was sure a series of visitors in the field would slow up the work. I often consider this period of work far more difficult than my job in Africa. I had to do all my own cooking and camping, besides my geological work, with no natives to help me. I was far more alone than in Africa, surrounded by my blacks. I was trained for any kind of solitude, consequently, and never succumbed to the effects of the lack of companionship which preys on so many of the whites in the tropics. I really enjoyed working alone, for I had learned how to have my work absorb all my interests and keep me sane.

The West, then, was my real training school for survival in West Africa. I had learned how to depend upon my own resources. The luxuries of servants, a good tent, chairs, tables, and lamps—not to forget a bed—made Africa possible for one who had learned to work with the minimum of comforts.

In the summer of 1929, I went to the International Geological Congress which was held in South Africa. I went alone, ahead of the others, so that I might spend more time in South Africa than was allowed in the schedule of excursions arranged for the geologists who were coming from all parts of the world.

I have often wondered what sent me to Africa, anyhow. Mostly a sudden inspiration, a desire to see parts more remote than the West. Also a feeling of futility which had grown on me in New York when struggling through the final form of my thesis manuscript. I was tired of social conventions, worn out with looking down my microscope.

South Africa, as seen on the Congress excursions, with its mines and scenery like our West, made me feel very much at home. We progressed slowly northward from Cape Town, eventually reaching the Congo, and real Africa. Here the Congress broke up, followed by a scattering of the participants in every direction. I jumped at the chance to have a glimpse of bush life, and planned to continue northward to Egypt, visiting some of the more remote places in Central Africa. I found I could travel most of the way with two geologists who were also going in that general direction. This simplified the transport situation in places where lorries or boats had to be resorted to. We pursued black Africa along one of the Congo tributaries, and then had a glimpse at some of the few surviving uncivilized parts of the world in Uganda and the Nile watersheds, where the natives are still naked heathens, and where giraffes and elephants are not myths. Africa was at last a live country to me, one which could be traveled in, studied, and liked. I was sorry to reach Cairo and the European world, where I cast aside my sun helmet and shorts.

When climbing Table Mountain, in Cape Town, I had met the man who was later to become my husband. He first noticed me when I scornfully refused help while climbing up a bad place. His only remark to a friend was: "Whew! What an independent woman!"

Then one clammy day that very December, at a London registry office, we were married by a man who looked as if he had stepped out of Dickens—long, dripping nose, high collar, blue-veined hands. Not to mention the dark alley itself, somewhere behind Covent Garden, where the great yellow limousine belonging to the American vice-consul, who had come to witness the ceremony, couldn't squeeze in.

I had always felt that I was not cut out for marriage. But where career and marriage could go on, hand in hand, that was different. We were both geologists; and a geologist is accustomed to sudden decisions and many partings of the way.

We began our married life with great ambitions of conquering Northern Rhodesia together, when my husband should return to his job, with the British Foreign Office, of mapping the Congo boundary. But this was not to be. My husband was suddenly transferred from Central Africa to the Gold Coast, West Africa. And he had to sign a contract that he would not take his wife. It was found that the red tape could not be cut, even if I was a geologist. Rules are rules.

I was not to be downed so easily, however. As long as I was not with my husband on the Gold Coast, apparently no one cared where I went. He might be given an armed guard—and I couldn't go with him. But it didn't matter if I went to a wilder place, with *no* guard. So I made up my mind. I would go to Sierra Leone, which was also in West Africa, and do geology on my own. It was only a thousand miles away from the Gold Coast—and we could go out on the same boat. I chose Sierra Leone because it was a country which had barely been scratched, geologically speaking. It had been called a land "with no mineral resources" until 1928, when the embryo Geological Survey had reported iron ore, gold, and platinum. They knew very little of the extent of these deposits. This in itself was a lure, for I should find plenty of problems to work out. Besides, Sierra Leone was still scorned by all except one or two hardy miners who were just trying to feel their way. It was truly one of the untouched spots of the world. This, then, is a brief sketch of my history up to the time when I set sail for Sierra Leone.

My impressions of West Africa are recorded in the following pages. The incidents are real; only the names of the white men are fictitious, with the exception of Major Junner, Dr. Stammers, and Holmes. If the reader feels that Africa is just one snake after another, that is my impression, today, as I sit down to recall my experiences. It is only the startling things that stick in one's mind. Behind the lines lie days of monotony—perfectly normal existence in the tropics. A tired feeling. Heat. Oppression. And a constant pushing forward through the same heat, day after day; just a struggle against nature and the native mind. Perseverance and interest in my work were the things which brought me back, sane.

Part I

TREKKING FOR IRON

SIERRA LEONE

AUSPICE BRITANNIA LIBER

+++++	Railroads
———	Roads
- - - -	Trails
wwwww	Route of the first tour barbed

Scale 0   50 Miles

Map labels:

Great Skarcies R.
Little Skarcies R.
Kaballa
Seli R.
Lake Sonfon
Bintimani 6390
Nerekoro
Kulia
Sankan Birya
Maranda
Mabonto
Masumbiri
Makeni
Port Lokko
Seli R.
Magburaka
Makelei
Sefadu
Marampa
Matotaka
Makali
Makong
Jaiama Mission
Freetown
COLONY
platinum mine
Teben
Pujehun
R. Sewa
Gandorhun
R. Meli
Kailahun
Bauya
Pampana R.
Lago
chromite mine
Bo
Kenema
R. Sewa
R. Moa
Bonthe
R. Mano

Inset map (Africa):

S A H A R A
GAMBIA
FR. GUINEA
SIERRA LEONE
LIBERIA
IVORY COAST
GOLD COAST
DAHOMEY
NIGERIA
Lagos
CAMEROONS
ETHIOPIA
C O N G O
0 — 0

CHAPTER ONE

FREETOWN

SIERRA LEONE! The mountains of the lion! Freetown!
Hitherto, they had been only names on a map of Africa;
now, as our boat steamed into Freetown harbor, they became
real. Eleven days out of Liverpool, and, quite fittingly for my
first view, the high mountains of Sierra Leone were draped in
clouds, and thunder roared like a veritable lion, for this was
late October, and the rains were just ending. Flashes of lightning zigzagged back and forth as the thunderstorm sped
toward us across the water. A torrential downpour reached us
just as we dropped anchor. The uproar was terrifying. Through
the descending water, Freetown, with its gray, tin-topped ware-
houses, its cathedral, its stores and government buildings, took
on a strange look, as though one glimpsed another world
through a curtain of time. As suddenly as it had come, the
storm stopped. There was a momentary lull, and then arose a
great clanging of bells and shouting of natives. The landing
barges had arrived; one cannot dock at Freetown.

As I leaned over the rail, watching the lively scene, it didn't
seem possible that at last I was really at my destination. I
thought of that day, now seemingly so long ago, when Jock, my
geologist husband, had burst into our London apartment, with

the announcement: "I've signed the contract to go to the Gold Coast, and I can't take my wife. It's no use, Kay, making any fuss; there's no way out of it. It's absolutely necessary that I go and the government won't let me take you."

I had been completely taken aback. I was a geologist, just as he was, and now I couldn't go simply because I was a woman. I was furious—at him, at the British colonial government with all its rules and red tape, at men in general. This was not the first time I had been told, "You can't go; you're a woman." If I could only make them understand that being a woman was not necessarily a drawback. I would go—perhaps not to the Gold Coast, but to some place just as difficult. I got out the map of Africa.

Along the southern coast of the great western extension of Africa, on the east side of the Gold Coast lies Dahomey, and on the west side is the Ivory Coast, but they are both French territory. East of Dahomey is Nigeria; that is British, so it presented possibilities to be investigated. West of the Ivory Coast are Liberia (independent) and Sierra Leone, British colony and protectorate. My choice would be Liberia or Sierra Leone. I began making inquiries, and the more I learned about Sierra Leone, the more I became convinced that here was just the opportunity I wanted.

In the first place, I liked the name, especially after I discovered that the country was not called the "mountains of the lion" because of the prevalence of that beast. As a matter of fact, few lions have been found there, because they prefer more open country. No, it had been christened Sierra Leone by Pedro da Cintra, a Portuguese explorer, in 1462, and, according to early writers, had been so designated because of the picturesque range of hills, rising to about three thousand feet, which form the peninsula whereon stands Freetown, the capital of the colony and the only port of the country. From certain angles these mountains do resemble a crouching lion. Another tradition declares that the name was given because of the "continual roaring of thunder on the summit, which is often enveloped in clouds." It didn't really matter which was correct; either explanation pleased me.

As a geologist, I was attracted by the opportunity to do pioneer work in new country. Before 1928, the country had been considered as without special mineral worth, but in that year, a reconnaissance trip into the interior had been made by Major N. Junner, now Director of the Gold Coast Geological Survey, and traces of gold, iron, chromium, and platinum had been found. There was rumor of a three-karat diamond having been picked up. As a country of unknown mineral wealth, it presented unlimited possibilities for study. Perhaps I would find gold or iron or some other valuable ore in quantity sufficient to make any one of them worth mining. Where could I find a better place to prove that being a woman was no handicap to doing worthwhile geology?

Moreover—and this was important—there seemed to be no objection on the part of anyone in authority to my going to Sierra Leone and doing as much geology as I pleased. So, Sierra Leone it was.

Luckily, Jock approved; Sierra Leone is ever so much nearer to the Gold Coast than England is. Besides, he had discovered that an American wife, particularly a New Englander, was apt to have ideas of her own that were difficult to change. So he helped me get an outfit together.

Upon inquiry, I found that Sierra Leone has about a thousand miles of roads—some good and some bad but passable, at least in the dry season, which would be the period of my stay. So I decided to take a Ford car and be independent as to transportation, rather than hire lorries driven by Syrians, which was the alternative. I would work out from the roads at first, studying the geology over a wide area, familiarizing myself with the general problems; then I could decide on some area to study in detail. Accordingly, I carefully planned my equipment for several months of work so that I could pack all my belongings into the car.

In the midst of all the flurry of getting ready, I somehow managed to find time to take a short course in tropical hygiene. The course is given to nonmedical persons at the London School of Hygiene, so that anyone going to the tropics may learn the best methods of combating tropical disease.

It had been decided that I should go out on the same boat with Jock, disembarking at Freetown, while he went on, two days farther, to the Gold Coast. I half expected a last-minute slip-up, as we drove the Ford on the loading wharf at Liverpool. A polite official took charge of the car. The immigration officer bowed us past; he didn't even glance at my visa. Sailing time came; slowly, the steamer got under way. I breathed a sigh of relief, but it was not until the coast of England faded from sight that I could persuade myself that I was really off on my big adventure.

Lack of spontaneous good cheer among the passengers marked this trip as different from any I had hitherto taken. These voyagers were not off for a gay time; they were going to Africa on duty. Most of them had been there before; that was obvious from their faces, resigned and set. How different from a transatlantic sailing! Momentarily, I wished I were heading back to the good old States. Why had I been so silly as to insist upon Africa? Well, it was too late now; I must make the best of it.

North of Madeira, rough weather kept me below, as it did

most of the others, except a few sturdy men like Jock, who, being Scotch, refused to part with even one meal. Beyond Madeira, however, the sea was so smooth that I could hardly believe it was the same ocean.

On my right, as I lay in my deck chair, was a baldish gentleman, with a kindly face and the air of one used to commanding. When he found that I was bound for Sierra Leone, he constituted himself my guardian, for he had served under the colonial government of the colony since leaving Oxford, many years before. First he had been an assistant district commissioner in a small town, far away in the interior, before there had been any roads. That was in 1896, when England took over the interior for the first time, designating it as a protectorate. Later, he had been promoted to the office of District Commissioner—he spoke of all the officers as D.C.'s—and now he was stationed in Freetown, in the capacity of a senior administrator, at the top of his chosen profession. He had watched the railroad push its way into the interior, and had seen the network of roads grow.

"The natives of the interior have not yet been touched by the effects of civilization," he said. "They are exactly as they have ever been, primitive, exasperating, and at the same time likable. The government policy is to preserve the native customs, to help the chiefs rule, and to assist in the administration of justice and the development of the country's resources."

We had many interesting conversations about this strange country to which I was going; and with each one, I became more and more convinced that I had made a good choice, in spite of the warnings I had received about Sierra Leone being hot, humid, low, reeking with malaria and tropical disease, and inhabited by a people some of whom, it was whispered, still practiced cannibalism. My neighbor was an old man; he had been out there since his youth, but he still looked the picture of health. He didn't seem to fit the picture of the "horrible hole" to which everyone assured me I was going.

"Why is Sierra Leone called 'the white man's grave'?" I asked him, a bit timidly.

He looked sad at my question. Many of his colleagues had died, he told me, and he himself was troubled with malaria, but he had been lucky. The country would probably never be free of disease, but the ravages of fever could be held in check with quinine.

"Young lady," he looked at me sternly, "be sure to take five grains of quinine every night. If you do, you need not be afraid of malaria. Quinine in the blood will kill the germs caused by the Anopheles mosquito, which is the carrier, and which is abroad only at night.

"Another thing. Always boil all the water that you use. This is most important."

Many times, later, when I heard of white persons ill with malaria and dysentery, I thanked my lucky stars that had placed me beside that good adviser on my first trip out.

Day by day the weather grew warmer, the sea grew smoother, and our energy grew less and less. The heat made us sink back into our deck chairs, oblivious to everything until sunset brought relief. The books I had meant to read slipped to the floor; the letters I had meant to write remained nebulous; my energies were limited to consuming cool drinks. I lost track of time. Then one day we sailed into the harbor of Bathurst, the port of the small British colony of Gambia. There we got a foretaste of what we might expect all along the West African coast late in October—heavy, humid, lifeless air, so enervating that no one even asked whether or not he might go ashore.

"Is it as bad as this in Sierra Leone?" I asked my neighbor of the deck chair.

"You can't expect it to be very cold in low country only six degrees north of the equator," he replied. "This is the best time of the year to be coming to this coast. The rains will soon be over; and when it rains in Sierra Leone, let me assure you, young lady, it rains. Freetown itself has a hundred and ninety inches, or sixteen feet of water, a year. It is in the same latitude as Addis Ababa, in Ethiopia. Most of Sierra Leone is only one hundred to two hundred feet above sea level. Only in the north and around Freetown are there mountains. To the north, there is a high plateau, with high peaks, the highest being Bintimani (sixty-four hundred feet above sea level). Around Freetown the mountains rise to three thousand feet, making it one of the beautiful harbors of the world. Back of the mountains, which make up the backbone of the peninsula that is the colony, are low-lying jungles, or 'bush.' Soon, hot dusty winds from the Sahara, known as the harmattan, will start sweeping down across the country. Then the rivers subside, the ground dries up, and travel is easier from November to May, when the rainy season begins again."

From Bathurst, we headed for Freetown. The night before arrival there, a heavy tropical thunderstorm came up suddenly in the evening. The stewards rushed around, shutting portholes, but we were rendered speechless and motionless by the grandeur of the spectacle. Some hours later when we turned in, Jock opened the porthole for a breath of air, but the sky still looked ominous, so he closed it again.

It was so hot and stuffy that it was some time before I got to sleep. Suddenly I was awakened by an exclamation of rage, and, switching on the light, I was greeted by a sorry sight.

Jock's bunk was directly below the porthole, which he had evidently failed to clamp securely, for the full blast of a wave had forced it open and had thoroughly drenched him. Six inches of water swished back and forth across the cabin floor. Frantic ringing of the bell finally raised a sleepy-eyed steward, who came to life at the ludicrous sight we presented. Our clothes, which had been laid out—and most of my wardrobe was there, waiting to be packed in the cool of the morning— were taken to the drying-room. Nine months later, when I unpacked my "civilian" clothes for my return to England, I found my silk dresses in ribbons, literally eaten by the salt in which I had carefully but unwittingly laid them away.

That morning, as we dropped anchor in Freetown harbor, a much perturbed purser sought Jock and me. Some mistake had been made. Our Ford was labeled to get off at Freetown. Fortunately, he knew that Jock was going to the Gold Coast, so he had rectified the error just in time. It took fully fifteen minutes to convince him that the car was to be unloaded at Freetown. Finally, he went away, shaking his head sorrowfully, obviously much mystified and not yet convinced. There must be a mistake. Women who went out to West Africa with their husbands stayed with their husbands; a husband and a wife bound for different ports was unthinkable.

With the thought of the unconvinced purser in my mind, I had decided not to leave the boat until I saw the Ford go over the side. While we waited, we watched the mailbags, then the crates and luggage being swung out in great nets to the waiting barges. Finally, the dusty body of the Ford was deposited on a barge. I was relieved, for I had feared that at the last moment the purser would decide not to be an accessory to such an unheard-of offense against tradition.

But even yet I could not go ashore; we had to wait for government launches to bring the customs inspectors and immigration officials aboard. I did not mind waiting, for the harbor about us presented an amusing scene. Negro mammies, in gay-colored shapeless gowns, which looked more like nightgowns than street dresses, crowded in tiny boats alongside, offering oranges for sale and some sticky-looking balls of food, which the native Krooboys, who had come aboard to do the heavy work of unloading, evidently found greatly to their liking.

Natives of Freetown flocked out from shore in their kayak-shaped canoes, hollowed out of tree trunks. Fishermen by trade, they had learned that steamer passengers were profitable customers. One old fellow in particular amused us. The natives called him "Uncle Joe." He came solemnly arrayed in a tall stovepipe hat, a parson's collar topping his black body, bare save for the native breech cloth. Periodically, he burst forth in song, the dulcet strains being "Hallelujah, I'm a bum." His grand array did not make him less eager than the others to dive for pennies; it was fun to see him carefully place his prized hat in the front of his frail craft and then dive overboard. Uncle Joe had probably attended some mission school, for, when the rain of pennies slackened and his steamer audience began to tire of the scene, he burst into a long harangue, which was a perfect caricature of the old-fashioned revivalist manner.

Word went round that the officials were ready to stamp passports. I held my breath while the black official squinted through his thick glasses, hunting for my visa. Suppose he wouldn't let me land; suppose he shared the purser's horror of a wife going to a country other than that for which her husband was bound; suppose— He looked at me, and my heart sank. But what he said was: "Is your husband in the government employ?" My "yes" was perfectly truthful. Apparently, there was nothing more to say. There was no more difficulty; I had found the open sesame to West African travel— "My husband is in the government service."

As I turned away, my landing papers all in order, the head of the Mines Department of Sierra Leone stepped up. He was a young man whom we had met and liked in London, and I had written him to let him know that I was coming out. He was keen to make Sierra Leone into a great mining center, and, as he talked about the things he hoped I could do, I caught something of his enthusiasm. I could count on his co-operation, that was sure, for he hoped I would be able to unravel some of the geological problems. Perhaps I would find some new mineral deposits. He would do everything in his power to facilitate my traveling in the country, he assured me. He had already obtained the Governor's sanction to my trip. His optimism was contagious; his trust in my ability as a geologist most flattering. I hadn't expected it; everyone else had been so discouraging. So I was almost gay as I said good-by to Jock and boarded the launch with my guide.

Jock's face and waving handkerchief grew smaller and smaller as we sped across the water to Freetown. The dock was teeming with black faces, but I was hurriedly ushered past the customs shed to a waiting car. A "boy," clad in white duck and resplendent with brass buttons down his immaculate vest, jumped out and saluted smartly as we appeared. It was another year before I discovered just what I had been spared by this kindly attention, and what a difference it made to a "happy landing" if one came welcomed as the wife of a government official and not as an ordinary traveler.

CHAPTER TWO

RED TAPE

MY IMPRESSION of Freetown, as we were whisked along wide macadam streets leading up from the dock, was of a crowded native metropolis. Portly mammies swept along with their gaily colored skirts and aprons brushing the ground, always balancing something on their heads—perhaps a few chickens in a calabash (the native reed basket), perhaps a great pack of dirty clothes. Brilliant yellow and purple silk bandannas covered their kinky hair and added another note of color to an already vivid ensemble. I caught glimpses of pickaninnies—who "are just pickins in this country," I was informed. Some had on filthy rags; others looked spotlessly clean in white togas; still others scampered about with no man-made fabric to hide the shining bronze of their little bodies. Men in voluminous gowns such as the Arabs wear, or simply in a shirt with its tails floating in the breeze, sauntered along. I noticed that most of the natives were barefoot, although here and there I saw one with sandals or slippers. Obviously, he belonged to the aristocracy.

Not all the streets were macadam; some were dirt—or rather, red mud. We went on, past buildings, narrow ones and wide ones, big ones and little ones, but all of them low, with gray roofs, many of corrugated iron. Only the government offices towered above the others, a mass of gray cement with arched doorways.

Suddenly I saw a huge cottonwood tree in the middle of the street. The fan-shaped spread of its radiating roots reminded me of an octopus or an umbrella blown inside out. I had never before seen such a huge tree nor such spreading roots. Beneath it stood a black policeman in khaki uniform with bright red trimmings, who saluted smartly and waved us on. My conductor told me that the cottonwood was one of the landmarks of Freetown. Government offices, stores, churches, native dwellings, as well as the official residence of the Governor, known as Government House, were here near the water front, my guide explained, but most of the English population lived six miles away at Hill Station on a spur of the mountains, eight hundred feet above the main town. It was healthier there and quieter. In the old days a narrow-gauge railroad had plied back and forth, bringing the white men to town; now, cars and a good macadam road most of the way had caused the railroad to be abandoned.

"Freetown is slowly becoming a modern city," he said. "We have electricity in our homes as well as in the government buildings and the stores. A good water supply is collected in reservoirs fed by mountain streams. Perhaps some day we shall have a proper sewage system, to raise still higher the already vastly improved health record of the place. I expect, though, that the native market will always remain an open-air, free-for-all barter place. I don't mind telling you I hope it will. Anyhow, the many French, German, and Swiss shops that have been opened do not seem to have changed the volume of business done in the markets."

Soon we began to climb steadily into the hills. I smelled the earthy odor of freshly wet soil and saw trees laden with yellow

The Gold Missus.

Fode, the cook (left), and Amadu, my personal boy, with Buster in front of a cook-house.

bananas and green plantains. There were many palms and even a pawpaw with its cluster of large green balls as big as ripe coconuts. We had climbed at least five hundred feet, when we swung round a bend in the road, and I caught a view of the town below, with the moist tin-topped native dwellings shining in the sun, and the old barracks on a small hill in the center of the town standing guard as a gloomy reminder of the days when many soldiers were necessary to keep order in the colony.

On we went, past the neat entrance to some gray cement houses, obviously belonging to white persons, presumably English, for there were gay flowers in neat beds. I looked at these dwellings with especial curiosity, for my guide had brought me an invitation from Miss Carey, an Englishwoman who was in charge of education among the Negro women in the colony, asking me to stay with her while I was in Freetown, and I wondered what kind of place she lived in.

We continued to climb: past more houses; past the new barracks, where a black sergeant was drilling his equally black men; past the rambling community clubhouse; past more houses, this time boxlike wooden structures standing high on steel frames, obviously antiquated. This was "Fug Alley" I was told, an amusing corruption of "Fog Alley," named because of the prevalence of mists on that ridge of the hills.

Finally, still higher up the mountain, we drove into the grounds of a yellowish-white cement house, its door almost hidden by a huge scarlet bougainvillea. This house, too, was raised from the ground on great cement piles.

A boy immaculately clad in white duck opened the door, ushering us into a room bright with colored chintz, which seemed to be doing its best to overcome the darkness of the heavy mahogany furniture. There was also a real rug.

"All government quarters are furnished with this heavy

stuff," my escort whispered, as we sat waiting for our hostess.

A curtain was pushed aside; before me stood a little woman with a merry twinkle in her eye and a cordial greeting on her lips. Under the influence of her quiet, matter-of-fact air and cheery smile I found myself relaxing gradually from the tense excited feeling I had had all day. Here was a home; I might almost have been back in England, only we sipped orange juice, not tea.

Miss Carey was different from most of the women I met in the tropics: she had a job of her own, and she had not come out to this country merely as a husband's excess baggage. She was in the tropics helping the natives organize and standardize their schools. About her was a purposeful quality that I found later in a few white nurses who were doing for the body what Miss Carey was endeavoring to do for the mind. Miss Carey's was a fine intellect; she had fought her way and achieved results in spite of vigorous opposition.

When I spoke of getting to work soon, my hostess and my guide both laughed and assured me that it would be "several days" before I could possibly expect to leave Freetown.

"But don't worry," Miss Carey said. "There'll be plenty for you to do before you start. It will take some time for your goods to get through the customs. Then you will have to make arrangements to have your car shipped to the interior. There are roads here in Freetown and on the peninsula, and there are roads in the interior, but between the two systems lie the mangrove swamps, across which all travel at present is by the railroad. Besides, you will have to have boys, and you had best select them here where we can help you. All this can't be done in a hurry. Time means little enough in the tropics, as you will find out before long."

She was right. It took time, and lots of it, to settle the merest detail. Not that I felt like hurrying, but my mind kept telling me I should. It was weeks before I could let things move along without being upset with the slowness. As a matter of fact, I don't think that I ever really learned the lesson of letting things take their course, for I found myself, when weary, in a state of irritation at the natives' apparent lack of purpose. Probably that was just my New England conscience pricking me.

First of all, I had to have a "personal" boy and a cook. To a white person in the tropics, these are as necessary as his toothbrush. Miss Carey told her boys what I needed; that was sufficient advertising. The next morning at eight, the sight of several dozen solemn applicants overwhelmed me. How in the world was I to select the right ones! They were all black; some were tall; some were short; most of them were thin; all of them wore the ingratiating look of one who hopes to be chosen. To my horror, I saw more and more black boys coming. Then Miss Carey appeared and quietly took charge. After slowly looking them over, she motioned to a shy-looking, rather small fellow to step forward.

"His name is Amadu," she told me, in an aside. "His credentials are nothing remarkable, but I know him. He has a reputation for loyalty to his former 'white missus' that makes me think he is the boy you should have. The boys at the hospital do not like him, because, when his 'missus' was sick, he commandeered hot water and special delicacies for her, without regard for whom they might originally have been intended. If all I hear about him is true, he is just the one you should have."

So Amadu became one of my African family. A cook was harder to get. Finally, and rather reluctantly, Fode was chosen, not because we liked him, but simply because we couldn't find anyone we liked better. His recommendations were far from encouraging, and, despite a perpetual grin, he looked a villain. The minute I hired him, I began to dislike and distrust him. Miss Carey warned me against showing any of this feeling toward a cook unless I was prepared to fire him. "You can't give a cook warning, in this country," she said. "If you do, he will probably poison your food before he goes, as a slight token of his displeasure. When you fire him, see that he goes right off, without a chance to get near your food."

Having selected my boys, I endeavored to complete my shopping, part of the time with Miss Carey and part of the time with Amadu, who had soon established himself as one I could trust. In the fun of watching the shifting colors, the chatter and calls, the laughter and good-natured gaiety which characterized the leisurely trading of the natives, I almost forgot what I wanted. Amadu tried to teach me how to bargain, but I soon gave it up and left him to do the dickering, while I watched. He enjoyed it; so did I.

But boys and shopping were the least of my worries. I could not get my goods through the customs. Finally, I found that the powdered milk was causing the delay. I had brought it out from England, for, of course, one cannot keep fresh milk in the tropics. For no reason that I could see, it aroused much suspicion in the minds of the authorities. In desperation, I asked that a can be opened and sent to the chief of customs, who had refused to believe that milk could be a powder. I strongly suspected that the natives wished to sample such a delicacy, and my suspicions were confirmed when the can was returned, its contents obviously much diminished. However, as a gesture of recompense, all my cans of milk were declared free of duty, although the rest of my food supplies were subjected to the required twenty per cent tariff.

The authorities did a thorough job with my boxes. My automatic revolver was scrutinized, and my cartridges counted. But my goods were finally passed, and I was able to organize my loads.

Life in Freetown was by no means all customs formalities and shopping. Such tasks occupied our mornings. After lunch, I quickly fell into the habit of taking a siesta. About four o'clock we had tea and went for a swim at a delightful sandy beach, protected from marauding sharks by an offshore bar. Then we drove to the near-by golf club, where the white population gathered at that hour. In the evening we dined out or Miss Carey had a few friends in for dinner. It amazed me to go out to the kitchen, at the back of the house but separate from it, and find her cook preparing a five-course dinner over a few sticks of wood, with tin lids for a stove top and an oven made of a four-gallon can. The food was good, too; better than many a meal prepared on the latest model stove with all the gadgets to which the modern housewife is heir.

It did not seem possible that this could be Sierra Leone, against which everyone had warned me. Freetown, with its mountains and sea, with its colorful, leisurely life, was delightful. Underneath the laughter, however, I detected a note of forced gaiety. Those who had been out there long were sallow-faced and tired-looking. They seemed to do very little, compared to the activities of people I knew in England or in the States. Only a few—and they had not been long in Sierra Leone—seemed to have any energy.

"It's the tropics," they told me, "and you'll look and feel just like the rest of us, or worse, after a few months. Why any sane white woman wants to go out into the bush and do what you are going to do is more than we can understand."

"Just another crazy American notion," I could almost hear them say to one another.

Then at last came the day when everything was ready. Supplies were all bought; loads were all prepared; the red tape had been cut; the Ford had been dispatched on a flatcar to Kenema, a hundred and eighty miles east of Freetown; its keys had been registered and handed to the black mail-man in the caboose. There was nothing left for me to do but to say good-by to this pleasant life in Freetown and begin my work. I was sorry to leave the delightful seclusion and peace of Miss Carey's friendly home; I knew I would miss the gay chats with her and her friends over the inevitable cup of tea or glass of orangeade. Now there was nothing to delay my departure; I must leave next morning.

CHAPTER THREE

HINTERLAND

WHEN I REACHED the railroad station at seven that bright cool November morning, I found Amadu and Fode guarding two huge wooden trunks, which, they explained, contained their own personal goods. For a moment I was too astonished at their impudence and too exasperated to speak. What did they expect of a Ford? Their faith in its elasticity was supreme; all week they had been helping me carefully apportion bundles that would tax it to the limit, and they had been told exactly how much space their individual bundles could take.

"You'll have to leave your trunks somewhere near the railroad," I said to them, firmly and sternly. "You can't take more than the small bundles you were told you might bring."

Sullenly, they ushered me along the station platform, past a line of high-standing wooden cars, which looked as though they had been running ever since there were railroads, to a first-class compartment. It was labeled "first-class compartment," so it must have been one; to me, it looked more like an empty baggage car than anything else. In it, my deck chair stood in solitary grandeur; in this country, one used one's own furniture, even on the train.

When I had made certain that all my loads were safely aboard the train and the Mines Department clerk had given me the checks and my ticket, I retired to my baggage car and waited for the train to start. I waited and waited. Amadu produced sandwiches, which had been put up the night before, and dispatched Fode to the engine for a kettle of hot water from the steam exhaust, with which he proceeded to make tea. Just as I was getting nicely through this informal breakfast, the train started with an awful jerk, which upset not only the tea, but also the equilibrium of a wide-eyed native audience that had gathered at the windows to watch this strange white woman—"a missus without a master."

In time, I became accustomed to the open-mouthed, wide-eyed wonder which my advent never failed to arouse among the natives of Sierra Leone, but at first it was very disconcerting. I felt as though I were a freak at the circus or one of the strange animals at the zoo.

As the train pulled slowly and jerkily out of Freetown station, Amadu and Fode waved good-by to several dozen "relatives"—at least, they assured me they were all brothers. I found out later that all members of the same tribe are "brothers." When the ruins of the breakfast had been cleared away, my two henchmen retired to their third-class coach and a day of excited jabberings with the crowd of blacks who filled the coach almost to bursting.

Our destination was Kenema, only a hundred and eighty miles from Freetown, but the trip took two days, necessitating a night stop at the railroad resthouse at Bo, a hundred and thirty-six miles from Freetown. I had wondered how any train could take so long to go such a short distance, but I soon found the reason. We jerked along, stopping frequently and at many places where it seemed as though the only excuse must be that the engine needed a rest. No sooner would the train stop than my car would be surrounded by a crowd of curious natives, who gazed at me fixedly and voiced their astonishment in plainly audible ums and ahs.

After we left Freetown, the railroad skirted the three-thousand-foot mountains of the peninsula, following the Sierra Leone River, which is more of a tidal bay than a river. The tide was out, and long snaky roots, which had been covered when it was in, stood out baldly, like gnarled stilts, supporting a leafy foliage high above the water line. Some of them had bulblike protrusions that looked like partly grown horns. These were the mangrove swamps, which formed a narrow belt between the highway system of the interior and that of the peninsula. I had to use the railroad to get across them, and, having gone to the trouble of taking the train, I had decided not to get off as soon as possible, but to take full advantage of it as far as I conveniently could.

Gradually, the even green of the mountains faded in the distance; we were in low flat country. Grassy patches within the swamp became more frequent until at length we had left the swamps behind and were moving through the jungle. I had always pictured a jungle as terrifying, but this one looked peaceful and invitingly cool to the hot occupant of the baggage car. It was like a great dark green awning between the earth and the sun, the monotony of its color unbroken save for the black tree trunks. The trees were tall, and from the branches great ropelike creepers hung to the ground. I could see no moss, only ropes and leaves, smooth, green, shining leaves. At intervals, an opening in the high green curtain was made by "low bush," cut-over regions, rank with struggling shrublike trees, matted together until it didn't seem possible that any human being could penetrate the underbrush. Then palm trees, topping masses of smaller trees which resemble a thick growth of hardwood. Then a small farm region, with bananas and scattered palms. Then an agricultural station, with neatly arranged rows of palms—acres of one size, acres of another size—all for a flooded market. Or possibly it was a type of reforestation.

Then more jungle, with the highest trees of all—the mahogany, king among the scrubby, feathery-leaved acacias, and cottonwoods. I knew them by their straightness, their height, their smooth-looking trunks. Then a small swamp, with beautiful, lacy, fernlike creepers enfolding the low bushes. White and red splashes of color in these low places appeared to be leaves, not flowers.

As the sun rose higher and higher, the heat grew correspondingly greater and greater, until its intensity overcame my curiosity and I pulled down the shutters and sank back in my chair, unable to think of anything except how hot it was. Besides, there was a dreadful monotony to the journey. Ever the great green forest shut us in, with here and there a clearing where we stopped with an awful jerk, which sent my chair skidding across the bare floor of the car, and, before I could get myself to rights, the window filled with black faces. The stops seemed interminable; evidently the engineer was determined not to move on until he had seen and greeted every one of his friends, and he appeared to know every person in every village we passed.

The villages consisted, for the most part, of a few native huts grouped around a central open space. I soon discovered that it took no more than two or three houses to make a "village"; or the buildings might number fifty. In the main, the native hut was a round, mud-walled enclosure, with dirt floor and high-pitched, thatched roof, with no opening except the door.

It was purely sleeping quarters, for the housework—cooking and washing—was done out of doors.

About noon, I was suddenly awakened from a doze, into which I had fallen from sheer exhaustion, by a more violent lurch than usual. I gazed out into the dense forest. This couldn't be a village; something must have happened. As I peered out of the window, I could see that apparently everyone on the train was jumping out of the windows and dashing off into the jungle. What did it mean? Ought I to jump out and run after them? While I was debating what course to pursue, they had all disappeared; there was nothing I could do but wait and see what happened. I waited anxiously. Fifteen minutes passed, and then, finally, I heard a great shouting. Presently, the entire mob returned, triumphantly bearing a buck, a creature much like the European deer. The engine had hit it, but had not hurt it enough to prevent its running away. The engineer had jammed on the brakes, and the pursuit was on.

After the poor creature had been heaved into the mail coach, we moved on again, but at every stop there arose a great clatter and what seemed to be the beginning of a fight. Evidently there was some argument concerning the division of the spoils. The next time the train stopped in the jungle and the natives all rushed off, I expected to see another buck join his dead brother in the mail car. But this time it developed that the engine was out of water. The black passengers made up a procession—not a bucket, but a hat, brigade—and, after several trips to a convenient stream, actually succeeded in filling the engine so we could move on.

Lunch consisted of oranges, bananas, and pineapples, purchased en route, for when lunchtime came I was too hot and fly-bitten to be able to bear the thought of anything but fruit and a cup of tea.

It was almost dark when we reached Bo. Every minute I had been getting hotter and dirtier and more exasperated with myself for starting on such a trek. A cloudburst, just before the train drew into Bo, was a relief. In the rain and the darkness, Amadu and I somehow managed to find all my loads, and got boys, who were wrangling over the privilege of earning the porter's penny, to carry the stuff across the road to the tin-roofed railroad resthouse where I was to spend the night.

The resthouses along the railroad were built and maintained by the government, serving the purpose of hotels. They were usually comfortable cement houses, quite in contrast to the small mud resthouses in the more remote villages. The lack of any kind of sanitary hotel in a place like Freetown meant that the government had to maintain a resthouse even there. The suite to which I was shown in Bo had a bedroom and a bathroom, which, however, had no running water. Amadu brought me a five-gallon tin of lukewarm water, which he said he had heated in the kitchen. I felt better after a sponge. A feeble lantern tried its best to dispel the gray gloom of the grimy cement walls. Outside, the rain continued with unabated zeal. I ate canned beans, and crawled into bed. I had carefully placed everything far away from the barred windows, for I had been told that the thieves in a railroad town did not stop at bars, but used hooks and poles to fish out what they could get. The door had been bolted; I had nothing to fear.

It seemed as though I couldn't have been asleep for more than five minutes when I was startled by a knock on the door. It took several seconds for me to realize that it was Amadu, and he was saying that I would have to hurry, if I wanted to catch the train. I had overslept, and it was only by dint of frantic hurrying that we managed to get the loads down to the train in time. I had meant to get up early and see what a town upcountry looked like, but Bo would have to wait until my next visit. I had to be satisfied with the railroad resthouse and station. The train, too, merely rested here, I found, for it was not a junction; the single track just went straight on to the east.

When Amadu brought my tea, he said that the Ford had gone on up to Kenema by freight the day before. Everyone in Bo knew about it, he announced proudly, as the train lurched out of town.

We reached Kenema by eleven, and there on the platform to meet me was a white man. I was as pleased to see him as though I had left Freetown a week ago instead of the day before. He was an official: I could tell by the blue band on his helmet.

As he came forward to greet me, I saw him suddenly smile, but I was quite unprepared for his greeting: "I see you've taken Dr. Stammers's course in tropical hygiene."

"I did take it," I answered, "but how did you know?"

"The aluminum paint on the underside of your helmet. I see you've done a thorough job of it, too."

We both laughed. I had done a thorough job of it. Dr. Stammers had recommended aluminum paint for the inside of the crown, but I had also covered the inside of the brim, thinking that if the paint acted as a deflector of the sun's rays for the head it would do no harm to have it perform the same service for my neck.

"By the way, I'm Brown," he added a bit belatedly. "I'm the District Commissioner's assistant, and this is my retinue," indicating a group of fifteen or twenty natives. "They're all from the local jail, but don't let that alarm you. They'll carry your loads up that hill to an empty house that has been set aside for your use. You'll see it as soon as we get around the bend."

While I saw to the loading, Brown went to see about getting

the Ford off the flatcar. It took some time for the men to get the loads divided to their own satisfaction, but at last they started off. I watched them out of sight and then realized that Brown had been gone a long time. As minutes passed and still he failed to return, I began to grow apprehensive. Finally he appeared, looking grave.

"What has happened?" I called before he could reach me.

"The keys to the Ford are missing," he replied. "We couldn't get it off the flatcar, so I've had it switched onto the siding. Are you sure the keys were given to the baggageman?"

"Well, I didn't actually see them into his hands, but I have a receipt," I said.

He smiled at my faith in a scrap of paper, and said we had better go up to the house now and worry about the keys later.

"You're going to have lunch with me, if I can persuade you," he said. "As a matter of fact, I've already told the boys to prepare for two, so it won't do to start an argument."

I assured him that I had no intention of starting one and that I should be delighted to accept his invitation. He led the way along the dusty trail, lined with the gray-spotted trunks of trees —"Rubber," Brown told me, when I asked what they were.

At the top of the hill, I was ushered into a cement house. It was one of half a dozen barracklike buildings erected by the government to house any officers who might be stationed at Kenema. Here, I found Fode and Amadu struggling with the mass of boxes which the prisoners had helpfully deposited in a heap in the middle of the floor; they had then departed without more ado.

We paused only long enough for me to wash my face and hands, and then Brown escorted me to another house, as like mine as two peas in a pod. It was furnished in the usual manner of government houses, all in heavy native mahogany. The table was nicely set, and the food excellent.

Brown proved to be a most amusing host, regaling me with stories about men who had forgotten important items of luggage, all of them aimed, I could see, at relieving my embarrassment at having lost my only set of car keys, Jock having absent-mindedly sailed on to the Gold Coast with the duplicate set on his key ring.

After lunch I returned to my house, to sort out things and take a siesta before returning to Brown's for tea. Tea over, Brown suggested revolver practice at a range he had had set up. I got my automatic from its hiding-place in the bottom of a tin trunk, and we sallied forth. Brown missed badly, but I had better luck, hitting the tin can every time. Brown's boy stood staring at me, his eyes growing bigger and bigger. When we had finished, Brown picked up the board from behind the can, and pointing to the holes in it, he said to the boy, "You go to the village, and tell all those thief-men that missus will kill them one-time, if any man goes near her. Savvy?"

"Yes, sah, I go one-time," he answered, dashing away.

He evidently told one and all a fine tale about the "devil gun missus have," and thereby added to an already rapidly growing reputation, which, wherever I went, I found had preceded me. I kept the weapon out of sight, as a rule, but thereafter the cleaning of it never failed to arouse much interest and lively chatter among my boys.

"You missed on purpose," I accused Brown, as the man sped toward the village. "But who are the 'thief-men'? And what does 'one-time' mean?"

"One question at a time," laughed Brown, ignoring my accusation. "One-time means many things—immediately, surely, hurry up. Just now I meant that you would surely kill them immediately, and that he was to hurry and tell the villagers. Thieving is a lively evil all along the main routes. You must keep a sharp lookout, and never fail to have a fire kept burning at night by a guard you can trust. I've known any number of white men to be cleaned out completely, some of them even to their underwear.

"Why, our own D.C. had a tough experience. He was spending the night at a resthouse along the railroad, having just returned from trek. With him, he had two great iron money boxes, containing about fifteen hundred pounds of head-tax money. Before retiring, he put all the money in one of the boxes and chained it to his bed. On top of the empty box, he placed his gold watch and his false teeth. The thieves eluded his guard, and made off with the heavy empty box—false teeth and all. Of course, he had saved the tax money, but he had to wait six months before he could go back to England and be fitted with a new set of teeth."

It was dark when Brown stopped at my house to escort me to the District Commissioner's house, where we were both invited to dine.

"You can't imagine how grateful I am to all of you," I said to the D.C., his nice English wife, and the two other white men, who, together with Brown, made up the whole "station"; and I sank with relief into an upholstered chair and glanced around at the shining brass trays and the queer native ornaments which made this house, not the usual stiff government dwelling, but one of charm.

"Oh, yes, we can," they chorused. "We've all been through the same mill."

As we chatted gaily, I found it hard to realize that I was in

A boy standing on the trail in the midst of a jungle of mahogany and tree ferns.

A native beauty parlor. The central figure is braiding her companion's hair, while the girl on the right is spinning thread.

the midst of a tropical jungle, far from England. The talk was of England and of Freetown, interspersed with tales of this strange country, into which I was to journey still farther.

Kenema, they told me, was an agricultural headquarters as well as a government administrative center for this part of the protectorate.

"Agriculture?" I asked in some surprise. "I didn't know there was any."

"Of course, you Americans might not call it agriculture," laughed the D.C., "but it is all that the native does that could be honored by such a term. Perhaps it might better be designated as 'shifting agriculture.' You'll see plenty of evidence of it as you go out in the bush. The native has no plow. His only tool is his swordlike machete, which he wields with a quick wrist motion.

"The soil is very fertile, so the native has only to go out and pick a spot, hack down the bush, burn over a small section, scatter the seed, and cover it lightly. They do not know about the rotation of crops, but they have a system, old as man, whereby they achieve the same results. After several years, or in many cases only one year, of planting in one place, they move on to another, leaving the old field to revert to bush."

"But what do they plant?" I persisted.

"Oh, rice is the principal crop; it is the native's staple diet. Enough rice is grown in the country so that tons of it are exported each year, together with palm kernels, palm oil, piassava, ginger, kola nuts, pepper, and peanuts."

"Tell me more about the people," I urged.

"You are now in the country of the Mendes," he responded, "numerically, the strongest race in the protectorate. They make excellent carriers, as you will very soon find out. Oddly enough, although they are a great tribe, they have no tribal head, but are divided into about seventy paramount chiefdoms. Each of these chiefdoms is entirely independent of all the others, not even the slightest form of federation being maintained. The chiefdom is a complete unit, and the paramount chief acknowledges no tribal overlord. Theoretically at least, he acknowledges the British government, and, as a matter of fact, holds the government in awe and acknowledges the authority of government employees. You'll have nothing to fear; they know the government will punish them if a white person is molested."

"Then you don't think I'm an utter fool to be going out into the bush?" I asked with astonishment.

"Not at all," he replied in a matter-of-fact tone that was vastly encouraging after the skepticism with which the white persons of Freetown had viewed my future.

"You make me feel much better," I said. "In Freetown, everyone raised his eyebrows and said a woman couldn't live in the bush alone, that the natives would do all sorts of things to me, that I would surely be taken ill. I'm sure they think they will never see me again."

They all laughed.

"That's another old story," said Brown, "and it's just like all other stories. There are rules to follow in living in the bush. If you follow them, you'll be all right."

Then they told me many of the things which my friend the Commissioner had told me on the voyage out, of life in the bush. I listened carefully, cheered once more by the faith and matter-of-factness of those who really knew this strange Sierra Leone.

When, at length, I followed the glow of Brown's lantern back to my house, I found that Amadu and Fode had succeeded in straightening out my mound of equipment, and had my camp bed, a chair, and a table set up, giving the place somewhat of an air. My portable tub was full of water, and after a sponge bath I crept under the mosquito netting and was soon fast asleep.

CHAPTER FOUR

TENDERFOOT IN THE BUSH

THE NEXT MORNING I was up early, anxious to see Kenema. Brown soon appeared, and we started our search for the missing keys in earnest. I had thought that I could find an extra set among my luggage, but a thorough search convinced me that Jock had failed to turn them over.

"Cheer up," said Brown, when I had disconsolately admitted that I didn't have another set, "perhaps they'll arrive on the next train. That will be tomorrow night. In the meantime, you can do anything you like so long as you stay with Sanka."

"Who is Sanka?" I asked.

"He's the court messenger, who has been assigned to you."

"The court messenger?" I asked, still more bewildered. "Sounds like a comic opera."

He then explained that the order of court messengers was, in reality, the native police force. There are about three hundred members in the entire protectorate, a certain number being attached to the office of each District Commissioner. Their duties include escorting the D.C. when he travels, supervising carriers, acting as messengers, guarding specie, assisting in the collection of taxes, escorting prisoners, and, in short, fulfilling all the functions of a police force. The members are recruited from the

West African Frontier Force and the West African Regiment, and competition is keen for every vacancy. The natives have a wholesome respect for authority, and the court messengers, though unarmed, as the embodiment of authority, enjoy tremendous respect among their fellows.

In answer to Brown's call, there appeared a husky native, resplendent in a blue uniform with red trimmings and a wide black leather belt. On his head was perched a red hat which looked like a fez without a tassel. He could speak some English, so we managed to get along very well. It made me feel strange not to be allowed to go around except with a personal bodyguard, but after the novelty had worn off I found Sanka good company, and he had an excellent sense of humor.

Sanka having been properly presented, Brown left me to my own devices. I set out at once on a tour of inspection, with Sanka close at my heels. There was a large rubber grove in the town, and I watched the prisoners removing the milky fluid from buckets set to catch the drips from tubes inserted in the trunks. "For all the world like maple syrup," I thought.

Sanka next conducted me to the village market. Rice, the staple form of diet; plantains, green-looking bananas, kola nuts —bitter tasting things, which the natives regard as a great delicacy—cassava root, sweet potatoes, groundnuts (peanuts), tiny tomatoes, red and green peppers, pawpaws, and oranges. These were all spread about on the ground of a wide central square. The native merchants bowed politely to my guard, and the vendor of kola nuts offered him some of his wares, which Sanka promptly accepted. They seemed to have some of the staying properties of gum or tobacco, for he chewed and chewed, spitting out a thick purple stream which reminded me of tobacco juice. I bought some oranges—or rather Sanka bought some for me—receiving two dozen for twopence (about five cents). In my ignorance I expected Sanka to carry them home, but he grandly ordered them sent; it was beneath his dignity to carry things. I soon learned that if anyone—white or native—wished to maintain his dignity among the natives, he must never carry anything or do anything for himself.

Sanka taught me many things besides the maintenance of dignity. He instructed me in values and prices, information which proved valuable long after I had said good-by to him. The cook, in addition to his duties as a preparer of food, attended to the procuring of food. I didn't trust Fode from the beginning, and I had been told that cooks lived on their masters. I knew from his shifty eyes that Fode would cheat me, but, thanks to Sanka's instruction, his depredations were not as great as they might have been.

Fode was paid three pounds a month, which is high pay for a native. Amadu, though he did far more work than Fode, at first got only a shilling a day, or about a pound and a half a month. This was the regular pay for any labor, except in the more remote places, where a boy would carry a load all day for sixpence. Amadu's position as personal boy gave him higher caste even than that of the cook. He ranked next, in the natives' code, to the court messenger.

Fode led a life of ease at Kenema, for the four white persons saw to it that I was invited out to every meal except breakfast, which was sketchy, anyway, and was no test of Fode's ability as a cook. It was really embarrassing, for I couldn't repay my kind hosts: first, because my equipment was for one only, and I felt diffident about even suggesting the possibility of borrowing, and second, because I feared that perhaps Fode couldn't really cook, and I disliked to find it out when I had company.

One evening Brown invited me to play tennis, for wherever Englishmen were stationed in Sierra Leone, one of the first things built was a tennis court. And here, Brown triumphed over me in great style, for he had been on the team at Oxford, I found out later, and I play the merest dub of a game. We had a lot of fun out of it—or at least I did, for it couldn't have been very exciting for him. He did get his exercise, which is one of the reasons for playing tennis, and he politely said he had enjoyed himself.

And all this time the Ford just sat in solitary glory on the flatcar, its maroon body gleaming under the daily polish lovingly given it by a boy who had been assigned to me to do odd jobs. It looked very nice, but the doors refused to open without the keys and the windows were tight shut.

When the next train arrived, two days later, and still no word of the errant keys, I sent a wire to Jock, to rush the other set to me as fast as possible. Then there didn't seem to be anything more to do except to wait, as patiently as I could, until the set arrived from the Gold Coast, which would be a week, with luck. But perhaps his set wouldn't arrive either; perhaps they, too, would be added to some native's collection of juju trinkets. In the meantime, that stubborn Ford was costing me fifteen dollars a day just to let it sit there in the Kenema railroad siding. The railroad didn't pass flatcars around for nothing.

Brown decided he could do something to save me money, anyway, so he commandeered all the prisoners, and by a process of prying and pushing, lifting and shoving, the car was lifted off onto the ground. Still no keys. Telegrams were sent to postal clerks all along the line. Yes, the keys had been registered and witnesses had seen them put on the train. Then they had vanished.

At last, in desperation, after having consulted all the carpenters and trinket makers, Brown found a man who said that he could open locks. He was a queer-looking fellow who might almost have been confessing rather than announcing an accomplishment. Whatever his past, he did know how to open locks, for after several hours of work, the doors yielded. Then with the help of a native lorry driver, he fussed with the wires and connections, and finally announced that the car would run. To start it, all I had to do was to connect two wires.

To celebrate this victory, Brown drove the car into Kenema, down the main street, with much tooting and clatter, out across a footbridge so narrow that there were only about three inches to spare on each side, and up to my house with a flourish. Everyone stopped and stared, for the only other cars in the town were the trucks used by Syrians for transporting goods.

Now, I could really move on. I would start early tomorrow. My stay in Kenema had given me a chance to explore the near-by hills and look at the rocks, so my week had not been wasted. I had found out something of the difficulties attendant on bush travel. For several mornings, I had risen early, donning my khaki shorts and light-weight wool khaki shirt, on the back of which was buttoned a spine pad, to keep my spinal column from the sun, for it is through one's spine that sunstroke often comes. The spine pad is a wadded pad which buttons across the shoulders and again above the belt, thereby protecting with a layer the whole of the spine, especially that part of the shoulders on which the sun beats. Then, with my army-type sun helmet, which had a long extension to protect the back of my neck so that I wouldn't get sunstroke when leaning over to look at rocks, I was ready to trek into the forest. Already the jungle had left its mark. My knees and arms were striped with cuts from the so-called sword grass. This was all my own fault, for I had sleeves which could roll down, as well as shorts which could be let down, the latter having a six-inch hem held in place by buttons. I hadn't bothered to cover my knees or arms the first day, never dreaming that the innocent-looking grass through which we passed was cutting my skin. Sanka first drew my attention to my bleeding arms and legs: I had only felt perspiration. Alarmed, he pointed to my cuts, then to the sword grass: "It no be fit for white man," he muttered. Undoubtedly he was right, for his own skin showed not the slightest puncture.

But in spite of the sword grass and the thorns, I loved the forest, its beauty, its quiet, and the feeling of aloneness which it gave me. Yet I was never alone, for Sanka always accompanied me on these rambles. The early hours, between six and eight, were the nicest. Then it was possible to walk without a sun helmet, and I could swing forward, not yet weary and stumbling over the rough ground. The shiny leaves of the thick foliage looked almost like laurel and felt cool as my bare knees brushed them. The creepers were a game, to be dodged successfully. The treacherous sword grass could be avoided either by jumping over it or by holding my notebook in front of my knees. The backward drag of the leg, which I soon mastered, became a habit at this time of day, thereby preventing the sword grass from giving a final vicious cut just as I cleared it. I learned how to avoid thorns instinctively. Many plants, especially the dainty-looking fern and palm, have thorns on them as part of their protective mechanism. No flies or mosquitoes were about at this early hour—just beauty in the forest and a new vista, with every bend of the path, beckoning forward into the jungle; on, into a clearing, where the natives had brushed a farm; a momentary view of distant hills and a breath of fresh air, instead of the musty, damp, rotting smell of the forest. Very little life stirred as I walked along. I felt at one with the world, a world which went on forever, with now and then a village in a series of close-ringed huts, huddled together as if afraid of the vastness of the surrounding forest. Occasionally a bird, startled, flitted past, its color matching the gray-greenness of the trees; the bright-colored birds were visible only in the clearings. All the life of the woods, sensitive to the least sound, had word of our coming long before we were in sight. There was quiet as we passed.

Only the monkeys were too curious to let a stranger go unchallenged. How they scolded at me! Perhaps I seemed different to them, for they never bothered with the natives. Most probably the unprecedented noise made by a white person was what attracted them. They wanted to make sure who I was and why.

Once there was a loud chatter, a hitting of chests, then silence. It was a troupe of chimpanzees, Sanka said. When the leader of a troupe of monkeys spotted me, there was a whistle-like call, followed by an excited chattering in all directions. This was the call for the troupe to break up and scamper for safety. When I finally passed near where they were hiding, I could spot a pair of eyes peering down at me. I could see the body quiver but make no move. Erect and rigid, tail stuck up straight, ready to direct flight in any direction if I should prove an enemy. Tightly clasping a limb with all fours, head bent down, with a wise and scornful smirk, as if saying, "You poor soul, only two feet to carry you; helpless, for whom a path must be cut. Just watch me, anywhere, up and down, the forest is mine." Indeed, I felt like an intruder as I sat down on a log and watched them move toward me, pause while they studied the strange creature, then away, as if I were not worth further trouble.

As the day grew hot and oppressive, the forest seemed to pant with the heat. Even the monkeys succumbed. We turned homeward. I was no longer interested in my forest friends, nor in the rocks. My high hobnailed boots weighted me down.

I had planned my trip with the D.C.'s help to cover as much territory as possible near the roads so that I might study good cross sections of that part of the country. Now that I was to start next day, a farewell dinner was given in my honor. After dinner, maps were again brought out, and final arrangements for forwarding my mail to certain points along my route by special messenger were gone over. It was then that the D.C. announced that he couldn't let me go with just Amadu and Fode. He said I must take a court messenger too. I had already acquired the D.C.'s dog, a huge Airedale named Buster. I needed a watchdog, and anyway the D.C. was going on leave soon and someone would have to take the dog. I had mentally calculated the expansive qualities of my car, and had decided that I could manage with Amadu and Fode in the front seat, and Buster on the baggage piled in the rear. But what to do with another man? In vain I told the D.C. I could manage without a court messenger. He was adamant. Finally I gave in, on condition that he would pick a thin man for the job. He kept his word. A veritable skeleton appeared the next morning and saluted smartly. He did not look as though he would be much protection, but he was certainly thin. He said his name was Abou.

I had had breakfast at dawn, and was busy supervising the packing of my goods when Fode appeared, looking horrified. He could never find English words when he was excited, so I followed him, wondering what had happened. He gazed fixedly at the car, and looking in his direction I saw that something was wrong with the tires. Flat? Bulging? What was it? As I drew nearer I saw that great swarms of driver ants, literally millions of them, were clustered on each wheel, on the tires, and all over the ground. I had been warned about driver ants, the scavengers of tropical countries. They move in armies, billions at a time, filing along in a black line, twenty or so abreast, held in rank by large warrior ants, pushing them along, keeping them in order. Sometimes it takes half a day for one of these armies to pass. Food, refuse, anything in their way which is edible disappears in no time, as the hordes surround it, spreading out in a clearing, then pushing off in battle array to a new field. Dogs and even people have been devoured alive by these jungle pests.

They are eating the rubber, I thought, and could have wept with vexation. We went to open the car door but couldn't get near it, for the ants swarmed up our legs, and we did a merry dance before we could get rid of them. There was nothing to do but wait and watch helplessly while the ants ate the tires and left the poor old car sitting on its rims.

I had said good-by to everyone the night before, planning to get off early. I had promised myself I would make no more trouble for Brown, but now there seemed nothing to do but call for his help again. He came running up, as excited as I. Neither he nor the boys had ever seen such a sight before. As we watched, long-faced, Amadu noticed a few long dark ribbonlike lines under the car.

"They go for bush," he cried excitedly. Sure enough, the driver ants were winding off, slowly but steadily. For a solid hour the file went on, until at last the tires were bare and—wonder of wonders—still whole. The ants had merely spent the night there! The boys swore that driver ants never sleep—that they had never before seen them sleep. Whether it was something about the rubber—perhaps it was warm and dry—I shall never know, for it never happened again.

When the last ant had gone, the loading began; Brown

superintended the job and did a good one. He discarded the tent; I would just have to depend on resthouses, and leave the tent at Kenema for the present. Fode was put in the back seat and around him were piled bedroll, boxes, bundles, odds and ends, until the pile neared the roof. A two-foot hole was all I could spare for Buster. She was shown this hole, gave it a knowing look, and crawled up, delighted. All the leftovers were piled up on the running board.

Finally, I climbed in, followed by Amadu and the slim court messenger. Brown repeated his instructions that I must positively keep to my schedule as planned. Otherwise, I might find the resthouses occupied, and if word came to Kenema that I had not reached a stated town by a certain date they would send out a search party. I realized then that they felt me to be a great responsibility. They were not used to having women geologists working alone in the West African bush.

We were off at last through the forest, traveling along a dirt road which was well packed and narrow. As there was no traffic, it took only a few hours to reach Lago, the town near the chromium deposit which was just being opened up and was my first objective. I stopped at a store owned and run by a French syndicate. This was one of a chain of stores scattered along the railroad, and the man in charge, a Frenchman, was the chief local trader. I was politely received, and told I might leave my car in the company's shed while I trekked up the near-by mountain to the mine. It seemed funny to be talking French, away out here on the edge of the jungle.

Abou took charge of the loads and turned them over to carriers who had been sent to meet me from the mine. Life was easier than I had anticipated.

CHAPTER FIVE

CHROMIUM

WE WERE READY to start in a few minutes, our retinue advancing in single file through the village, the carriers singing as they moved, balancing my bulky bundles on their heads. Abou managed everything perfectly. He brought up the end of our procession, strutting along, waving a stout stick, apparently quite able to handle the situation.

A mile or so beyond the village, I heard a noise of many voices, as though a crowd were pursuing us. The shouting and sound of running drew rapidly nearer. Startled, I quickened my pace. What was going to happen? I had studied the map carefully and knew there were still several miles, including a steep climb up a mountain, before we could reach the chromite mine camp. There was no use trying to get away from the mob; we must face them and hope in some way to placate them. Beads of perspiration stood out all over my forehead; was my stay in Sierra Leone going to end before it had fairly begun?

The crowd caught up with us. Abou looked slimmer than ever, and for a moment I longed for Sanka, my stalwart guard in Kenema. Abou spoke with authority and great dignity to the first man who caught up with us. After a moment's conversation, he turned to me and said, "The woman chief na village come to greet missus. Missus go wait."

So that was it. I wondered what the proper procedure was. I had forgotten to ask. As we waited, the men and children crowded around, eying me solemnly and exchanging remarks which, of course, I could not understand. Now I knew how the freaks at the circus must feel. I tried to appear unconcerned under this unswerving scrutiny, but was relieved when the chieftainess came. The crowd drew back respectfully. We stared at each other for several moments. Obviously, she was as embarrassed as I. She hadn't much in her costume to distinguish her from the other native women, for in her hurry to see the white woman, she had not stopped to put on any of her finery or the symbols of her position. She was perspiring freely, and her disarrayed pigtails stuck down from a striped silk bandanna which was tied around her head. Her only other clothing was a blue and white native cloth wound around her body. Despite all this, she bore herself with that undisguisable something which marks the leader, whether man or woman. I wasn't much to look at, either—khaki shirt, shorts, hobnailed boots, and golf stockings; my head was hidden beneath my sun helmet. I couldn't help wondering if I were as great a disappointment to her as she was to me.

On a chance, I extended my hand, and she brushed my palms twice. Evidently this was the customary greeting—the equivalent of a handshake. She spoke in a very soft voice, and Abou, now in his element, standing at attention beside me, translated.

"The chief, he presents his compliments. He pleased to greet big chief."

"Tell the chief, missus glad to see one woman so fine chief," I replied. "She pleased that a woman makes such a fine chief."

This apparently was just what I should have said, though I felt that Abou enlarged upon my words, for he spoke at great length and apparently with eloquence, for everyone, especially the chief, seemed tremendously pleased.

Then followed questions as to where I was going, how long I was going to stay, how I liked her country, until I knew exactly how a visiting celebrity to the United States feels when the reporters question him as he sails up New York harbor. At that time I was not versed in the art of cutting short a meeting of this kind, so we stood there at least twenty minutes before I had the bright idea of shaking hands again. Apparently this was the signal for departure, for the chieftainess turned and beckoned to a follower, who produced a calabash filled with rice, four eggs, and a fine-looking rooster. This was a "dash," a gift of friendship, about which I had been told. I was expected to return the compliment with a dash of money. This was a regular part of the ceremonial connected with visitors. Later, I discovered that a chief frequently gave me food I did not need, just because he desired my money dash. I tried a policy of returning such white elephants and found that the chief did not mind. I did not know what to do with the chieftainess's present, but Abou solved the problem by volunteering that the boy who was carrying it take it up to the mine for me. I produced three shillings as my dash. Abou gave me back one shilling, saying that two would suffice. I was somewhat embarrassed at this, but the chieftainess did not appear to be in the least upset, and we parted friends.

As we walked on, I asked the court messenger if there were many women chiefs. His answer was that there were a few, for inheritance was often through the chief's eldest sister. If she had no sons, she herself might be elected chief, as was the case here in Lago. Abou went on to tell me a little about the native

Individual resthouses in the hinterland for the use of visiting government officials or other white travelers.

Abou and Sanka, "court messengers," with Sanka's family in their Sunday best.

government, explaining that small villages are ruled by head-men. Several of these headmen are ruled by a chief of a larger village. Ruling over a great number of chiefs is the paramount chief. He is a real king, having a province which covers a com-paratively large area containing many villages. He is all-powerful. Sometimes there are several paramount chiefs in a tribe. They are responsible to no one except the government District Commissioner, to whom they are answerable for the good behavior of their people. The paramount chief is spoken of as "the chief." He collects taxes for the government, obtain-ing a certain portion of the five shillings head tax for his trouble. Most of the chiefdoms are inherited, the number dif-fering from tribe to tribe; some few are elected. I gathered that the chieftainess I had just met could be put in the class of headman.

Abou and I soon got ahead of the carriers. All this time we were climbing, shut in by trees; suddenly we came out into a clearing on the mountainside. This was the chromite mine camp, which consisted of four buildings—a good-sized, grass-covered mud house, a tiny kitchen, a boys' hut, and a tool shed. There was no one in sight except one boy, who stared. He made no move to greet me, so I walked into the house. It consisted of two rooms, separated by an open space over which the thatched roof extended. The open space was dining room, liv-ing room, and workroom combined. One of the rooms be-longed to Smith, the white manager of the mine, who was out of camp when I arrived, so when the carriers came I took possession of the other section of the building. Smith's boy brought me an orange squash—a sweetish, preserved concoc-tion, into which he siphoned soda.

After I had cleaned up a bit, I sat down in a comfortable camp chair, and looked out across the clearing. There were a few palm trees, but all the weeds had been carefully pulled up, leaving bare a red soil, which contrasted strikingly with the dark green background of mahogany trees. Beyond, miles and miles of green blanketed the world as far as I could see. Away to the east were hills, which the boys said were in Liberia. No roads, no villages could be seen: only this green forest carpet, stretching away to the sky line. Life was very pleasant.

Suddenly my reveries were cut short by a scurrying noise and a digging of nails into my legs. I was too paralyzed to move, and called for a boy. He appeared, just as a furry beast arrived in my lap.

"That na mongoose. He no bite."

I was relieved but still somewhat suspicious of the strange, long-nosed creature, furry, like a woodchuck, but smaller, which sat on my knee, wrinkling his snout at me and evidently prepared to regard me with distrust. Another clutching, and a second mongoose arrived to look me over.

"He na brudder."

"Any more?" I asked, not daring to move.

"No sah."

Having decided that I could be trusted, the little animals snuggled down behind my back, between me and the canvas chair.

After a short time, Smith arrived, introduced himself, and called for tea. He was a much younger man than I had expected and lacked the beard with which my imagination garbed the solitary miner. Much to Smith's annoyance, his boy served him first. The poor boy was puzzled when he received a calling-down for following his natural instinct of serving his master first. Smith passed me a cookie, which I took and held idly. Suddenly it was snatched from my hand and off it went down my leg, in Mr. Mongoose's mouth. His bright-eyed brother gave my hand a gentle nip to remind me that he needed a cookie, just as much as did his brother.

"These saucy beasts expect to be fed first," laughed Smith, "missus or no missus."

And before we could go on with our tea, the boy had to give them milk from a tin and some cookies. Dusk was on us before we finished. As soon as the gasoline lamp was lighted, the rascals crawled up on the table and curled around its base, sleepily yawning in the warmth, while Smith and I argued at great length whether they were "mongeese" or "mongooses." We did not settle the argument, as there was no dictionary in camp, but when I got to such luxuries I looked it up and found "mongooses" correct. As I lay awake that night, under my net, I could hear them exploring the grass roof, hunting for snakes. They are one of the few animals that delight in killing snakes. Swift and clever, they dart in at the snake's throat, miraculously avoiding the fangs.

Although called the "chromite mine," this place was not a mine yet—merely a prospect being explored. Smith showed me the workings, where trenches and pits were uncovering the chromite. Chromite is not a common ore, but is a valuable one, increasingly in demand as an alloy for use in making chromium steels. Hence, the company who owned this mine hoped to be able to find sufficient quantities for export. As chromium is rare, and the ore had been exposed in a network of trenches, I spent a whole day studying the deposit and the rock surrounding it. The following days were put to advantage in the near neighborhood by following the various hunters' trails that radiated into the forest from camp. Most of these trails were poor, but a few boys with machetes could clear the way in front of me as fast as I could walk; when I wanted to go where there were no paths, they would slash through the creepers and undergrowth. This took much longer, but we struggled through, even if it took all day; time was nothing.

Smith knew a lot about mining and geology, and at night we discussed the various problems that had arisen. Five days of this gave me confidence. The tropics were not so bad after all— a little hotter and more humid than I had ever experienced; more thorns and insects; thicker soils; many poisonous snakes, but always a boy at my side to do the killing. I found I was standing the heat better each day; at night I took five grains of quinine and slept under a net. It was not hard to develop a routine of rising before dawn so as to set out with the first light. I could work steadily in the cool hours of the day and often until late afternoon, without becoming exhausted. I found that I liked the life, the natives, and the work.

The time allotted to my stay at the chromium mine passed quickly. When I headed back to Lago, I felt like an old-timer, a hardened "Coaster," as the white people who go out to West Africa are called. The chieftainess did not even come out to see me, for I was an old story by now. She had satisfied her curiosity. But the villagers were on hand to watch us pile into the Ford. We were off for my next stopping point, forty miles away, where there was a resthouse in the village of Gandorhun in which I was to stay a few days. Abou knew the country well, so I didn't have to get out my map. When we reached the village, Abou directed me to pass through to the far end. We drove between rows of round thatch-roofed mud huts, with here and there a tin-roofed store, until we left the limits of the town; beyond was a pointed, thatch-roofed hut set off by itself. This was the resthouse, I was informed. The railway resthouse seemed like a hotel compared to this small mud structure, perched in the middle of a well-cleared grass plot.

The resthouses upcountry were all thatch-roofed mud houses,

in all states of repair, maintained by the various chiefs for the use of government officials visiting their districts. Each chief was responsible for the condition of his resthouse. In fact, he was ordered to build it by the District Commissioner, who was stationed as the head of that particular province or locality. The D.C. usually picked a convenient spot, on a well-drained bit of land, away from the noise of the village. Then a round, or sometimes square, mud structure with an especially high, thick roof of thatch was built. Attached to the resthouse, sometimes by a small covered passage, was the cookhouse, where the cook established himself, native-fashion, built his wood fire, and cooked as well as he could. As all government officials carried their beds, chairs, and all their equipment with them on trek, the houses were unfurnished. Other white people besides government officials might take advantage of these resthouses, but they were expected to give the chief a small dash for the maintenance of them.

No sooner had we descended from the Ford than the few carefully barred windows and the two doors of the resthouse were opened by the chief's messenger, who arrived almost as soon as we did, for the chief had seen the car go through the town. A veranda to serve as dining room and a small kitchen hut completed the establishment. The term "kitchen" is capable of wide interpretation, I discovered. Any place where cooking is done is the "kitchen." Even if it was only under a tree, Amadu would speak of going to the kitchen. This resthouse was maintained for the use of the D.C., who visited this particular district once or twice a year, to hold court or collect taxes.

Before we had had time to do more than look around, the chief himself arrived, with a bevy of followers—women, their heads crowned with calabashes of water from which the liquid slopped down over their faces, and boys with straw mats. The water was presented to the cook, and the mats were scattered about on the mud floor, to make the hut look more habitable and to keep down the dust. While the chief watched eagerly, Amadu and Fode, supervised by Abou, unloaded the car. Buster sniffed the chief, and, deciding that everything was all right, chose the central mat, right in everyone's way, and promptly went to sleep. My bed, canvas table, and camp chair looked rather pathetic, stranded in the middle of the big room. Most persons had more baggage than I. The Ford, with real glass windows, made up for my lack of loads, however, and made me appear as important as other masters who had visited there in the past.

Abou spoke fiercely, and everyone disappeared in the direction of the village. I was informed that the chief would return later, bringing me a dash. After eating, as I sat lazily looking out from my veranda dining room, I heard a low monotonous chant from the kitchen. It was Amadu, washing the dishes— he never let Fode touch them. Over and over again the slow wail rose and fell. I wondered what it could be and finally made out the words:

"My mother is dead,
My father is dead,
We have no bread today."

Strangely enough, Amadu usually sang this when he was particularly happy and contented!

I felt sluggish and lazy; it was much nicer to sit still and dream than to stir about. This would never do, however, if I was to study the country about here in three days, according to my schedule. So I sent for Abou, who was finally found in the village; he appeared to be a little put out when he found that his duties for the day weren't over.

Having put my camera, compass, map, notebook, and first-aid kit into a shoulder-strap knapsack, I gave them, together with a three-pound sledge hammer, to Abou. He took the bundle reluctantly, and off we started.

As we passed through the streets of the village, between two rows of thatched houses, Abou grabbed a young boy out of the crowd. The boy recoiled at the touch of the hand of authority. I heard a few words, and the boy's look of alarm changed to a grin of triumph, as he shouldered the knapsack and rested the sledge hammer on his bare head. So that was the game! Forced labor, perhaps, but it didn't look very reluctant as it trotted behind us, ragged shirttail—his only garment—streaming after him. Abou next acquired a machete—I didn't see from whom. This is a sharp-bladed steel knife, resembling an elongated meat cleaver, which is used for cutting down trees, creepers, or any obstructions, big or little. Probably he felt safer with this protection.

I was glad to get away from the village and onto a path. The village was dirty, though from a distance the little round and square huts, with their pointed thatched roofs, were picturesque and did not suggest the squalor which surrounded them. There were flies, chickens everywhere underfoot; the heat of the sun beat down, with no trees to break its strength; and the ever-present mobs of staring natives, who pressed close to look at this strange white missus. Poor Buster didn't like villages either, for the goats chased her and native curs barked and tried to fight. She ignored everything, keeping close to my heels. She, too, was relieved to leave all this behind and get into the woods, where her hunting instincts took her off the path, her shaggy coat protecting her from the thorns, as she crashed noisily through the dense growth, telling any lurking animals that she was coming, long before she reached them. She was awkward and noisy, just as I was, not like the soft-footed native and his sly dog, both of whom were versed in jungle lore.

We stepped out briskly, for this was a well-traveled trail, with no creepers to interfere. Bare rocks were not common, but whenever we found an outcrop, I'd have the boy knock off a fresh piece in order to see what it really was like inside. They all looked alike on top—dark green, mossy, fungus growths covering them. Besides the rocks themselves, I studied their position in relation to the country as a whole. I took measurements with my compass, to the awe and wonder of Abou and the boy, who regarded the instrument as some powerful magic, or juju. The wonder of it showed in their faces as it was gingerly handed to me whenever I asked for it. I did other things which seemed strange to them—most of the rock fragments which they had knocked off I threw away, but some distinctive types were carefully labeled and wrapped in paper bags from the supply in my knapsack. Sometimes I wrote notes in a book, after looking at the rock, as a record of my observations.

I had been so engrossed in my work that I was surprised when Abou suggested that we had better return if we were to make the resthouse before dark. We hurried back, but it was quite dark before we reached the house, where I was greeted with the welcome "Baf leddy" (bath ready) from Amadu. My square canvas tub had been set up, and I made short work of the sponging, which was what a bath really was. This ritual accomplished, I completed the ceremony by putting on my pajamas, my mosquito boots, and over them a blouse and skirt, and I was dressed for dinner and the evening. For an appetizer I had orangeade, with which I tried in vain to kill the bitter taste of the evening dose of quinine.

And then Amadu brought in "chop" (food). For me there

was chicken soup with rice. It was good. While I sipped it, Amadu appeared with a strange-looking dish in his hand. "Buster's chop," he said. And surely no dog ever was served with a fancier dish—a series of chicken bones, arranged concentrically on top of a great bowl of rice, and scattered about were odd pieces of chicken fat and skin. Buster crunched the bones and made way with the rice, hearty approval written all over her satisfied countenance. I had forgotten to give orders concerning her food. But the boys knew that when master ate supper, master's dog also ate. This was the custom of the country. A dog was an excuse for more rice in the kitchen, I was to learn; a chance for the boys to live a little better themselves. So they liked Buster.

After supper, the chief, a wizened old chap, attended by the whole village, made me a visit. I received him, sitting in my deck chair, and he sat down on a stool which someone produced. He liked Buster.

"He be big too much. He be fine past all. Missus go dash him to the chief?"

So that was the game. I parried by asking if he wanted to "chop" Buster.

The crowd laughed, and, although the old chief assured me that he had no such intentions, he rolled his eyes and I thought I could see his mouth water as he looked at sturdy Buster, for in this country they ate dogs.

I looked over my stock of dash, and selected two bracelets, made of brightly colored celluloid squares, strung on elastic. The chief accepted them, politely, but didn't look as if he really felt particularly pleased. Then suddenly he discovered that the elastic snapped. He pulled at the bracelet and snapped it back, his eyes getting bigger and bigger. There was no longer any question as to his delight with the gift. The last I saw of him that night he was skipping down the road like a child, despite his obviously many years, snapping the elastic, and followed by his pleased and wondering retinue.

As soon as the chief left, Abou appeared, holding a great blue trench coat, and informed me that he was going to sleep at my door. Brown had given strict orders not to leave me night or day, and he meant to obey. He was accompanied by a native, who was, he said, the watchman. So he curled up out on the veranda, and the watchman built himself a fire just beyond. The excitement of being out on my own and the strangeness of it all kept me from sleep; I lay there listening to the snores of the court messenger, Abou, doing his best to drown out the chant of the bullfrogs and the rasping of the crickets, while the flickering shadows of the watchman's fire added an un-canny aspect to the scene. That was the last night I allowed him to sleep within earshot.

Four weeks passed with this same routine, resthouse to rest-house. One day was much like another. Gradually, I was get-ting the picture of the area as a whole, so that when Christ-mastime came I was able to leave this section of Sierra Leone, feeling that I knew its general geology fairly well.

Before going to Sefadu, where I planned to meet Miss Carey for Christmas, I visited Kailahun, going from there to the place on the Meli River which marks the spot where French Guinea, Liberia, and Sierra Leone meet. The river looked like any other torrent, but it marked an invisible dividing line between countries. I could have stepped across the river on stones and been in Liberia.

At Kailahun, I saw the Kissi pennies for the first time. These are thin iron rods, sixteen inches long, twisted and forged by hand. They are the currency of the area, being interchangeable in the three countries. A dozen of them make a shilling. I watched a native parade into market carrying on his head a squealing pig, neatly bound with raffia, and return home, with the pig replaced by a great bundle of these pennies. It would not be easy to steal a fortune under such circumstances.

This was one of the few places left where bartering was done with tokens. Elsewhere, English money was being rapidly introduced or straight barter was carried on. Gone were the days when the natives buried their few pennies under a tree. At least, they were gone wherever mining had sprung up. And the change from barter to coinage took place overnight. Yet in many places the rate of exchange was still something like this:

$$12 \text{ eggs} = 1 \text{ fowl}$$
$$3 \text{ fowl} = 1 \text{ duck}$$
$$6 \text{ ducks} = 1 \text{ goat}$$
$$3 \text{ goats} = 1 \text{ cow}$$
$$2 \text{ or } 3 \text{ cows} = 1 \text{ woman}$$

Women were rated as the most valuable marketable commodity in the native's land.

CHAPTER SIX

CHRISTMAS

I FELT LIKE an old-timer the day I drove out of the forest country, northward to Sefadu. It was six weeks since I had said good-by to Miss Carey in Freetown, and now it was almost Christmas, and we were to meet at the resthouse in Sefadu. As I approached the government headquarters of this northern province, I found this to be high, open country, with picturesque, bare, granite hills covered with great rounded boulders. Elephant grass, thirteen feet high, reminding me of cornstalks, waved gently as far as the eye could see, the brownish-green tops looking like a western prairie scene. Above the grass, here and there rose isolated, flat-topped, thorny trees. This was the so-called "orchard bush" country. As I drew near Sefadu, I saw a large house, high on a hill, artistically surrounded by beautiful vines and carefully landscaped gardens. This, I knew, would be the D.C.'s house. The messenger pointed out the barracks, a row of round mud-covered huts at the base of the hill, fresh in new whitewash. Even the native village was well planned. It was clean, with no foul odors. Sefadu impressed me greatly, perhaps because it was so well laid out and was not shut in by the steadily encroaching jungle, ever seeking to reclaim its own.

Lane, the D.C., welcomed me cordially and ordered tea served on a little terrace overlooking the valley. I might have been in an English garden except for the strangeness of the bright pink and yellow flowers and the noiseless, white-clad blacks, scurrying in and out, anticipating every demand of their master.

"Miss Carey will be here in a few days," said Lane, "and I've asked all the white men, mostly traders, between here and the railroad to come and help us celebrate Christmas in style."

"Mercy," I cried, "where will you put them all?"

"It isn't as bad as it sounds," he said with a laugh. "All the white men are only five. The court messengers are making a tennis court for our amusement. And the villagers are putting up some shimbeks there on the hill."

"Shimbeks?" I queried.

"Come, I'll show you."

Shimbeks turned out to be low palm-leaf shelters, temporary affairs but quite adequate as shelter. In addition, a "bari," which is something like a summerhouse, had been constructed. It is round, without side walls, but with a heavily thatched roof and a low, fencelike wall, or balustrade, to give it an artistic finish. Miss Carey and I were to have the resthouse.

Dinner, by candlelight, with a centerpiece of vivid poinsettias, took me completely out of the tropics. Lace doilies on a shining mahogany table, a victrola being played—this must be England. And spinach to eat! I ate ravenously. Lane enjoyed my delight.

"Spinach," he explained, "occurs as eleven varieties of greens, and is anything from the tops of sweet potatoes to edible grasses. But it is all spinach to us."

He called the boy and ordered that "spinach" be served at every meal. When the boy looked startled, he said gravely:

"The missus is different from an English missus. She comes from a strange faraway tribe who eat nothing much but spinach."

The boy looked at me strangely, but bowed, and every meal thereafter I had spinach. Lane told me that when his wife had been out she had made him eat spinach until he was sick of it, and when she had left he had ordered that spinach was never to be served again until a missus came.

For a long time we sat there talking, mostly of England and the world outside Sierra Leone, for Lane was hungry for news. My two-months-old news was recent to him, for he had been isolated in Sefadu for almost a year.

Dawn was just streaking the eastern sky the next morning when Lane's boy appeared at the resthouse to say that his master was going on a tour of inspection and would I like to go, too. I was just about to set out to do some geological reconnaissance work, but I accepted the invitation. After we had inspected the shimbeks, the tennis court, and the barracks, Lane turned to me and said:

"Wouldn't you like to drive over to Jaiama? It is only ten miles away, and the mission is run by your fellow Americans. They are looking forward to seeing you."

"What fun!" I said.

"More fun for me than you can guess," he replied. "You see, usually I have to go alone on my motor-bike. A ride in a car will be a real treat. Let's eat breakfast right away." I was Lane's guest for meals, on his insistence. He hated to eat alone.

Breakfast over, off we went, with a court messenger, Buster, and Lane's two dogs on the back seat.

The Americans were from Kansas. And if Sefadu was Africa according to English ideas, Jaiama was Africa according to American. They welcomed us with unfeigned delight, and showed me the mission and the new village that was being built, the carpenter shop, and the sewing classes. They insisted that we stay for lunch, and when I found myself at a table with a big dish of fruit salad, with lettuce and real mayonnaise, I was so happy I could have danced a jig. When I voiced my delight, my hostess looked pleased and assured me that she had personally washed the lettuce three times in potassium permanganate solution, and that I need have no fear about eating it. Lane looked askance at such a combination of food—fruit salad, lettuce, and mayonnaise—no wonder Americans seemed queer. And then, to finish up in style, we had an apple pie.

Lane and our host discussed the dictionary of the Konno language—this was Konno country—which Lane, master of many native dialects, was writing. All too soon it was time for Lane and me to return to Sefadu.

While we waited for the guests to arrive for Christmas, I managed to get some geological work done in the country surrounding the settlement. Here I had my first encounters with elephant grass. During the driest season—in January and February—when the hot Sahara winds (harmattan) blow off the desert from the north, the grass dies, and great fires frequently sweep the region.

"Then you can just walk anywhere," said Lane. "But since now is not then, I shall send six boys with you, to flatten down the grass so you can walk."

So we set out, the boys crushing down the grass, just as do the elephants who inhabit the country to the north. It was hard work finding a rock, and those that we did find were all granite.

On the second day of our explorations we came to a river, across which was swung a queer-looking structure, over which the boys scampered like monkeys, but which I found somewhat precarious. It was what is known as a "hammock bridge." High above the water, great creepers, bound together in a net-like structure, are swung across the river from one great mahogany tree to another on the opposite shore. Bamboo poles, tied together, form the footwalk. It looked thoroughly unsafe and decidedly rickety. I would have preferred to use a hollowed-out tree-trunk canoe, but there wasn't any. Neither was there a raft. It was far too deep to be carried pickaback, as was my usual method of being ferried across a small stream. There was nothing to do but to cross. I felt, as I swayed in the branches, as though I could never reach the other side. The water looked very far below. But at last I was over. Buster started, but turned back, preferring to swim across rather than take such chances.

Miss Carey arrived by lorry, which carried the mail, after a two-day train trip from Freetown. The other guests turned up Christmas Eve. Never have I seen a man as excited as Lane was over their advent. He couldn't be blamed, surely, for he hadn't seen so many whites since he had left Freetown, eleven months before, and he did love company.

After a gay dinner, Lane decided to open his Christmas mail, so we all gathered on the terrace and helped him perform his pleasurable task. After he had opened his personal presents, there were gifts for all the members of his household. Mrs. Lane had forgotten no one, not even the mission children, whose gifts were sent off immediately by messenger.

The various members of his household were summoned and were presented with their gifts. The personal boy's wife received some beads, which caused her to grin broadly. She got down on her knees before her master, bowed her head twice to the ground, and begged him to send thanks to the missus for the beautiful present.

The cook's wife wept—never in all her life had she seen

Miss Carey and Buster against a background of elephant grass at Sefadu.

Native women preparing chop.

such beautiful cloth as the missus had sent her for a gown. It was black silk with a flowery design in gold thread, and fresh off a Manchester loom. The woman stared at the pile of silk, tears streaming down her face. Lane told her to drape the cloth around her, so we could see how it would look. Handing the bundle to the cook to hold, she undid her skirt, unknotting it in front, and before we realized fully what she was doing, she began removing layer after layer of different-colored petticoats and skirts, a pile collecting at her feet, until Lane, in consternation, commanded her to desist. Evidently, she had reached the proper layer by this time, for she stopped, and wound the dazzling gold and black about her. The boys' eyes popped at the beauty of the gaudy material.

Lane turned over the arrangement of things for Christmas Day to Miss Carey and me. It was a busy time for us, for we meant to do the day and ourselves justice. Late in the afternoon, accompanied by a court messenger, we went out to pick the Christmas decorations. These consisted of shiny leaves and red berries, which we tried to arrange so that they resembled holly. Then we had garlands of delicate fern fronds, which we strewed on the table and the mud walls. Poinsettialike flowers and some white-leaved plants completed the floral decorations. All we lacked was mistletoe, for which we could not seem to find a substitute.

The dinner itself was a triumph. At Lane's request, Miss Carey had brought a huge box, packed in ice and sawdust, from the cold-storage plant at Freetown, and in it we found fresh fish, a turkey, butter, English tomatoes, and—final joy— cranberries. Lane's own garden produced a little poor lettuce, but it made a good garnish for salad. Miss Carey produced the Christmas pudding, which her mother had sent out from England. This was served with burning brandy, to the delight of the guests and the dismay of the poor scared boy whose lot it was to carry it. There were drinks, too—cocktails, and wines during dinner, and whisky for the men after we two women had retired to the living room.

When the gentlemen rejoined us, there were gifts from the mission to be opened. The one which gave me the greatest pleasure was a box of popcorn. The others, unfamiliar with this great American institution, regarded my enthusiasm apathetically; but when we moved out to the bari, where a campfire had been lighted, they watched with amazement the transformation which the unexciting little brown kernels underwent. The poor court messenger, who had been delegated to shake the pot in which the corn was popped, thought the kernels were bewitched, and would have run to the village if Lane had not restrained him. Even when he saw us eating the white flakes without any visible harm, he was loath to try a kernel. Once tried, however, he seemed to enjoy it, for his eyes sparkled when he was given more. Now, at last, he was a partaker of the white man's magic. What tales he would have to tell!

We lingered around the dying campfire, watching a glorious full moon set as the sun rose.

The three days that followed were happy ones for all of us. Miss Carey and I planned the meals, trying to make them as much like home as possible. The men played tennis, and then came in to afternoon tea, just as if they were in England. All too soon, the time came to part.

It was decided that Miss Carey would drive as far as Bo with me, and that we would send our loads by lorry to the train, accompanied by Fode and Miss Carey's boys. Amadu, Buster, and Abou would be our escort. When crammed into the back of the car, together with duffel bags of beds and bedding and food for a day, the poor little Ford didn't have an inch to spare. We reached Bo at four-thirty, the longest trip I ever took in Sierra Leone—a hundred and fifty miles in nine and a half hours—after a cramped, hot ride. The train arrived at five-thirty, but no boys and no loads. They had missed the train! This was a fine mess, but Amadu, with his usual efficiency, directed us to the railroad resthouse, and some white officials gallantly came to our rescue with food for the evening meal.

At seven the next morning, I waved good-by to Miss Carey, as the train for Freetown slowly moved out. I hated to see her go, for I had enjoyed the visit, but I had so much to do that I had no time for regrets. She had brought me word of the Governor's decision to permit me to map the iron ores in the closed area, far to the north of the country where I had been. This was the area, some thirty miles long and twenty miles wide, which the head of the Mines Department had discussed with me in Freetown. I knew that he was anxious to have this region properly mapped.

Reports of iron ore had caused various English mining companies to make inquiries. The government had closed a large area to prospectors, and an adequate map, showing the exact location and the extent of the deposits, was urgently needed. The head of the Mines Department had sent a letter by Miss Carey stating that I was to map the ores, starting as soon after January first as possible. She had brought me maps, such as there were, which would do for base maps. She also brought word that a headman, Johnny Boy by name, who had been on trek with white men before, and who spoke English, would meet me at Magburaka, the railroad station nearest the deposits, to help with my carriers. The work would take me six weeks at least, all on my own in the untouched interior, where few white men had ever trod, and probably no white woman.

After I had seen Miss Carey off, I made the rounds of the various government officials at Bo, to find out anything I could about the iron ore region.

Before leaving Bo, I visited the government hospital to see if I could find something to cure my legs, which were covered with horrid raw sores caused by the sword grass. The doctor in charge gave me some salve but said he thought probably they would not heal until I left the tropics. He was right. But on my two subsequent trips I had no such trouble, so that evidently I built up an immunity, which made me feel that all my suffering had not been in vain.

I made arrangements for Fode and my loads, which would not arrive in Bo for another thirty-six hours, to be sent on by train to Magburaka, my starting point. There was no use in my waiting, so I set out that morning by car. Amadu, Buster, and I bumped over eighty or ninety miles of very poor highway to Magburaka, the place of waiting, having no especial difficulty beyond a few breathless moments as we crossed a temporary bridge which seemed in danger of ending its career at any moment. The ferries didn't worry me in spite of the hazardous drive down steep riverbanks onto unrailed wooden rafts, which natives pulled across the rivers by hand pulleys. I was shown the place where the black chauffeur of a wealthy native chief had neglected to put on his brakes in time, and had driven his new Chevrolet car over the raft into the swift current. Much perturbed, the chief had wired to Freetown for help, saying pathetically, "My motorcar is drowned." It was reported that the guilty chauffeur had promptly disappeared into the bush and was never seen again, fearing the vengeance of the chief.

CHAPTER SEVEN

TREKKING FOR IRON

FOR ME, Magburaka signifies "waiting," as every time I went there I had to wait for something. On this first trip, Fode and my loads, together with the boxes I had left weeks before at Kenema, managed to miss the connections at the railroad junction, after being sped forward from Bo, and arrived two days late. As Abou had been sent back to Kenema from Bo, I thought I was through with court messengers.

At Magburaka, Johnny Boy, with a show of perfect teeth in his delight at the prospect of an important job, met me. Momo Limba, a new court messenger, also joined my retinue, for I was doing government work now, and a court messenger was issued to me as a matter of course. Johnny Boy, I found, had been especially picked because he had trekked with a geologist at least once before. He made a good headman, but I never quite trusted him. Momo Limba was an old and trusted government servant. He spoke the language of the country into which I was going and, besides being of invaluable assistance among his own countrymen, turned out to be a delightful old character. He immediately assumed command of my camp, getting the rest of my retinue to wait on him.

Beyond Magburaka I found that the road extended, more or

less hesitantly, for fifteen miles to Mabonto, where it would be necessary to park the car and trek into the interior with carriers. After much waiting, we finally managed to get all my stores as far as the Mabonto resthouse in two trips. I was glad to get away from Magburaka, because it was the hottest place I had yet seen; even the evening thunderstorm didn't seem to clear the air. Mabonto wasn't much better, but at least I wasn't just sitting around waiting for something to happen.

At Mabonto I was confronted with a fresh problem: I had to engage carriers. After assembling my stuff and carefully apportioning the loads so that each man would not have to carry more than sixty to eighty pounds on his head, I found that I needed sixteen carriers. Accordingly, Momo Limba and Johnny Boy departed to commandeer the necessary helpers. Evidently everyone in Mabonto knew that "Missus" was going on trek and thought it would be nice to go along, for in half an hour the two returned, followed by dozens of would-be assistants. I was somewhat taken aback, but I remembered that Lane had told me that the thing to do in such cases was to line them up and gradually eliminate the undesirable until I had the required number. First, I picked out all those with sores and those with scars which told of bad sores. That eliminated all except about thirty. Next, I looked at their necks and eliminated those with sinewless throats, as they apparently were not in the habit of carrying loads. Then out went the puny, then those whose eyes looked diseased or as if they could not be trusted. Then I looked at their hands, just to see if they bore evidence of work. One fellow refused to show his right hand at first, and when he was forced to show it, I discovered that he had a large gash, obviously not due to disease. He evidently thought that I was looking for cuts, and great was his amazement when I took him.

Finally, the choice narrowed down to the requisite sixteen, whose names were carefully written down. I asked each one what his tribe was, and found I had representatives of four of the main thirteen tribes—Temne, Mende, Limba, and Yalonko. They were all good husky-looking specimens, and grinned their appreciative pleasure when told to report the next morning at dawn and to bring their mats and bundles with them. They promised to be on time, and begged for an advance in order that they might "chop" that night. Momo Limba said "yes," for I had their names and he knew them. Anyway, it wouldn't be much to lose, so I gave each of them threepence.

Johnny Boy, Amadu, and Fode, likewise, wanted advances, probably for a final fling that night, before setting off for the bush, so I gave them each three shillings. Momo Limba said he had plenty of money. Later, I found that he never needed money: he was such a big man among his people that everyone fed him for nothing and did everything possible to win his favor. In the Limba country, as in any other tribal territory, all members of the Limba tribe are brothers. They were all proud of having Momo Limba uphold the honor of the tribe by his position, for a court messenger is the highest position a native can reach—possibly because he wears a uniform, and the uniform makes the man in Africa as well as anywhere else.

Everything seemed ready for my first real trek into the bush. Even the Ford had been cared for. Momo Limba had arranged with the local chief to look after it in my absence. A large bari (the central meeting place in the village) had just been completed. It would be just the place for the Ford, the chief thought, for it would never do to leave such a fine car out in the weather. So a section of the wall was removed, I drove in, and the wall was immediately rebuilt. The chief viewed the result with evident pleasure, and his eyes lighted with anticipation when I promised him a long ride in the car on my return.

Everything went off like clockwork the next morning under the direction of Johnny Boy, and satisfaction fairly oozed from him as he helped boxes of food, tent, cook boxes, kerosene, and miscellaneous packages up on the boys' heads. Off they started, he bringing up the rear, with a great walking stick, his badge of authority, held proudly at his side. He had orders to pitch camp that night in Nerekoro, fifteen miles by trail.

Momo Limba and one boy with my knapsack, hammer, and machete accompanied me as I followed the loads, slowly, for I studied the rocks as I advanced and made digressions from the path whenever I saw a rock sticking out of the brush. Poor Momo Limba! He was no longer a young man, and although he trotted faithfully along beside me, he would sit down with evident relief, sigh wearily, and mop his brow whenever I found an outcrop of rock to study. He was a thoroughly trustworthy court messenger, but he was used to going on short treks with a D.C., spending whole days at a time lolling about the village where the D.C. held court. The D.C. at Magburaka had not realized the pace I would set, or he would have sent a younger man. But Momo Limba tried his best to keep up with me.

It was about four o'clock when I arrived at Nerekoro, to find that Johnny Boy had the camp all ready. I had said that I wanted to be outside the village, but evidently his ideas of what was outside were not the same as mine. When I dragged in at the close of a hot day, I found that my tent had, it is true, been pitched on the outskirts of the village, but close to two dilapidated huts, to my horror. As I appeared, a goat emerged from under the fly of the tent, and a dozen chickens had to be shooed out before I could get in. It was too late to do anything about it that night, but I summoned Johnny Boy, who obviously expected praise for his judgment in the selection of a camp site, and told him sternly that he was never again to set up my tent within sight of a native village. He found it hard to understand why I failed to agree with him that this was an ideal camp site. Here was a great spreading tree—which was shedding the red petals of a tuliplike flower all over everything—in the midst of a clearing. All he had had to do was to set up the tent and dig a trench around it for drainage in case of a thunderstorm—and there usually was one, even in January, in this part of the jungle. Moreover, it was handy to the village, so that he could gossip with his friends, at the same time feeling that he had the camp under surveillance. With some difficulty I convinced him that I wanted my camp made where it was necessary to brush entirely new ground, that I did not like unclean soil, full of jiggers, hookworms, and other things which swarmed about the native huts, especially where the animals roamed.

When it was time to go to bed, Momo Limba produced his greatcoat and many mats and laid himself down under the fly—orders, I suppose, from the D.C. A boy from the village sat huddled over some logs he kept pushing up into the center of the fire. In spite of this guard, I had great difficulty in getting to sleep. All around me I could hear the creeping life of the great forest. Near at hand the animal scavengers of the village roamed about, picking up odd scraps, and frequently getting into noisy disputes over some particularly juicy morsel. If I had been in the United States, I should have thought they were skunks. Queer rustlings, whose origin I could not determine, disturbed me every time I got partly asleep. I was told the next day that wildcats and leopards come every night to get scraps.

Then, just as I was dropping off from sheer exhaustion, the

drums started: "Dum, dum di dum, dum, dum di dum." Momo Limba rose and left the place. The drums stopped beating. Soon he returned and once more lay down. The next day he told me that villagers had no right to have a dance without asking my permission. If a white man sleeps near a village, the villagers are expected to secure his consent before having a dance.

Bleary-eyed and tired, I rose at sunrise. I could hear Amadu filling the canteens and my thermos bottle with water which had been boiled the night before and left standing to cool. All the water had to be boiled hard for five minutes; even muddy water was then safe to drink. It was difficult to keep a filter clean on trek; besides, filtering wasn't important. I took tea, morning, noon, and night, in preference to the lukewarm muddy fluid that was water.

Camp having been struck and the chief having said good-by, Johnny Boy set off with the carriers, while Momo Limba and I, accompanied by a boy to carry my knapsack, set off for the river below, where, according to the information I had gathered at Magburaka, a prospector had taken up a claim.

We wandered a mile or more along the riverbank before we came to the place where he was working. Our appearance startled him, to say the least, for he hadn't seen a white face for months. He was hospitality itself, and after a cup of tea showed me his claim, his rough sluice boxes, and his boys, who were panning gold by hand. He was working under terrific odds, but like all inveterate gold seekers, he knew that everything was going to be fine. He had gold; he showed it to me, his tired, fever-ridden eyes gleaming with joy. He was sure this was going to be a bonanza. Then he would get enough to go home to England and live in comfort the rest of his days. It was the same old story, told with the same faith and enthusiasm which marks the prospector everywhere. But he needed machinery to cope with the water-saturated soil; his equipment was entirely inadequate to meet the floods which came every few days. Somehow I knew he would never give up until forced to stop.

Months later I heard what happened to him. A few weeks after I was there, he was stricken with blackwater fever. His money had given out; his boys ran away with everything he had, as payment for their labors. Only one boy stuck to him and literally saved his life by careful nursing and by sending for a doctor, a Negro with a University of Edinburgh medical degree who was stationed in the small government hospital at Makeni. He had arrived by a forced march and worked over him night and day for five days, despite the fact that he knew he could not be paid. After the crisis was past, the prospector was carried to Magburaka, where a kindly man and woman of the Public Works Department gave him clothes and helped him to get down to Freetown, whence he was sent back to England by the government as a D.B.S.—distressed British subject.

The third day out from Mabonto, Momo Limba got sick. I doled him out ten grains of quinine and sent him to the near-by village to sleep off his fever. He stayed in the chief's hut for three days, and when he rejoined us I suggested that in the future he stay in camp and manage things for me and thus release Johnny Boy, who could act as my interpreter. I told him also that it was foolish for him to sleep by my tent. Momo Limba was delighted, and thenceforth things moved along much better. Johnny Boy proved a stalwart creature who could follow my pace without difficulty.

We were pushing steadily northward, and Momo Limba was useful in more ways than I had expected. The farther we went, the poorer were the farms, and the more trouble I had in obtaining food for myself and the carriers. The oranges were gone, and the bananas were not yet ripe. Chickens were scarce, for the natives kept their skinny stock for the eggs. Rice was obtainable, but expensive, for the new crop had not been picked, and the natives never had enough to carry them through the "hungry" season. This was principally because the chiefs commandeered any surplus stock in order to send it down to Freetown, where it sold for a good price. My boys had to depend upon buying food in the villages near which we camped. They never carried food for themselves.

I found groundnuts the most useful food in that country. With a little chicken stock, Fode could make a peanut soup that was very tasty. Groundnut stew—chicken, rice, and anything else we had on hand—was a daily dish, thanks to Momo Limba's wanderings about the countryside. He had a way of persuading the natives, guarding their crops of rice on the little hillside farms, to sell him a chicken and to give him a few vegetables—okra or sweet potato tops, which made excellent greens—or a few eggs. And Momo knew a bad egg. He'd hold an egg in his clenched fist and squint through it at the sun. If he could get light through, it was a good egg; if not, he kept it for himself.

It was an egg for breakfast which caused Fode's downfall. I wanted some salt for the egg, and Amadu announced that the salt was "finished." I could not believe my ears, for I had purchased a ten-pound bag of salt at Magburaka, and I knew that I couldn't have eaten ten pounds of salt in two weeks. Without a moment's hesitation, I discharged Fode. Momo and Amadu chased him out of camp, right in the middle of breakfast, giving him no chance to poison any of the food before he left. Weeks later, I learned that Fode had been selling the salt to the carriers, bit by bit, childishly thinking I would never notice its disappearance. I sent my most trustworthy boy to Magburaka with a note to the D.C., asking if he could send me some sort of cook. In the meantime, Amadu did what he could to fill the gap, mostly with the aid of a large part of my stock of canned goods.

Amadu was fitting into bush life fairly well by now. At first he had been clumsy and slow and loath to take any initiative. Several times I had threatened to send him back to Freetown, but his tears and prayers to be allowed to stay—he knew he would never get another job if his missus sent him back in the middle of a trek—finally won out, and I gave him another chance. He took great pride in the fact that he was my personal boy, and waited upon me with the devotion of a dog. I felt that he wouldn't desert me, no matter what happened, and it was good to know that he would stand by me in a pinch.

Camp had settled down to a regular routine. A day or two was spent at each camp site, then we moved on for a few miles, so that I could make a geological map of the country. As we moved northward, it was easy to trace the iron ore, once I had found the belt of iron, for it continued systematically, usually being exposed high up along the ridges. There were gaps, to be sure, where the thick red soil of the tropics—laterite—covered everything; but, always, up some winding stream course, I would again find the iron ore. Back and forth we went across the country, a gang of boys cutting a path through the underbrush. Soon they got so they recognized the ore—or at least they knew what I was after—and they became as excited as I whenever we picked up the trail again after losing it for a time. They were even more delighted if a few specks of gold turned up in the pan, when I stopped to wash some stream gravel.

I was pleased at the interest the chiefs took in the work. I thought at first their desire to help me was real, but one incident showed me how careful they were to guard their own secret knowledge of mineral wealth from the white man. I was told that there had been native smelting of iron in a certain locality and that they had made their own weapons up to recent times. The government had been obliged to suppress this custom in the interests of peace. One old chief, upon being questioned, reluctantly promised to lead me to the old workings. I was hopeful of finding more ore. We wandered aimlessly about the bush. The chief became more and more evasive, and I gradually realized that he had no intention of leading me to the place. I saw I was wasting my time, so dismissed the chief, and cut systematic traverse lines through the region, covering the territory as I was accustomed to doing. Just by chance, one of the lines crossed some depressions which looked suspiciously as if they had been made by man. We combed the neighboring bush and came upon some primitive-looking kilns made of mud, with piles of low-grade iron ore waiting to be smelted. These were some of the abandoned workings for which I had been on the lookout. But what surprised me was that the natives had used such low-grade ore, when the near-by hills contained quantities of ore of a much higher grade. I sent the chief a piece of really good ore, with a message that if he ever took up smelting in his country again, he should use material like the sample rather than the poorer quality used by his people in the past. He sent me a dash of bananas, rice, and oranges, so my advice was evidently appreciated.

CHAPTER EIGHT

ALONE IN THE BLUE

O NE NIGHT WHEN I had camped at least a mile away
from a small, remote village, I heard the tom-toms start.
When Momo Limba appeared to ask if I would permit the
dance, I said "yes," for that seemed a safe distance—I little
knew what tom-toms all night would mean. When he suggested
that I might like to see the dance after supper, I readily
acquiesced. He told me that he thought it was an initiation for
three young women into the Bundu Society, the secret society of
the women. The people would be glad to have me come and
watch. I was curious about the Bundu Society, for I had only
heard about the Poro, or men's society, and what the women did
was much harder to find out. In fact, when questioned, the boys
always hedged their answers. I knew that the young girls went
into the Bundu Bush, or the grove sacred to women, for many
moons, as the boys did into the Poro Bush, usually during our
winter or the season between crops. The women were trained
by a few old hags in the ways of women, were taught to sing
and dance, and were circumcised. This gruesome habit was an
old institution in this part of the country, having grown up
long ago, so the report goes, because a man from a far-off tribe,
whose women practiced circumcision, married a woman from

the West Coast and, horrified to find she had not been circumcised, returned her posthaste to her father.

The wife of a medical officer, with whom I was discussing the Bundu Society, told me that her husband knew of cases where women had bled to death as the result of this barbaric custom of cutting away the skin. She also suggested, as there is no health basis for doing this, that possibly it was merely the sadistic desire of the old hags to mutilate the younger girls just as they themselves had been. The old hag women, whose use in raising children was past, apparently doted on torturing the young girls put in their charge. No anesthetics were administered either to the men or to the women, but they were made as drunk as possible before the operation. None of the women was supposed to leave the Bundu Bush until all healed. That is why they remained away for many moons. Or if they returned, as they did toward the end of the ceremonies in this vicinity, they painted their faces with thick white clay and wore shawls over their heads, so as not to be recognized. When they returned to their people, there was a great ceremony— dancing, drinking, and much rioting. Although in some parts the medical men were persuading the young boys to go to hospitals to be circumcised under anesthetics, there was no way of inducing the women to go.

Exactly why this dance was being held, I could not tell. My boys were just dumb about it when questioned. Three women were being initiated, I was told. Probably they had just reached maturity, because it did not appear that they had just come out of the Bundu Bush. Possibly they were being given in marriage, but my boys did not think so. Of course, this was Limba country, so perhaps my boys, all except Momo, did not really know. More than likely they knew, but just would not tell for some reason.

Locusts descending on the upland.

A camp in the bush.

I listened to the tom-toms and singing while I was eating supper. Then Momo came up with a lantern and got me safely across the river, pickaback. A way was made for me to see into the inner circle, which was lined with women for the most part, wildly clapping their hands, stamping their feet to the rhythm of the drums, shouting, swaying, and looking thoroughly pleased with the three girls who were dancing. One girl appeared to be the leader, for she was doing most intricate steps, principally in a crouched position. She seemed to have terrific endurance, staring blankly ahead as she twisted her supple body in sensuous rhythm. The other two left her the whole cleared circle, when she got really started. She waved her arms, holding, as a shawl dancer does, a blue and white "country," or native hand-made, cloth, which she twisted and turned gracefully as she moved around the circle. Her only clothing was a cloth wound about her waist to make a skirt, and a string of beads bobbing up and down on her gleaming black breasts. She had a new brightly colored silk scarf on her head, which kept her pigtails in place. She was beautiful, young, and lithe. Her body glistened with oil; her expression was as one entranced, her face a mask, as she seriously varied her steps, rose to an upright position, arms, hands, feet, and head always in rhythm with the monotonous, chantlike music. Finally, when exhausted, she drew into the rank of admiring women and old men, breathless, while one of the other girls carried on. The women wrapped her tenderly in the cloth and patted her on the back. In a few moments back she went into the ring to start even a lower pantherlike crouch, more intent than ever. Finally, after half an hour or more, the tom-toms stopped, as did some boxlike rattles on a stick, which seemed to be full of pebbles or beans and were shaken in time to the tom-toms. All the women gathered around the dancers and, talking loudly, disappeared down the trail. I was informed that the women were going to wash and that they would be back soon. The men gathered in groups and a couple of pipes, as well as a gourd of palm wine, were passed from one to another. After at least fifteen minutes, singing and chanting was heard in the direction of the river, and the women came into sight by the light of the moon, swaying and shuffling, looking much refreshed. Then the dancing began all over again, and continued until a youngish man, strong-looking and broad-shouldered, carrying something in his hand, stepped into the ring and called three times. He then burst into a long harangue, chiefly addressing a very old hag. Finally, he went down on his knees in front of the old woman, bowed low, and presented her with a long reedlike basket which, I later found, contained native salt, a thing of great value in these parts. He then went into the nearest hut, reappearing with a country cloth and a calabash of rice, which he presented in like fashion to the old woman, who seemed childishly pleased. After this he continued his speech, and when he stopped everyone gathered in groups, talking and laughing, while more palm wine was drunk and the old chief began hopping around like a child, offering raw rice to everyone, who promptly dipped their hands into the small calabash which he carried. I tried to ask whether the young man was the husband of the girl, was he going to marry her, but all my questions brought out a stubborn "no savvy, missus" from the usually bright Momo Limba. Soon the dancing circle formed again, and the girl continued her dance. She would dance all night and maybe the next day, Momo informed me, or "until she tire," then the other girls would have a turn. I decided I had had enough, and headed back toward camp, hardly noticed, as the circle closed in on the dancer, who was becoming more snakelike in her arm waving and crouching posture, never moving a muscle of her tense face.

That night I could hear the distant pulsing of the tom-toms every time I turned over in a restless sleep. They were still going while I ate an early breakfast, and on my return that evening, a feeble pounding could still be heard, rising later to a louder note, but finally stopping entirely about dark. More than twenty-four hours of almost constant dancing!

We covered, on an average, twelve miles a day as we went north, the country gradually becoming more open, grassy meadows and burned-over land more and more extensive, with thick forest only along the waterways. I was glad to be in open country, for the bush, where I was never able to see out, was becoming oppressive. It became more and more difficult to find villages near which to camp, and finally one night we could find none. This was a hardship for the boys, who made it a rule, after I had finished with their services for the night, to go into the village to sleep, leaving a fire guard on duty. At this camp, however, the nearest village was at least five miles away—too far for them—so they decided to put up temporary shelters of grass and palm. It was four o'clock in the afternoon, and they had had a long hard day, but they insisted that they needed shelter lest the leopards get them. They had made a clearing in the elephant grass for my tent, and at its edge they built a shimbek. I tried to get them to cut the grass away in order to make a bigger clearing, for the grass was dry, and I was afraid of fire. But they were tired, and after cutting a slightly bigger space, they quit.

I went to bed with a queer feeling of unrest. The harmattan was strong and dry, and the air was suffocating with smoke from distant fires. I lay awake for a long time, hearing the boys jabbering in their shimbek and bullfrogs in the near-by stream making the loudest croaking I had ever heard. Finally I dropped off to sleep only to awaken suddenly, feeling stifled. Then I heard a sound which for a long terrible minute paralyzed me—it was fire. I had once been caught in a Montana forest fire, from which I barely escaped with my life; the sound of it—the quiet crackling, hiss, snap—I shall never forget. The watchman had fallen asleep; the boys all slept. I shrieked. At my cry, the boys appeared, like animals startled from their lairs. No need to tell them what the trouble was. They began stamping the grass back from the tent, slashing, piling heaps of it up in the cleared space, down-wind from the tent. Our campfire helped to light the work, gleaming on shining black backs jerking up and down.

Across the stream, the grass was burning fiercely, its heat adding to our discomfort and terror. A lane was cleared to the stream, and backfires were started. Momo Limba and Amadu poured tin after tin of water on the tent, and grabbed at every stray spark. Suddenly, a spark leaped across the stream. The blaze moved toward us. Luckily for us, the enlarged clearing and the backfires saved the camp. We watched the flames make their way around the clearing and knew the danger was past.

In the morning we followed the path of the fire northward, and beyond the burned hills we came upon a green valley. Two weeks previously it had been burned over, but already the green grass was sprouting profusely. Even as we rejoiced in the fresh greenness, the locusts came—straight south from the Sahara— thousands of them, right for this field. Hour after hour, the brownish-green bodies and vibrating wings darkened the sky. Before I could believe it possible, the grass had disappeared, together with everything else that was green. The trees were stripped. My boys were delighted and scooped up great handfuls of the pests for their supper. The natives pound the bodies and get a salt extraction, according to Johnny Boy, or roast the legs of the insects. The boys were much amused to see me recoil as the creatures swarmed about my helmet and shoulders. But there was no escape, so I tried to ignore them.

In a few hours, when the work of devastation was complete, at a signal from their leaders the locusts rose straight up above the field, and after circling about for fifteen minutes, they were off for the south, to wreak more havoc.

Many times we saw animal tracks—occasionally those of a leopard, but more often those of buck or of "bush cow," a pygmy type of buffalo, which the natives fear, for they are ferocious when disturbed or attacked. Many of these bush cow tracks were fresh, as if the animal had walked ahead of us. Once we came upon tracks in the mud, with bubbles still oozing through, as if the animal had only just lifted his foot. And there was blood! Everyone stopped. Consternation was written on the boys' faces. I examined the ground ahead; there were no other marks of blood. Then I saw what it was. The animal had severed a creeper which had dripped red sap into the tracks. I showed the boys what had happened, but they were not convinced. Maybe it wasn't real blood, but it was a warning to them; they must never cross the path of a bush cow where there was blood. So we turned back and cut a line through the forest elsewhere that day.

Such superstitions were constantly interfering with my plans, but most maddening of all to a geologist was the sacred bush around the villages, into which no white person was permitted to go under any circumstances, for it is the haunt of those initiated into the secret societies. Iron and gold might lie all over the ground, but I couldn't even set my foot into this territory. I could sleep by a graveyard and defy almost any other custom, but not this one.

One day Buster disappeared. We hunted and whistled without results. The boys scoured the woods, and after an hour's hunt they found her, standing quietly with a noose around her neck, patiently waiting to be freed. She had followed a hunter's fence—a thick barrier of thorns, cutting straight across country—and had come to the little opening which is left as a trap for wild beasts. She had started through, but the noose had sprung. Luckily, Buster was large and heavy, and she knew better than to struggle. Evidently she thought this was just a new type of leash, but she was glad to see us and wagged her stub of a tail excitedly.

Johnny Boy frequently expressed his regret that I had not brought a gun suitable to shoot game. My automatic was packed away in the bottom of my tin trunk, forgotten by now, for there was nothing to fear from the natives in these remote places. Occasionally a chief's hunter, carrying his old-fashioned "Dane" gun—dating from at least 1850—brought me some guinea fowl or a small buck, which were a treat and varied the diet dished up to me by the new cook who had been sent to me by the D.C. I rarely saw a buck, just heard them crashing ahead. But one day I came upon a beautiful waterbuck—tall and stately, with long straight horns bent slightly backward, and a soft brown coat with a few stripes. We eyed each other, my boys wild-eyed with excitement, for such specimens are not common. Then he slowly turned, flipped up his white tail, leaped over the undergrowth, and was out of sight in three bounds.

Almost more than anything else, we dreaded the driver ants, for they could clean up the entire camp unless they were diverted. At night the watchman scattered ashes in a circle around the tent, for the ants hate ash, which smothers them. If they came on, in an unending line, and pushed through the circle, hot ashes had to be gathered, and burning twigs were pushed in their way until the line was diverted. Buster usually dashed off into the bush and circled around, coming back into camp long after they were gone. They often crossed our trail when we were on the march, and if by any mischance the carriers stepped on the line and broke it, we all ran ignominiously, the boys jumping about and wildly pulling the burning creatures off.

Almost six weeks passed before I reached the north end of the area which the government had closed to prospectors; the iron ore outcrop had ended—but I had followed it for thirty miles. I circled back on the west side of the same range of hills, but found no trace of the ore. It seemed best to return to Nerekoro, where I had started, and try to pick up outcrops of iron south of the closed area.

Not far from Nerekoro, a messenger, sent with mail from Magburaka, met me with an official telegram which stated tersely: "Urgent. Return Freetown immediately." That was all. What had happened? Had the government changed? Didn't they want me any more? Had bad news come from Jock on the Gold Coast? If only officials who sent telegrams would give an inkling of what the trouble was it wouldn't be so bad. I couldn't get tomorrow's train, anyway, so I decided to go on as far as Maranda, where I knew a British mining company was just opening up a placer gold mine. Then I could catch the next train, which left three days later. This would be quicker, and I could do some work on the way.

I got to Maranda the next afternoon and went up to the white men's compound, a row of neat huts on a cleared hill, beyond the town. No one was in. I hadn't seen a white face for six weeks, so was slightly disappointed. However, I was so fagged out that I consoled myself with the thought that I was too tired to see them anyhow. I ordered my tent pitched near the village, quite a distance from the miners' little cluster of shimbeks. Just about suppertime my whereabouts was learned by the four white men, and a message was sent down asking me to come up to dinner. I could not refuse, tired as I was; and, after I had made the effort, I was glad. It was fun to see white persons again, and I enjoyed their food immensely, not having had any fresh vegetables or such a variety of dishes for weeks. While we sat around after supper, the men smoking and sipping whisky and soda, the terrific din of approaching hordes startled us. A messenger came up panting, saying that the villagers were coming for palaver. I thought this an excellent opportunity for my retreat, excused myself, and hurried home by lantern. I went to bed and immediately fell into a deep sleep.

Some time later, I awakened slowly to the sensation of having my head slowly pounded in; instinctively, I knew it was the dreaded tom-toms. And so near! Every beat cut right into my tired brain, seeming to hurt my whole skull. I could have screamed at the idea of listening all night to this awful noise, for it was full moon and I knew from previous experience the natives would continue with their revelry for at least twenty-four hours. One night of this and I would be insane. I lay wincing for about fifteen minutes. I was dreadfully tired, but I felt I would move camp at this hour rather than endure the torture. The rhythm just ate into me until I cringed in time with the music.

I finally called to the never-understand-anything watchman whom I had at the time. He half rose, sulkily, from a reclining position by the fire. He understood English, but could not express himself in that tongue. Hence, when I ordered him to go to stop the music, he merely looked sulky and said, "I no be fit.

They no 'gree." All my boys knew I had a standing order forbidding tom-toms in any village near which I was camped. By now, I was roused to a point of fury. My stay in the bush had been too long; little things got on my nerves and almost drove me insane, depriving me entirely of any feeling of caution. So when the watchman did nothing, I crawled out of my net, clumped into my mosquito boots, put my raincoat on over my pajamas, grabbed my flashlight, and, followed by my timid dog, strode past the watchman, glaring at him, and marched down the path to the village. The watchman stood rooted to the spot, not budging after me.

When I reached the square of the village, I stood still a moment, hesitating. The silver moon lighted the white packed clay of the wide open space. Black silhouettes of pointed thatched huts ringed the horizon, blending into black trees. Before me, swaying bodies, in white shirts or tunics, flickered in the light of the moon, a weird cloud of dust rising from the swaying mass, keeping time to a rhythmic clapping and thudding of bare feet, with the unending "dum-dum-dumdum" of those frightful tom-toms. No, I could not stand it. I stepped into the moon-flooded space and spoke in a rasping, dry voice. Nothing happened. Nobody heard or noticed me. Wild with anger, I took the police whistle, which was always pinned to the end of my flashlight, and blew a shrill discordant blast. There was a sudden, dead silence, only the dust still moving, as hundreds of black faces turned and transfixed me. Instinctively, I felt I had done something awful. Hatred was written on every face, mingled with curiosity. But I had to carry it through, now I was there; I could not turn back. Not one familiar face did I see among those turned toward me—no Amadu, or Momo, only strangers.

Boldly I said, in the silence, "Haven't you more respect than to make all this noise, when a white woman's camp is right by your village? You must stop. Go to the next village. Anywhere, but go away."

A more complete silence, if such a thing were possible, followed my commands. I felt rather than saw the faces move a little nearer. I was powerless to do anything but stand my ground. I felt as if I were taking ether. Then, from their midst, a tall white-clad man moved toward me, doffed his little round white cap, bowed low twice, and said, "Yes, missus, we 'gree for stop." Then, turning, he spoke a few sentences to the tense group before me, while I still stood, facing them. The group moved, broke up, low murmurings arising here and there, and began to scatter. I turned, dazed, and wandered back toward my tent, still surprised that nothing had happened to me, and feeling a bit of a fool for having gone out absolutely unaccompanied by any boy of my own.

At last, I could sleep, and I didn't waken until I heard Amadu rummaging around among my supply boxes in the morning dusk. Not a word was said about the previous night. The boys, more silent than usual and terribly efficient, packed up, while I gobbled a hasty breakfast and left before the retinue, taking only Johnny Boy and one boy to carry my knapsack. There was not a person in sight when I hurried through Maranda—no staring multitude, just silence. My path wound past the outskirts of the miners' shimbeks. Only a cook's helper was in sight, for it was barely light, with a clammy mist over everything. I felt quite peppy, and we tore along, until at length we came to the point where I had decided to strike inland, over the mountain range, along a hunter's trail, to study the structure of the hills. The carriers, going by the much quicker road, met me at Mabonto that night, so that I could entrain for Freetown the next day, according to orders.

It was more than six weeks since I had left Mabonto and put my Ford car under the chief's bari, in the center of the village square. The chief was away when I arrived, but there was the good old Ford, sitting like a hen in its coop, waiting to be let loose. First, we had to pump up the tires. Then two native men came up, demanding dashes. They were the night watchman and the day watchman; the chief had told them to stay on guard all the time. I gave them each three shillings (this was a new graft) and they were satisfied.

A feeling of suppressed emotion prevailed, which I could not explain. I wondered if it were related to the events of the previous night. There seemed to be far too many people about, among whom were a number of fine-looking, tall, chocolate-colored natives, turbaned, with long flowing gowns. Momo said that these were northern tribes. Silently, they watched me drive the Ford, loaded to the brim, out of the bari and down the road toward Magburaka.

I had decided to spend the night in Magburaka. On arriving, I went to the D.C.'s office to see if he could explain the telegram. But all the white persons had gone to Freetown. There was no mail for me, so I telegraphed to the Mines Department in Freetown to find out whether or not I was to bring my things down with me. The reply came, "Leave loads Magburaka." I left Momo Limba with the loads at the resthouse and returned to Mabonto to pay off my boys and get Amadu and Johnny Boy. The carriers looked genuinely sad as I said good-by. They were really old friends by now. They liked working for a missus, they said, and would I take them back when I returned? They perked up when I said "Yes."Then we headed back to Magburaka.

The train ride to Freetown was hotter than the trip out, as I remembered it; probably because I had discarded my bush clothes and found myself decidedly uncomfortable in more civilized habiliments. Mobs of natives swarmed on every platform, boldly looking into the windows. Always the cry of "Na missus" rang out. Perhaps they were disappointed in me; I wasn't sure; but they seemed to be looking for something they didn't find.

CHAPTER NINE

WINDUP

IN FREETOWN, I was met by the chief of the Mines Department. His first words were, "I'm relieved to see you alive." I felt my conscience prick me, for I thought he referred to the dance in Maranda. But I soon learned that the natives in the eastern part of the province were in revolt. This was why I had been called back. As we drove up to Miss Carey's cottage, I gradually gathered that Adara, a Mohammedan in French Guinea, had preached for weeks on the borders of Sierra Leone, sending his messengers all over the country and causing unrest generally. Then, having persuaded his followers, of which he had collected several thousands, that he was another Mohammed and that he was immortal, he had launched a so-called crusade into Sierra Leone, with the object of freeing the natives from the white man's oppression and taxation. Troops from Freetown had been rushed to meet the oncoming hordes, and all white men had been recalled from certain areas. Freetown itself was defenseless, until the arrival that night of a battleship, which lay gray and silent, in the harbor. Freetown was quiet, but there was a prevailing feeling of uneasiness, for there was a powerful

Mohammedan element, and if Adara were successful all the Mohammedans might rise up against the whites.

News was meager, and we lived in doubt for two or three days. I wished I were safe in my tent in the bush, where no native would harm me. Horror spread across the Mines Inspector's face when I told him of the episode of the tom-toms a few nights before. He told me that this was the eve of Ramadan, a great feast night of the Mohammedans, and it was almost sacrilege to interfere with a celebration. Adara's messengers were rousing the people to revolt, for Ramadan is a time when the natives are in a highly emotional state. I found out later that the palaver which had been brought to the Maranda miners' camp had been a request to be allowed to celebrate Ramadan. The miners had not dared to refuse the request, and the multitude had returned, jubilant, to drink and dance by the light of the full moon, until I stepped into their midst, unsuspecting, unarmed, and angry. No wonder I felt as if a feather dropping my way would have meant my being blotted out. The absolute preposterousness of my appearance, its suddenness, and my brazen demand to have them desist, the very fact that I was unaccompanied and at their mercy, may have made them give in, for had not Amadu told me they all called me a "big chief" and that I was known as "the Gold Missus"?

At last, news came through that the tide had turned. Adara was dead, but Holmes, the young officer in charge of the detachment of soldiers seeking him, had been cut down in an ambush and slaughtered. Later, exact facts drifted through. Adara had marched east, unresisted, his ranks growing daily. He had sent an order out saying that any man in shorts (meaning a white man and his followers) who crossed a certain bridge should be killed. Holmes, with only two or three scouts ahead, followed by his regiment of blacks and a white sergeant-major, crossed this bridge and had been cut down instantly by natives hidden in the tall grass. The troops turned tail, but the sergeant emptied his revolver into the attackers before retreating over the bridge. One lucky shot had killed Adara. However, it was some time before he could be positively identified, for, swathed in his yards of Arabic wrappings, no one had ever seen his face very closely. Besides, being immortal, he had preached that he could not die. Hence the unrest among his native followers continued for some time.

Freetown was very quiet those days, especially when the report of Holmes's death reached town. I longed for the bush, and waited impatiently for the opportunity to return to my interrupted work. At first it was fun to be with white people in town once more, but I soon tired of the unending round of dinner parties and a generally aimless existence. One night I awakened with an acute attack of ptomaine poisoning. Miss Carey hastily summoned a doctor, who tried in vain to diagnose my illness as some strange tropical disease. Civilization, not the bush, had laid me low.

When at length the Adara episode died down, I was allowed to return to the bush, although I was still weak from the poisoning. I decided to go to Kaballa, a high and healthy place in the extreme north, where I could be quiet. There I would write my report on the iron ores for the government, and rest a while. My car and goods had been shipped to the end of the railroad at Makeni, where a white member of the Public Works Department greeted me with the news that the bees had used my Ford for swarming purposes. He was having them smoked out and he hoped by morning I could get on my way.

I felt so much better the next day that I decided to go to Port Lokko and trek to Marampa to visit a small isolated iron deposit, which private interests had already begun to work. I took two days to go a mere twenty-seven miles—even accepting the luxury of a hammock for transportation, though I found walking far more agreeable and less tiring.

The mine itself was still hardly more than a prospect. I found that, unlike the iron deposit of the closed area, which was in the form of a great bed extending for miles, this was a hill, more or less circular in shape, consisting almost entirely of iron. The two white men who were running the place gave me a cordial welcome and listened eagerly to all the news of the outside world I could give them.

Returning to Port Lokko and Makeni, I continued my journey to Kaballa. After leaving Makeni the country began to change in appearance. It reminded me of the scenery near Yosemite, but without the great gorge. Granite peaks, three thousand feet high, isolated and rounded, stood out amid the low orchard bush and the elephant grass. After eight hours of hair-raising driving over bad roads and narrow, rickety wooden bridges, I reached the picturesque thatched resthouse which stood on the hill at the end of the treacherous, narrow dirt road. Kaballa was indeed a haven.

In the absence of the D.C., who was out on trek, his clerk extended the courtesies of the post. At teatime, the doctor's wife came to call. Her boys had told her that a "gold missus" was at the resthouse and she "just had to come and satisfy" her curiosity. I was delighted to see her, too, for it was pleasant to be having a cup of tea with one of my own sex. Apparently, word of the strange woman had spread far, for the following day the chief of the district appeared, clutching a handful of mud. He was quite sure it was gold, for he had seen yellow specks in it. I put it in water, and had to disappoint him with the verdict that the yellow was merely flakes of mica, not gold. He was crestfallen, but took my word for it.

The barracks as viewed from the resthouse at Kaballa.

Gate house entrance to a village. Food is placed at the entrance to appease bad devils.

Next day, the locusts descended upon us, and the lovely green grass disappeared in a twinkling, as did also the leaves of orange and lime trees, leaving the naked-looking green fruit dangling dispiritedly. Except for that sad happening, everything went smoothly and I finished my report within a week.

It was now the end of March. I felt rested and quite strong again, and decided to go back to Freetown by way of the gold prospects at Makong and Pujehun, where they were beginning to mine gold. I would also make a visit to the platinum fields near the coast. Then I would take a boat at Freetown and slip into the Gold Coast and visit Jock until he was ready to go home to England in June. It was nearing the rainy season, and I didn't want to be caught in the interior of Sierra Leone when the rains broke.

I decided to leave the next morning, but, as usual, circumstances ruled otherwise. When I went out to superintend the loading of the car, I found the tires were flat. No amount of effort would make the pump work. We put in new washers; we oiled it; we tried everything we could think of, all to no avail. I looked at the D.C.'s black clerk in despair. He returned my glum look for a moment; then his face lighted. A lorry was expected in two days; it would undoubtedly carry a pump. After two pleasantly idle days, the lorry arrived, but without a pump. There was nothing to do but sit as calmly as possible while the lorry went back to Makeni. The pump was sent out by special lorry the next day.

To reach the mine, I could drive as far as Matotaka, where I parked the car. From here, I trekked into Makong, about twenty miles of the worst going I had had. It was unusually hot and humid. I found conditions primitive at the mine, which was still mostly great plans. Makong was just beginning to produce gold in paying quantity from placer deposits or gravels which were proving widespread and rich in ore. The mine consisted, at the moment, of an odd sluice box here and there for washing the gravels. "Leats," or trenches, to bring the water from near-by streams, were being dug. Machines were being installed, but it was slow work. It would take six months for man power to bring in the gasoline engine for the great excavator.

I found Mr. Babcock, whom I had met in London, at the mine, with two other white men established in native-made mud huts. The area around the camp was infested with snakes. Before supper we killed a black mamba, a deadly variety which spits poison through its fangs in a fine spray. It lives in trees, as well as on the ground, and is greatly feared by the natives. Later, I computed the snake population at Makong as seventeen black mambas to the square mile, this figure being based on the number Mr. Babcock and I encountered in old prospect holes of the vicinity.

That night as we four whites sat down to supper, we became conscious of the faint sounds of a feast in the near-by village. We had just finished the soup course, when, suddenly, a wild-eyed headman came panting up to the table and blurted out a story of "bad men go burn village." Wren, the manager, jumped up, eyes dancing at the thought of some excitement, put on some heavy boots, and grabbed his ever-handy revolver, thrusting it into a holster and fastening it to his belt. Clutching a horsewhip in his right hand, he called back over his shoulder, "If I don't return in twenty minutes, come along, Parker." Parker waited five minutes only, and, as the noise became louder, he jumped up and went off with his revolver. Mr. Babcock, despite my desire to go along to see the fun, somehow dissuaded me, saying that it could be nothing; he was not going to bother to go down. So we sat, silently, listening, looking at each other and wondering whether we should go along or not. Mr. Babcock kept insisting that it was better to "stay put" until Wren sent word of what was happening.

It was half an hour before the two men returned, dripping with perspiration, shirts torn, hair ruffled. Wren had a cut on his face but was smiling, thoroughly pleased with himself. He told how he had descended into the village—lashed right and left in the dark with his whip, grabbed native black legs as they scrambled up roofs, having no idea what it was all about. Aided by Parker and surrounded by a gang of the mine's own headmen and boys, he hit out in every direction. At last things quieted down, no houses having burned down after several futile attempts to set fire to the thatch with burning brands. The riot was merely a feud between unfriendly Mende and Temne tribes, a Mende having sold salt to a Temne at a price considered exorbitant, the two finally coming to blows. The whole village took sides, as the Mendes swore they would burn the huts of their Temne enemies. Anything might happen when these tribes got aroused, for they really loved a fight, whether they knew what it was about or not. The village was saved only by some freak of fortune, things quieting down as suddenly as the trouble started. Mr. Babcock decided he must soon build a native compound for the laborers. This would at least segregate them from the villagers, and certain sections could be put aside for the different tribes in an attempt at segregation, for the peace of the mine.

From Makong I trekked nineteen miles south to Pujehun, which was being developed by the same company, but, having been begun earlier, had made more progress. What impressed me most at these two places was the manner in which seemingly impossible obstacles had been overcome. The forests had to be cut. Natives, who had never seen a wheelbarrow and promptly put it on their heads after tiring of pushing it, had to be trained.

But I saw that mining had come to stay in Sierra Leone. This English company meant business; they were getting the gold.

At Bo the Ford was again loaded on a flatcar, and Buster was relegated to the D.C. to await her master's return from England. I boarded the Freetown train once more, but at Waterloo, twenty miles from Freetown, I got out. This was the starting point for the platinum workings. Up two thousand feet, we climbed to the Pass over the small range of mountains behind Freetown. That night in a delightful tin-roofed resthouse, I listened to the "mountains of the lion" roar, while the raindrops hammered on the roof over my cot. An early start down; the sparkling sea coming nearer; a refuse heap of boulders to mar the scene—these were the platinum workings. The natives were picking out the platinum by hand from washed pebbles and putting the dull nuggets into cigarette tins. Platinum is even heavier than gold, settling quickly to the bottom of a hand-sluice box. Great boulders, as much as six feet in diameter, were pried out of the stream bed, and under these they found the platinum, brought down by the steep torrential streams which tumble into the sea from the high hills.

It was with a feeling of quiet satisfaction with these months of treks and geological study that I finally turned my footsteps toward Freetown. Mingled with this was a feeling of relief and thanks for having been allowed to see so much and return safely —in good health.

The quickest way to reach Freetown from the platinum workings was along the shore, a two-day trek over broiling sands and through picturesque fishing villages. There I found, not the untouched, marveling native of the hinterland, but a scoffing, proud race. I had trouble with carriers; they wanted more pay; they wouldn't go farther without it; they would not obey me.

Luckily for me, a native policeman had been detailed in Water-loo to accompany me to Freetown. This was a precaution thought necessary after the recent uprisings. With his khaki uni-form and gun, his belt lined with bullets for my protection, he was a real guard, although far more ineffectual than an unarmed court messenger upcountry. He threatened and cursed the car-riers, until finally we reached the end of the longest, hottest beach trip I ever made, and camped under some trees which overhung the sandy shore. No "brushing" to make a camp site here; my tent was pitched on the beach. And, best of all, the rocks jutted out into the water, forming a natural pool protected from sharks, where I had a fine swim before teatime.

The next morning, we struck camp early, for at ten I was to be met by a car on the road. We walked through a colony vil-lage, set in a grove of mango trees laden with their oval orange-like fruit. There were orange trees, too. The place looked quite civilized: the wooden houses had tin roofs; some even had a second story; most of them needed repairs. There were tumble-down wooden churches. On through a strip of cooling forest we went, at length coming to the macadam road, where we found the car which was to take us to Freetown.

In Freetown I found that Miss Carey was away on govern-ment business. The resthouse was full, I was told, and when I sought my friend of the Mines Department for advice, I found that he was in the hospital. I had been told that a woman shouldn't stay alone at the hotel, but there did not seem to be any alternative. The room I was given was musty. The bed smelled sour. The floor was dirty, the mosquito net torn. I wished I were back in the bush, and that wish gave me an idea. I sent for Amadu to bring my loads, put up my own cot and net, and set out my canvas bath and chair. This was more like home. I sat on the balcony and watched the passers-by. How different these natives were from the simple bush native, with his few wants, owning only the clothes on his back.

But even my own cot couldn't insure sleep that night. My room was over the bar, from which raucous laughter and cursing, accompanied by the breaking of glasses, continued until a late—or rather, an early—hour. Finally, I closed my eyes from sheer exhaustion, feeling stifled between four walls—a tent or a mud hut was so much cooler. Even the buzzing of the mosquitoes on the net could not keep me awake.

It seemed as though I couldn't have been asleep for more than two minutes when roosters began crowing in the back yard, to be answered by others down the street. Then I heard a dreadful screaming, as though a child were being whipped. Then chattering and excited jabber. Silence let me drop off to sleep again, but only for a short time. The noise started again. Then light came, and with it the church bells, which seemed to be everywhere. I had no idea there were so many churches in Freetown. The bells called forth the natives, whose merry laughter annoyed me —they must have slept through all the racket which had kept me awake. I envied them and wished for the bush, where none of the noise was human. There was nothing for it but to get up and dress. I resolved to do something drastic before another night came. When Amadu arrived with hot water, he looked sleepy-eyed, too.

As soon as the government offices were open, I went to the large cement building, several stories high. Going from one office to another, I tried to find someone who would help me. The third man I talked to was upset at my story. He got out his car and drove me to the resthouse to find out what was what. Sure enough, there were two vacant rooms, and one of them was immediately reserved for me. The native clerk I had consulted had simply decided not to bother his head about resthouses for a mere woman. As soon as Amadu had shepherded my baggage from the hotel, I went to bed and slept all that day in the peace and coolness of this old barracks on the hill, for the resthouse had been converted from the abandoned officers' quarters. Around the base of the hill, the buzz of the city droned, far away and undisturbing.

Amadu wept when I paid him off; perhaps I would never come back. I didn't know. The Ford was put in storage, to be picked up on my return to England. The next day, with my personal boxes and my tent, I boarded the boat for the Gold Coast.

The boat was a strange world. I felt as if in a dream when I took a bath in a real tub and ate meals reminiscent of a life which had vanished moons ago. The food seemed wonderfully delicious, and I looked in amazement at the other passengers who were complaining bitterly.

The haze which characterized the end of the harmattan hugged the earth so closely that the captain had difficulty in finding Monrovia, the capital of Liberia, where we were to land two missionaries. Finally a point was sighted, the boat idled in slowly, and the surf boats pushed out, proudly bearing flags which looked like the American emblem, but contained only one star and ten stripes. We stopped only two hours.

The next day we pulled in behind the breakwaters of Takoradi, the protected artificial harbor of the Gold Coast, where I was to land. The boat did not dock here, either, and we had to put off in tenders. Snappy black officers, efficient and quick, took control. I was a little worried. Would I be allowed to land? Would they guess I was coming in against rules?

"Is your husband a government official?"

"Yes."

"Pass."

They had stamped my passport, politeness itself, and I was through. I drew in a deep breath and looked around. I was conducted through spacious, clean government sheds, past bags of cocoa, palm-oil kernels, and row after row of other produce ready for shipment. Outside, trainloads of manganese ore, used as an alloy of steel, were being brought down from the mines, to be exported to America and other places. Everything seemed to move like clockwork.

A car whisked me past neat-looking bungalows to the resthouse, situated in a town much like Freetown, but bigger, with more pretentious houses. The native garb was far more colorful than in Sierra Leone, especially the batik pattern of the togas worn by the men, reminding me of Indian prints. The resthouse was a veritable hotel run by the government; my meals were prepared and I did not have to unpack a thing, not even bedding. The view from my screened porch was across the sea, and I watched a smudge of gray, the boat which I had come on, moving stealthily away through the misty harmattan haze toward Nigeria.

The next day I went by lorry to Dixcove to stay at an old fort now used as a resthouse, where Jock was expected. The fort was an ancient Portuguese castle with thick stone walls, on a point above the pounding surf. My loads were dumped in a spacious chamber, and I settled down prepared to find even a long wait pleasant. And that night, Jock arrived.

In June we sailed back to England. At Freetown the Ford was put aboard and Miss Carey delighted us by turning up for lunch on the ship. She said that Amadu, in some strange fashion, had learned that I was on the boat, and had begged her to bring him, but she had had to refuse.

Among the passengers for England was Mr. Babcock, of the

Makong gold mines, sailing on leave. He asked me to meet the chairman of his company when we reached London. This I did, and was surprised to hear myself being offered a job with the company, to go out to Sierra Leone again, when Jock returned to the Gold Coast in October. I was a woman, to be sure, but I had proved that women were no liability in the tropics. Besides, I knew the ins and outs of the rocks of Sierra Leone better than any of their men. So it was settled, and I left London for my summer vacation with a happy heart.

Part II

QUEST FOR GOLD

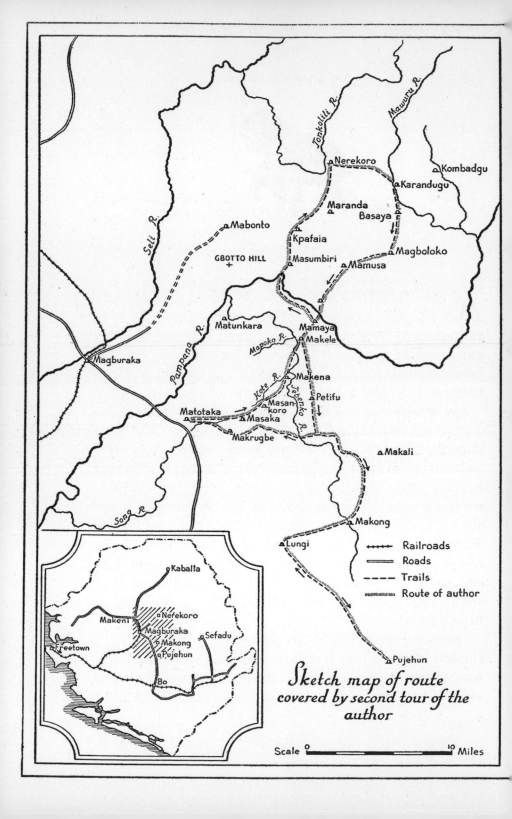

Scale 0 ————————————— 10 Miles

*Sketch map of route
covered by second tour of the
author*

CHAPTER TEN

MAKONG MINE

AGAIN THE HILLS of Freetown came in sight, the tops blanketed by clouds, as our boat slowly maneuvered to an anchorage. As we rounded the lighthouse point and caught a glimpse of the ramshackle buildings massed together, with the forests beyond, I realized that I liked this country of Sierra Leone and was glad to be back here once more.

The immigration officials came aboard, and we submitted our passports. I had less argument with the native in charge of immigration than did the other nongovernment people. It never occurred to him that a woman who had a husband aboard would be going ashore in the capacity of a wage earner. I certainly was not going to enlighten him. I had waited long enough in line already, hearing harangues over incomplete papers, and I feared delay if it were discovered that I was going ashore for a mining company. I knew this would be found out in the customs shed, and anticipated trouble enough there. So I hedged my answers, and slipped through unnoticed, hurrying away to find a launch to take me ashore.

Once clear of the ship, I felt my troubles just beginning; I climbed from the launch onto the pier, and was immediately surrounded by a perspiring mob of shouting natives. A white woman, unaccompanied and unmet, was a new kind of game for them. A carefully aimed kick here and there was what usually got the men to the customs shed, but I was dripping with perspiration, and just feeling cross. Besides, a kick from a woman would only have got a laugh from the natives. Chaos ruled. No one knew where anything was, or should be, or when things would arrive. The game was to spot your own luggage as it was dumped in the shed, have some boys pile it in a heap, and then hope to get one of the native customs men to clear it for you. I wished I were anywhere else; I felt weak from the inactivity on board ship the last ten days, and thoroughly nauseated by being suddenly dumped into that evil-smelling multitude under the tin roof. An odor of rotting fish added the finishing flavor. For a moment I wished that the immaculately clad Governor's wife and her friend, who had been sped ashore with all their baggage as soon as anchor had been dropped, might have just ten minutes of what the ordinary traveler had to endure. I recalled the ease of my own previous arrival.

Grasping a sheaf of papers which told me what I was to expect in that shed, I waited. My supplies had been packed and carefully numbered, so that a glance down the lists would tell me exactly what each box contained. Numbers one through fifteen contained food—odd numbers, flour, sugar, tea, sausages, peas; even numbers, milk, biscuits, sardines, and odd canned goods. Crates numbered sixteen through twenty-six contained an assortment of picks, shovels, prospecting pans, cooking pots, and so on. Some of these were for my own use; others were for the mining company I was representing. I was to send these to the main mine. Tin trunks, helmet case, lamp boxes, my tent, bedroll, deck chair—all added up to a grand total of forty pieces. Helpless! That didn't half signify how I felt, as the articles labeled for me began to be dumped in heaps in various places.

All this time I had been besieged by boys—tall boys, small

boys, fat boys, emaciated boys—all in their Sunday best, a sort of nightgown arrangement, some with round Mohammedan hats, others with stolen or borrowed felts; all polite at first, then officious when I continued to brush them aside. There was an incessant yelling of "Missus want headman." It always started that way, ending with "Missus want small boy"; the policeman on duty occasionally making a sally at the throng, hitting right and left with a long whip. The boys only swarmed around closer a few minutes later.

Just when I thought I couldn't stand it another minute, I suddenly saw a small, thin, weak, but clean-looking boy with a grin from ear to ear, trying unsuccessfully to get to me. It was Amadu! I almost fell on his neck, so overjoyed was I to see him. I had not expected Amadu, nor notified him; but there he was. It is curious how the boys one has employed on a former tour find out that their masters are returning and turn up on the dock. No white man ever discovers how they know that their masters are arriving on a particular boat. But a boy from up-country will not fail to come down in time. Whether some clerk in the government office had read on the sailing lists that I was coming on such and such a boat, and the word was passed along, I do not know. Anyway, it didn't really matter. All that mattered was that Amadu was there to take charge. My relief at being able to put myself into his hands was intense. We pushed our way back to the boxes, and at last I could sit on the counter, while Amadu stood guard over my possessions as they appeared. His grin was frozen by now, he was so pleased to have a job again with his former missus. He began to assert his authority, and scared away most of the others by telling tall tales that "his missus savvy plenty too much," that "she be proper master," while I longed for it all to end.

Amadu next produced a tall, domineering boy, and said he

"be proper cook for missus"; after I hastily looked at his references from former masters—notes undoubtedly purchased from a native clerk who could forge quite well—Amadu engaged him. His name was Lamina. By this time Amadu was almost swamped by prospective job hunters, so Lamina let out with his fists and a flow of what sounded like first-class cursing. At last a white man parted the throng, using his fists and heels effectively, and came up to me, asking if he could help me clear my pile of boxes, which was becoming bigger every minute. He turned out to be the head customs man, so things finally moved, and the black clerks, who had been almost rude before, suddenly became overpolite while their boss was in sight, immediately relapsing back into sullenness when he left.

After two and a half hours of waiting, I was told that all my boxes could not possibly be cleared that day; I must return the next day, for they would have to go into the matter of how much duty I was to pay on the food, as well as on the loads of machinery which had been sent out with me for the mining company. So I departed with Lamina and Amadu to the Mines Department office. There I found several telegrams and cables stating that I was to report first at the company's main gold mine at Makong. I was to stay there as long as necessary, and try to find out the source of the gold which they were mining in the gravels, before I proceeded to do prospecting in the "blue." That settled various difficulties, because at an established center I could get my equipment in proper order and repack my food boxes.

The Mines Department chief arranged for me to stay in the resthouse, for Miss Carey was in England on leave. I began to feel quite cheerful, now that I knew I should not have to repeat my stay at the city hotel.

The next three days were a hectic rush of clearing food and

General view of main paddock at Makong, showing gold workings. The bush has been cleared, and the gravels washed starting from the downstream side. The work is going on in the middle distance. Note the line of trenches at the edge of the forest in which water is being brought to the workings.

Roll call at the Makong mine at 6 A.M. with the mists just rising from the hills.

The "working face" where the gold gravels are collected in head pans to be washed near by.

The gold gravels being carried in head pans up a gangway to water which is brought to the workings in wooden sluice boxes. The water in the foreground is overflow water, and cannot be used in workings down the valley without pumping. The water is kept at a high level so that it can be used again.

machinery through customs, getting maps and a prospecting permit, and shopping for gasoline lamp accessories and odds and ends which I had not brought from England.

At last, train day arrived. I dragged myself down to the station at seven in the morning, feeling that I had been in the tropics for months. I was followed by my string of loads, carried on the heads of natives—a real cavalcade. An extra baggage car had to be shunted around for my goods, which thoroughly upset the baggage master. Everyone traveled with a lot of stuff in this country, but my array of loads and machinery was evidently unprecedented.

The train trip seemed endless, and even hotter than I had remembered. It was almost six when we arrived at Magburaka, to be greeted by the usual tropical thunderstorm. We were dumped—my two boys, my loads, and myself—in the midst of yelling natives. While I was wondering what next, an efficient-looking, well-dressed black, carrying a large umbrella, doffed his hat, and said he was the headman sent from the mine to meet me, and that a Syrian was waiting with his truck to take me by road to the Matotaka resthouse, ten miles away, where I was to spend the night. We took the necessary loads, leaving the others in charge of the headman, who would have them carried to the mine. I climbed up beside the dusky Syrian driver, who told me proudly in French that he had informed the native chief that a "missus" was coming that night, and to sweep the resthouse, have some wood on hand, and bring water. This was good news, for I was already feeling the damp chill, as the sun set, and was hungry.

The town of Matotaka was ruled by a powerful and famous paramount chief, Bai Kaferi. I was surprised to find him at the resthouse to greet me, looking very impressive with gold distaff, crownlike embroidered hat, gold nose ring, flowing gown, and umbrella. I asked him for a good watchman for the night, and got rid of the curious villagers as soon as possible, telling Bai Kaferi I would give him a dash in the morning. After hastily consuming a can of beans, it didn't take me long to crawl under my mosquito net and drop into the sleep of exhaustion.

It was still dark when I heard pans rattling in the adjoining kitchen, and I knew it was time to get up, for I had twenty miles to walk that day to Makong. I hated to put on my heavy hob-nailed shoes, but the trails might be slippery. I wondered how long my new golf stockings would fit my feet. They invariably shrank, for I had never been able to train Amadu to wash them properly. They were protection for my legs, and prevented blisters.

The sledge hammer was finally found. I never moved any-where without a boy to wield a sledge hammer, so that I could keep a record of the type of rock I was passing; it might prove a valuable aid to me later, in my prospecting work, if I mapped the rocks as I went along. I had brought out a surveyor's measur-ing wheel this time—just a bicycle wheel, with handle bars and cyclometer—which would give my distances in tenths of a mile. I had never been sure of my exact position when mapping the iron ores; this time I would make accurate reports about my work, and measure my distance from known points.

The small boy chosen to push the wheel was delighted with his job. He was the envy of the others, as he gingerly practiced pushing the wheel back and forth. I ate a hasty breakfast in the dawn, while Amadu and Lamina packed my bedroll and locked the various boxes.

Then came the lining up of the boxes, and the scramble for the lightest loads by the carriers, who had been sent from the mine. Eight more carriers were needed, so volunteers from the mob of onlookers from the village were requested. The crowd shrank back. None wished to carry a sixty- or eighty-pound box twenty miles. I appealed to the chief, who was watching the performance, telling him that I would not give him his dash until I saw my last box loaded on a boy's head. He would have to supply me with eight boys. He called his policemen, who vanished into the village, to be gone an incredibly long time, finally returning with a dozen emaciated-looking boys, all in rags and obviously more or less outcasts. Undoubtedly they were in debt to the chief, or were his slaves, and would have to pay him the shilling that they would earn that day. I chose six who looked as if they would not drop their loads after three miles and disappear into the bush. Then, as it was getting late, seven-thirty, and the sun seemed to have bounded upward and was already cutting through the mist, I had the boys' loads helped onto their heads, and sent them off along the trail, with the headman close behind, his stick handy to urge any laggards forward. This left me with two loads of chairs, table, lunch box, hammer, and knapsack of instruments. I needed two strong intelligent boys who would keep with me all the time, and who could carry me across streams if necessary. Amadu and Lamina, of course, carried nothing but my precious lamps, and these only as a great concession, for they were above being beasts of burden, personal servants rating highest in the native social scale.

By this time the chief was eying me with concern, for he had brought me a dash of two chickens and six probably rotten eggs, and so far I showed no signs of dashing him in return. When he realized that his dash was growing smaller as my temper rose at the lack of available carriers, he turned to two stalwart personal retainers and said they were to go with the missus, and not leave me for one instant. Grateful at this sudden turn of affairs, I handed Bai Kaferi three shillings, which he carefully counted before thanking me, a gleam of pleasure in his eye. I started out at a fast pace, with the whole village after me shouting farewell.

I was glad to lose my village escort after a quarter of a mile or so, and breathed more freely as I settled down to a steady pace in the shade of the dense forest. I passed my line of carriers resting in the next village. The headman was drinking palm wine, so I scolded him properly and told him to get a move on. I knew the performance of drinking palm wine and resting would go on in every village, but there was nothing to do except go ahead, hoping that the loads would turn up at the mine by dark. The two boys whom the chief had given me were good boys, and kept right at my heels, groaning audibly from time to time, hoping I would slow down. But I knew their tricks, and never even looked around. We crossed one big river in a canoe ferry, but I had to be carried pickaback across the other streams. Shoes are precious in Africa, and wet shoes blister one's feet. A native takes it for granted that a white person will be carried over water, so, although I could not talk to my two retainers, they automatically arranged with themselves about my transportation.

As the hours passed, my stops became more frequent. I rested at least half an hour for lunch under a big mahogany tree, my retainers exclaiming at the various implements from my lunch box. The chance to see what a white person ate, and the curious things I produced for this purpose, made the trip worth while to them. Their eyes got bigger and bigger, especially when I gave one the can from my sardines, and the other an empty grape juice bottle. They probably kept these as precious souvenirs, or traded them for food. The natives usually eat only once a day; however, if chance puts food in their way at other times, they are always ready to eat it.

It was four o'clock when I finally dragged into the Makong mine, just as the thunderstorm I had been anxiously watching broke. I was footsore and stiff, being badly out of practice, and the heat during the afternoon hours was exhausting. Glad I was to be greeted by Wren and Parker, who were still stationed here. They immediately offered me a chair and tea, plying me with questions about the outside world, from which they had been separated for twelve months.

Wren noticed that I looked cold, for my clothes were soaked with perspiration, and the coolness from the storm made me shiver after all my exercise. A boy was ordered to bring whisky and soda, and the inevitable quinine bottle.

Much to the concern of my two companions, I refused the whisky, thereby earning a long discourse about how I could never survive in that climate unless I filled my blood with alcohol. I laughed at them; I knew their country; they need not worry.

As there was still no sign of my carriers, Parker ordered his boy to fill his tin bathtub with hot water "one-time" and then produced a suit of clothes for me to put on.

I reappeared, revived, just as the first of my soaked carriers came out of the dark woods into the camp clearing. The loads were dumped in the spacious mud hut which had been assigned to me; this was a rectangular house built entirely of sticks and mud, newly whitewashed that very day. The roof, made of palm leaves neatly woven together into twelve-inch squares which closely overlapped, showed leaks in only a few places. I carefully noted the wet spots. One particularly nice feature about my house was the covered passageway to the kitchen, so that I could have my soup arrive undiluted by the rain. Another feature which had been installed for my particular comfort was an inside lavatory. The only thing lacking was running water. The central part of my house was open to the west, and had a delightful view.

The white men had invited me to chop with them, not just because my cook had not turned up as yet, but because any break in their usual routine was hailed by these lonely souls. At a camp such as this, with only two white men, it was customary for each to run his own establishment, and to eat separately. In the tropics, one's nerves become touchy after a while, and too much of anyone's society irritates.

My coming into camp was made a festive occasion, and the dinner passed most pleasantly; many tall tales were told with gusto, until I finally pulled myself, feeling quite stiff, out of my chair, and left them, happy for once, to continue their bigger and better yarns until the early hours of the morning.

I found my house topsy-turvy, for the carriers had struggled in by dark, dumped their loads anywhere, and left the tired Amadu and Lamina to straighten things out as best they could. Luckily, my bed was ready, and I could worry about the rest in the morning.

A terrific clangor woke me out of a deep sleep. Something dreadful must have happened. Then I realized that it was the rising bell in the laborers' compound. I hastened to get up, for I wanted to pick out, from the unemployed throngs that I knew would appear, a good crew of boys for my own work. A cup of tea and a banana were brought in by sleepy-eyed Amadu—he had probably sat up most of the night telling an admiring audience all the doings in Freetown.

As I came out into the bedlam of the compound, throngs of black faces eagerly turned my way, for word had gone round that the "missus" would probably want laborers. Momo Beer, the headman who had been assigned to me, appeared and saluted, saying that he "get plenty good boys for missus." I asked to see what particular boys he had chosen, lined them up, and quickly eliminated several feeble-looking ones, undoubtedly "brothers" of the headman, or possibly his "slaves," for all I knew. Then I looked around and picked a dozen ragged-looking, but powerfully built boys from the throng. The twenty lined up before me. They looked fairly promising, but I knew I should soon find out how they worked. Picks and shovels were assigned to my personal crew, and off we went to make the rounds of the mine.

At Makong, the gold is found in stream beds. The wearing down of the land has resulted in the concentration of the heavy gold gravels in the stream beds, making workable deposits known as gold placers. My job was to find out where these placer deposits came from. In order to answer the question, I had to map the rock formations carefully, sample certain rocks, and, in places where the soil was deep, have trenches dug to see what the rock was at depth. I reasoned that the gold might have come from the rocks of the higher lands above the streams or from reefs of gold across which the streams were cutting.

We passed through the now deserted compound in which the laborers slept—row after row of double mud houses with palm-thatched roofs, twenty-four rooms on each side. Each "room" housed one laborer, and as many wives, children, and relatives as he allowed to live with him. All the women and relatives were out preparing chop or getting firewood for the night, so the streets were deserted.

Several larger houses faced the compound. These were decorated with shiny kettles, lamps, gaily colored cloth, sparkling beads, and other trinkets to attract the native eye. They were the shops of the Syrian traders, men who supplied the growing mine with an endless supply of cheap goods, dumped in the colonies. The Syrians made a mint of money on payday, for a native either spends or gambles away his earnings. Money is so easy to get, and he needs so few things!

My boys greedily eyed the Syrian stores, knowing that they would soon have money to spend; but I hurried them on toward a great din of shouting and singing. When we reached the source of the noise, I found natives not mining in one place, but in five. Each digging is called a "paddock." These paddocks had a hundred and fifty natives working each of them—more than seven hundred boys in all. I visited and studied each paddock, and especially the high land between them.

On our approach to the first paddock, known as "the excavator paddock" because of a machine being used there, bedlam let loose. Work moved at a feverish pitch. A white person—male or female—meant a "master" to them. And a master meant that they must work. They could relax as soon as the master was out of sight. I went on upstream. Soon I saw a white quartz vein on a hillside. As quartz veins under certain conditions carry gold, I decided to test it. I set a crew of boys digging trenches above and below the outcrop, to see if it extended under the surface soil for any distance. While the boys were busy, I made a quick tour of the gold diggings, in order to get the general idea of the whole lay of the land before studying the region in detail.

The work of digging out the gold was fascinating to watch. The forests had been entirely stripped from the valleys; even the stumps had been burned. The complete removal of payable gravels was started at the lower end of the valley and gradually progressed upstream, leaving great boulder heaps and desolation behind. Every bit of the gravel was washed in order to collect the gold. A steep, even front, about eight feet high, marked the "working face." I could see gangs of boys, presided over by a gesticulating headman, cutting the gravel away, shoveling the dirt into pans which waiting boys then placed on their heads. These latter dogtrotted off over boulders and through puddles, up the banks—sometimes up inclines built of logs—to the troughs of running water, which every few feet extended downward from two great ditches to the sluice boxes, where the gravels were washed. The boys threw the contents of their head pans into the sluices, usually against a board, so that none of the precious metal was lost. Other boys shoveled the gravel on through the sluices, washing and removing any boulders too large to be carried down by the flow of water. The heavy gold settled to the bottom near the point where the gravels were originally dumped. The gold is heavy and is caught in irregularities in the bottom of the sluice boxes, which are specially constructed for that purpose.

Every day or two the water was turned off from the sluice boxes, and the gold was collected, together with whatever gravel lay at the bottom of the box. The gravel was then carried back to camp, where it was panned or washed once more; mercury, which has an affinity for gold, was used to collect the gold particles. Then, once a week, the gold and mercury were put in a great iron basin and "burned," in order to separate the mercury from the gold. This process always puzzled and alarmed the natives, for they felt that all their labor was going up in smoke. An enormous bonfire had to be built and kept going all day, in order to burn the gold properly and melt it down into small bars, ready to send to England.

The importance of having much water, steadily supplied to each paddock, was obvious. Trenches extended for miles, winding in and out of valleys, bringing the water from distant streams. They were almost level, with just enough grade so that the water would flow steadily.

The task of figuring out how to bring in water, without

pumping it, was a job in itself. At places where trenches could not be dug through the solid rock, wooden boxes were constructed; in extreme cases, iron runways were built at great expense, the sheets of iron being brought out from England, and carried to the mine, four boys being required to handle each sheet.

Study of the excavations in the valley showed a topsoil in which there was no gold. Beneath this were coarse gravels, which had been worked back and forth by the stream. Beneath

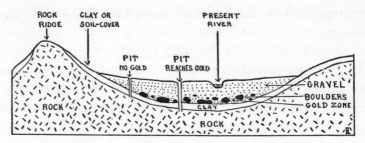

Cross section of stream valley to show the occurrence of gold and the best place to sink pits to test the gravels.

the gravels was bottom clay. Some of the clay contained gold, but most of the metal lay at the bottom of the coarse gravel, where it had worked down, as the stream churned up its bed and moved its materials back and forth. (A typical cross section of the gold-bearing river gravels is shown in the accompanying diagram.)

Every day for two months I worked at the main mine, visiting the paddocks where the gold was being mined, inspecting the clay the boys had reached—for one never knew when a clue might show up—visiting the piles of boulders that accumulated as the washed gravels were rushed through the sluice boxes, and carefully examining the fine sands found with the precious gold at the bottom of the boxes. Each aspect of the mining helped to form in my mind the picture of the source of the gold.

First, I had to make a map of the region, in order to understand the rock relationships and to keep track of the various gold-bearing reefs. As fast as the rocks were uncovered in the paddock diggings, they were recorded on my map, before the debris was heaved back and they were covered by twenty-foot piles of stones.

We constructed a rough plane table, such as surveyors use. Distances were plotted to scale; exact measurements were taken. New trenches were dug by my gang, so that I could see the bedrock in key places. Rocks were tested constantly, crushed to a fine powder, weighed, and washed, until I knew for a certainty whether or not they contained even a few grains of gold. These were weighed on accurate balances, and the value of that particular rock figured out mathematically. The work took two months of steady plugging, from early morning until late afternoon. In order to map the area beyond the mine, my boys cut straight lines through the thick brush and made trails up every stream. In this country, I could not move a foot off a trail without a crew in front, cutting a path with their machetes.

Trenches, trenches, and more trenches! The boys tried so hard to be helpful, but often they were more of a hindrance than a help. The day I came nearest to giving up was when I had been hunting everywhere for an important boundary marker—a great cement beacon weighing a hundred pounds—which had been placed by government surveyors in order to mark the exact corner of the company's mining claim. The jungle had grown so rapidly that all trace of it was gone in six months' time. I had boys scouting the vicinity where I knew it must be. Finally one boy, puffing and panting, struggled through the bush, carrying a great load on his head. One look, and my heart sank. A cornerstone in place shows exact north, according to the surveyor's calculations. It is a criminal offense to touch one. Smiling broadly amid his puffing, he deposited the cornerstone at my feet! Poor Kalfalla was so proud of finding the stone for which we had all been searching that I did not have the heart to scold him.

In addition to the heat and the insects, my days were made miserable by snakes, for which I soon learned to be subconsciously on the watch. They came into my hut. They turned up in boxes of food. I met fierce ones in the trenches, on the mine dumps, in the forest. With only one exception, the python, they were poisonous. The mambas I dreaded most of all, as did the boys, for if provoked, they spit poison to blind their adversaries, and a mere scratching of the skin with their fangs would allow a fatal dose of poison to enter one's system.

CHAPTER ELEVEN

LEOPARD PALAVER

BUT THE JUNGLE had other living creatures besides snakes, and white persons were always trying a new kind of pet. They were the one break in the routine of our monotony. Some were short-lived, some long. Some made us laugh; some annoyed us; others bit us.

Shortly after my arrival at the camp, a new man, Mr. Chequers, came from England to act as accountant. He was a jolly soul, who added Johnny, a nondescript gray monkey, to our menagerie. Johnny got into everything. He used to sit by the hour on his owner's shoulder, picking imaginary fleas from his master's half-bald scalp. Mr. Chequers found him very amusing until his pencils began disappearing. Then he discovered that Johnny was picking them up, as fast as they were laid down, and chewing them to bits. That was the end of Johnny's freedom. Poor Johnny sat, hunched up all day on the limb of a tree, grinning and chattering to draw attention.

Once we had a tiny, graceful little buck deer, but it lived with us only three days. Mongooses, civet cats, and even a python—the latter "disappeared" one fine day, and I suspect it was eaten by the boys—all had their brief hour.

But none equaled Sally. Sally was a tiny chimpanzee, six months old, perhaps, when she came to us. She was a spoiled child. She had tantrums. She stuck out her lower lip, and even sucked her thumb. She cried if she could not have her own way. She would not tolerate being touched by a black hand and screamed at the sight of a black face. Her master had to keep her in a barrel when he was at work. She loved to look in mirrors. She sat at a table and fed herself, being particularly fond of bananas. She liked to play with the pups. Her quaint charm finally won her a trip to London, where she was sold for twenty-five dollars.

The pups were my special pets. When I arrived at the camp there was a great black and white dog, named Jo, who looked like a descendant of one of Pharaoh's hounds, reigning in solitary glory. But I wanted a dog of my own, so I gave orders to Amadu to look for some pups. One day he appeared, grinning from ear to ear, and accompanied by two filthy men, their arms full of puppies. Dogs galore, aged three weeks, were deposited at my feet. I couldn't make up my mind whether I liked best a black and white, a brown and white, or a brown. When I asked the mining men to help me choose, they were equally unsuccessful, so I kept all three with the understanding that when I left the mine, Mr. Parker would have the black and white, Mr. Chequers the brown, and I would keep the brown and white, which I promptly named "Balto"—for the lead dog of the Alaskan team that carried diphtheria serum to Nome. Balto was a fuzzy pup, but he never grew up to his name. He remained nothing but an African cur with pointed, half-flopped ears, short hair, and nondescript tail. In a short time, the pups were grown up enough to follow me on their wobbly legs wherever I went, much to the amusement of the native boys. Always, they had to be brought home in a head pan on a native's head, for they became exhausted before we returned to camp.

Then there was the leopard. Wren had told the boys that he wanted a leopard for a pet, having spread great tales over his whiskies about the pet leopard he had once taken to England, scandalizing and frightening all his friends and neighbors. So one day a leopard arrived, brought by a chief who wished to obtain favor.

The beast was more than half-grown, at least six months old, and still in the original cage in which he had been caught. He was half-starved and spitting, trying to claw anything within reach. He was filthy, covered with sores where he had been bruised against the cage in his mad attempts to escape. Even Wren was a bit uncertain how to tackle this lively bit of fur. He waited until fortified with a good strong "sundowner" before putting on gauntlet gloves—gloves that were made of some heavy composition material to withstand terrific heat; then he had a great log brought and around it he tied a leather strap and a chain with a dog collar at one end. We three white persons stood at a safe distance; the natives retreated to the bush. Wren approached the cage with a heavy stick in one hand. He first inserted the stick, which was viciously attacked, chewed, and scratched. Then the beast's attention being diverted, he opened the trap door and grabbed the leopard by the neck, pushing its head down. The fight was terrific, but he squeezed the neck and hit the leopard's head against the bars, stunning it. Quickly he put the collar around its neck, removed the animal from the cage, and, thoroughly pleased with his work, went for another drink as the leopard gradually revived.

Then the fun began. The poor creature leaped and thrashed about in a circle, pulling at the chain. The collar held, and the log did not budge, but the boys' eyes popped with fear, as they watched this "bad devil." Small Boy was sent to fetch a chicken and returned shortly with a scrawny skeleton well plucked. No one, not even Wren, could get near the leopard without making it wilder than ever. Finally, a string was attached to the chicken's legs, and Wren threw it within reach of the beast. For a second, fury restrained the beast, then with a bloodcurdling half spit, half growl, it leaped on the chicken and bit it furiously, slapping it with its paws. Finally it settled down, suspiciously crunching, finishing all but the head, and licking its chops and paws.

Still no boy would come near our part of the compound. It was getting dark and beginning to rain. I felt sorry for the beast and thought it should have shelter from the rain. I approached within reach of the chain, turning my flashlight on the yellow eyes of the leopard, which spat at me in most unfriendly fashion. An empty box offered possibilities as shelter, so I kicked it near, being careful to stay behind the closed end. With a leap, the animal attacked the box, only to find itself inside the three walls. Here he stayed, apparently content, for whenever we approached, blinding him with a flashlight, he just spat and did not make any move to come out. There he still lay in the broiling sun the next day, when I took a look on returning from my rounds to the mine. I found a mat and cautiously flung it over the box from behind, with no result beyond the usual hiss. The beast seemed to like the shade of the mat for he stayed motionless in his box. That night I pulled the mat off and flung a chicken over the front of the box. A paw grabbed, pulled it into the cage, and in three minutes there was no chicken left. Wren went to Freetown the next day, and it became my duty to care for this unwelcome pet, for not a boy would go within yards of this bad devil. He was too old to tame and had no desire to become friendly. Gradually, he grew to tolerate me so that I

Dumping loaded head pans of gold gravel against a board, so that none of the precious soil is lost. Workers below eliminate the boulders which are too large for the water to clear away.

Washing the gold in sluice boxes. The gold, being heavy, settles to the bottom within a few feet of where the gravels are dumped, and is caught in grooves at the bottom of the trough.

could throw sawdust, saturated with Lysol, into the box, hoping to cure the sores and disinfect the beast. In time, he would even let me put a forked stick into the cage and clean out the refuse. When Wren returned, he thought his beast quite tamed.

Then, one fine night, Wren and Chequers, having sat up over their whisky and soda until three in the morning, the subject of the leopard and his amiability came up. Wren dilated upon the pleasant nature of his pet and bet that he "could pat that damn pussy." Chequers bet he could not. They argued. Wren, to prove what he said, strode up to the pussy, his arms bare, shirt sleeves rolled high, no flashlight—no light other than the laughing moon. This time, Wren was wrong. The leopard waited until he leaned down to stroke it, then sprang at him. Wren retained enough presence of mind to grab the leopard's throat and hang on for dear life, but not before he had been clawed above his eye, his hands bitten, and huge gashes cut in his arms by the claws of the struggling beast.

I was wakened from a dead sleep by cries of fear and horror. Instinctively, I knew that the leopard had broken loose. I slipped into my mosquito boots, grabbed my automatic, and tore out, flashlight in my other hand. I saw Wren, perspiring and dripping with blood, but gamely hanging on to the struggling animal. I could not shoot the beast for fear of hitting Wren; but it was almost dead by now. An extra twist of the head, and Wren felt safe to let go. Chequers had just enough presence of mind to order Yunka to get some boiling water, for there was still a fire in Wren's kitchen where sleepy Yunka had been waiting for his masters to retire. Throwing Lysol in the water, he gave Yunka the job of bathing his master's angry wounds. I saw I was of no more use and slipped back to bed.

Wren had had a real fright. Fever and pain kept him in bed

all the next week. Send for a doctor? It would be four or five days at least before a doctor could come, and he would be dead by then if he were going to die of anything like lockjaw. An attempt to rush him by hammock to a doctor would be foolhardy. The trip would kill him in his present condition. So we all decided that the only thing to do was to have his wounds treated three times a day with hot water and a little carbolic acid. On the fifth day, he was up and around, arms swathed with wet bandages, looking yellower than usual, but recovering his confidence with every step. The next day he took a stroll through the village, swaggering a little, so that all the natives could appreciate what a powerful man he was, for had he not told the chief that he was the only man who had ever strangled a real live leopard? Awe greeted him on all sides; he had gone up another notch in native eyes. He had been feared before, but now not a soul would dare cross him, and he knew it.

Weeks later, when the final scab had come off, "Pa" Wren proudly displayed his scarred arms. Now he had a permanent record of his prowess in Africa and a new story to tell. However, when Mr. Babcock, now one of the directors of the company, came out to the camp with his wife, for a brief visit, it was quite a different story. We were all told to say nothing about it, for London would not approve. The first day, the guests accompanied Wren on his tour of inspection. With great care, Mr. Babcock began to instruct his wife in the ways of avoiding the sword grass, and, to impress the gravity of the situation on her, he pointed to Wren's arms and said, "You see, my dear, how really serious the sword grass can be. Just look at Wren's arms. Those scars are the result of having to walk through this vile sword grass. So do, please, be very careful." Wren did not blink an eyelid, and the lady was duly impressed. Later, on returning to camp, the visitor noticed the leopardskin carelessly flung over the woodpile and asked who had shot it. I could not refrain from answering sarcastically, "Oh, Wren, one moonlit night."

Another night, again at the zero hour of three, I waked from a half-sleep to hear loud calls for Small Boy. Apparently, Small Boy had finally succumbed to slumber after hours of running back and forth with bottles and new sparklets for the soda water siphon. Demands for Small Boy became violent, and finally the announcement that he would show Small Boy how to come, when called, was broadcast. In the bright moonlight I saw three swaying white-clad figures make their way across the open square to the servants' huts. Tipsily, the smaller figure in the center of the group pounded on the first door. No response—in fact, dead silence prevailed in the hut which I knew must be full of natives. Loudly, the smallest figure announced that he would show them. Heaving against the bamboo door, he pushed with all his strength, lurching in as the door gave way. Startled figures of women and children scampered out of all the huts. No Small Boy there. One by one, the doors of all six huts were either burst in or opened, the occupants pouring out, huddled in their country cloths, "pickins" (pickaninnies) crying and hanging on to their frightened parents. It was only the smallest figure that kept up the cursing for Small Boy. The other two trousered individuals hung back until, every corner having been searched, Wren turned back exhausted and was silently escorted to his hut, the effort having sobered him considerably. Next day I was the only one of the whites up bright and early for roll call. Weeks later, when the director made some inquiries as to the sanitary conditions and the overcrowding of the servants' quarters so near our own, Wren volunteered the information that he had made a thorough "inspection" one night in the presence of Chequers and Parker and had found everything satisfactory!

Christmastime drew near. My nerves were becoming a bit ragged, as these three o'clock episodes became more frequent. The boys were letting up on their work, because the "Big Master" rarely made rounds, and when he did, just did not notice the slackening up on every side. All of us were becoming short-tempered.

On his return from Freetown, Wren had boasted about getting Yunka out one night in front of the resthouse, at the railroad, and making him dance for his amusement. When Yunka's ardor slackened, Wren got out his revolver and fired it at Yunka's feet to frighten him into continuing. Poor Yunka danced for his life, with the crowd of natives growing bigger and bigger. Wren evidently did not realize that one false shot in his alcoholic state would have made the whole crowd turn against him and rip him to pieces, for one could almost feel the boiling hatred of many of the natives. It was only a matter of time before someone would come along and rouse the blacks to turn upon their masters. Before long the miner would have to listen to those who outnumbered him so heavily; the government was bound to step in eventually and introduce real mining laws and supervise what went on at the mines. The time was coming, and soon, when the natives would realize that these whites were bleeding them of their natural riches.

To celebrate Christmas Day, I slept late. I got up feeling depressed, to lunch in solitude, the three pups looking on and the quiet Amadu bringing in a plate of the now despised chicken. A boy arrived from next door, inviting me to supper in Wren's spacious new hut. I accepted gladly.

At four, Wren, Parker, and Chequers, with Johnny on his shoulder, paraded past my house, followed by various and sundry personal boys, all headed for the village, laughing and cheery. I hoped nothing untoward would come of the expedition. Shouts from the village could be heard with increasing frequency for the next few hours. At six, I saw a sorry-looking procession return. Wren's shirt was torn and dirty, his hair disheveled, and across his brow an ugly cut. Chequers stopped when he saw me, and, when I offered him tea, he gladly accepted. He felt very sad, for Johnny, in the excitement, had got completely out of hand and had taken to the bush. Gradually the whole story came out. They had made for the Syrian trader's store, and Wren had purchased a couple of cases of beer as a treat for his friends and a few chosen natives and Syrians. After they had consumed all the beer, Wren demanded entertainment, so a few natives were set to wrestling. Bored, Wren spotted a bull tied near-by and challenged any native to tackle this animal. No one volunteered, so he, brave Wren, the "ex-champion wrestler of his school," rolled up his sleeves and had a ring set for himself. Twice the bull tossed him; twice he returned madder than ever. The third time, he got the bull down, and, hanging on for dear life, amid the cheers of the natives, he finally twisted the bull's neck until it gave up. He strutted home, feeling and looking much the worse for wear. I told Chequers that I felt sure I would be a damper on any Christmas dinner, and that I thought they should excuse me. He agreed, knowing full well what a Christmas dinner with such a good start would be. Bottles were carried back and forth from the storehouse, until finally Wren had reached the high-spirited stage which made even him admit that I had better not come. At nine o'clock he sent over a deliciously cooked duck dinner, Yunka having outdone himself, knowing what would happen if everything was not perfect.

Earlier in the afternoon, Yunka had got up a band, consisting of his wives and all the servants, and paid me a Christmas visit, singing and playing on the native instruments. I was amused and not a little touched by this attention, and got out some Woolworth trinkets for his head wives as Christmas presents.

Having eaten my Christmas dinner by the moonlight with only the three pups for company, I retired early, only to be awakened by a serenade from four white men, another having arrived from the north just at dark. The singing of "Good King Wenceslas," "God Rest Ye Merry, Gentlemen," and all the other Christmasy things of their repertoire, made my throat feel lumpy. I looked out to see four white-clothed figures silhouetted against the dark forest.

With Christmas had come word that five new white men, all engineers, were being sent from London, and would arrive on New Year's Day. Anticipation of newcomers to the camp buoyed us all up. My prospecting around the mine was completed. I had made a map showing the gold reefs, and had plotted the formation from which the gold was derived. I could do no more than just putter around and waste my time, if I stayed on. I should have gone south to Pujehun, to prospect the mine there, but Wren said that he wished to show me around Pujehun personally, that he had to inspect Pujehun some time, and that I should wait and go down when he went. So I was still in camp when the five newcomers arrived, despite the fact that they very much needed the use of my hut. Wren took care of three of them for supper, Chequers and Parker fed the other two; then all congregated for a night of reminiscences in Wren's house. Every time I dropped off to sleep I was wakened by the call of "boy." I made up my mind to pack the next morning and go to Pujehun.

Relieved, I almost dropped off to sleep, when I heard a voice pass beneath my rear window, and, as it passed, a monotonous drone came, "Tell me, Fine Boy, have I, or have I not, had chop tonight." "Yas, sah, you done chop, sah." Again and again, the question; again and again the same answer, as the two passed out of hearing. Doubled up with mirth, I buried my laughter in the bedclothes, wondering what I thought was funny in this three o'clock remark.

At five-thirty, bright and early, after practically no sleep, up I got, called Amadu, and announced to a face that did not register any surprise that we were to go to Pujehun that day, and he was to begin packing at once. At six-thirty I sent a note to Wren announcing my departure. At seven, just as all my loads were lined up and my own boys began to return from the village, where I had sent them for their own bundles, a note from Wren demanded my presence in his hut. I marched over to face a very sick-looking, bleary-eyed, trembly-handed individual, dressed in a clean shirt, and with his hair slicked back. To the question of what was all this about and why my sudden decision, I announced that I was going on with my work as I should have done ten days before. He looked at me for a moment without speaking and then gave me carte blanche to do as I saw fit. So we parted, friends.

CHAPTER TWELVE

BAI KAFERI

WITH REAL RELIEF, I watched the boys shoulder their loads and start off over the mountain to Lungi rest-house. Hot and weary, I pushed on during the morning, reaching Lungi in time for lunch. Then, contrary to my usual custom, I had my bed set up, mosquito net fixed, and crawled in for a nap. I slept until six, then ate supper, and turned in for the night at seven-thirty. At five-thirty the next morning, rested and revived, I struck out once more, making record time to Pujehun. Momo Beer, my headman, sensed my feeling of hilarity at being away from the mine and pranced along in front of me for the first few miles like a freed monkey. Coming to a stream, he took his staff and started to vault over. Crash and kerplunk, Momo with all his dignity landed neatly in the deepest spot, his nicely carved walking stick floating downstream. The carriers, who had just come up to the stream, laughed uproariously as they watched the bedraggled Momo clamber out. After this disgrace, Momo kept to the rear, well out of my sight, for the rest of the day.

A surprised white man met me at Pujehun. Usually, he knew days ahead when a visitor was coming to his camp. Having spent a lonesome Christmas, he was overjoyed to have someone to whom he could talk.

Pujehun was the stickiest, sultriest place I had come to, so far. I started work early and stopped early, when possible. A few days sufficed for me to find out that the gold came from the rocks of the region and not from the quartz reefs. The gold-bearing rocks were already known, and it was now a matter of sinking shafts to see whether an underground mine was the best method of operation. This was the engineer's job, not mine, so, after a careful examination, I went back to Makong. On the way I passed a messenger, headed for Freetown, with four bars of gold, worth at least ten thousand dollars, carried in a small bundle on his head. He was accompanied by an unarmed government soldier. The insurance premium for gold sent out without armed guards was ridiculously less than the premium where an armed escort was deemed necessary. As yet, the natives did not know what to do with gold, if they had any. One day Mr. Chequers put down a penny and a nugget worth forty dollars and told the boy who was standing near to take either one. The boy took the penny! He could buy something with a penny, but the gold was just some white man's palaver.

Things at Makong had changed in the short time since my departure. I hardly recognized the place. Order and discipline prevailed, for Mr. Babcock, now a director, had arrived and taken control. Wren had been taken mysteriously ill, and had been bundled off in a hammock to Freetown and the hospital. Mr. Babcock and his wife had immediately moved into Wren's palatial residence and had sent the five new engineers off posthaste in various directions to start up new mines or to prospect thoroughly some areas reported as possible gold finds. The paddocks at Makong were humming, with not an idle native. The weekly gold output shot up to a high peak. Trenches were being dug, and a new gasoline pump was installed in the large flats so that work could begin there. The long-since abandoned excavator, a simple, gasoline-run machine used for a few weeks in the "excavator paddock," was actually being moved to new ground. This mechanical scoop, which could work a circular area of ground in record time, had been brought out from England at great expense, five months having been spent in getting it to Makong itself, literally dragged by humans through the jungle trail. Bridges had been constructed for its safe passing. After a delay in setting it up, it was abandoned when engine trouble developed. Wren had found all sorts of excuses to use the slow native hand labor instead of struggling with the problem of shifting the excavator about and repairing it when things went wrong. Now it was to wheeze again and draw mobs of admiring natives to watch the ropes pull out the long scoop, open its jaws, eat into the gold gravel, drag the gravel to the water, dump its precious load, and return for another jawful.

Mr. Babcock looked at my trenches, my maps, and my sketches of the gold reefs, and agreed that no more could be done at Makong. He also agreed that I could now go out to prospect for new territory, for the company would need more land as mining speeded up. I was given full sanction to go wherever I wished. The unknown, the unexplored places naturally were the most tempting and alluring—places I knew the government geologist had never visited, but places somewhat in the vicinity of the roughly mapped boundary of the granites and schists, for there I might reasonably expect to find gold. I collected two or three months' supplies before hitting into the "blue."

Chop boxes made of three-ply wood, light and strong, well padlocked, were made up in lots of three, so that three boxes could be carried for a month and then three more could be sent up from the main camp. Everything was in sealed tins—flour, sugar, salt, pepper, tea, butter, milk, an assortment of canned meats, consisting of lunch tongue, sardines, salmon, sandwich spread, and dried beef. I took only asparagus and peas for vegetables, together with a few cans of grapefruit and "fruit salad." These were heavy, though they came in small tins. I hoped to get bananas and oranges, as well as a few vegetables, along the way. Two boxes of digestive biscuits and one of Vita Wheat, the best bread substitute, two packages of Wheatena, and baking powder (a necessary addition to palm wine as a yeast substitute in making bread; for, as Lamina remarked, "Mebbe they no be power for them palm wine"). I intended to buy rice along the route or to send for it to the nearest villages, for this was the staple diet throughout the country. Besides, any chief would dash me rice at my request, as well as chickens and eggs, bananas, and vegetables such as sweet potatoes (if he had any). However, all these dashes must be repaid in a dash of money that would leave him satisfied. I finally added four bottles of grape juice to each box, as a special treat. The light things were scattered in the various boxes to equalize the load, each box weighing between sixty and seventy pounds when full. I knew that they would be lighter by the time we reached the bad steep trails, so that seventy pounds was not too much for a start.

The cook's box was carefully weeded out—all the pots and pans with which Lamina would part were eliminated. This cook's box was the biggest trial of the trek, for somehow Lamina would acquire more junk along the route. He hated to throw away a single bottle or can that he thought he might use some time. Accordingly, I had to have a regular weekly weeding out of the box in order to close it at all. My gallon canteen for boiled water was stowed with difficulty in a corner, and my big kettle was finally tied on the handle outside, as it was too large to put in the box.

My "office box" with a few consulting books, writing materials, maps, official papers, and money box, was carefully repacked, with a few clothes to balance things. Then my clothes box was examined until I was satisfied I had everything I needed.

One box had to be allotted for kerosene. The mine's carpenter had cut the top off two five-gallon tins, which were set in a reinforced crate with a padlock and a hinged cover. Inside one of the tins I put four one-gallon cans of kerosene, leaving space in the other tin for odds and ends such as rice, bananas, and food we would get in the villages. These were to be my chief water containers. They could be filled with water and heated on the fire. The cook insisted upon tying on top of his cook box two old five-gallon tins he used in the kitchen; he always stuffed them full of any chickens I bought, their legs tied together so that they could not escape. In camp, after getting water in the cans, he used them as a stove, building his fire in one, with the top for a grill, and using the other for baking. This sort of stove had all kinds of possibilities, depending upon what the cook wished to have me eat that day.

Finally, two loads of tools, picks, shovels, and head pans, as well as gold-washing pans, were made up. Each boy was issued a machete for his own use. At last we were ready, with no detail overlooked. I had even given my automatic a final cleaning, quite openly, so that my boys might see that I had the weapon, which they eyed with awe and alarm.

After a consultation with Mr. Babcock, it was decided that the paramount chief of the next chiefdom, Bai Kaferi, might be worth consulting. All the chiefs hoped that gold might be found on their land. Bai Kaferi was feeling piqued because

Alimami Souri, the paramount chief where the Makong mine was located, was having such a windfall. Bai Kaferi would like to have a mine started on his own land; he might even know of some likely possibilities, if I could worm the information out of him. This was a good starting point, for I had ideas of my own about where I wished to prospect, and Bai Kaferi's town of Matotaka was as good a place as any from which to begin. Besides, there was something in keeping fairly well in touch with the paramount chief for the first few days, in case I had trouble with my carriers, and I would be in Bai Kaferi's chiefdom for some time.

I had planned to get an early start, for it was twenty miles to Matotaka; but there was much to do. I had reduced my goods to sixteen bundles; sixteen carriers, previously picked, were counted off and allotted to me. Then I picked a strong-looking boy, Momo the First, as a personal helper who would carry me across rivers, push my cyclometer wheel, and carry my knapsack. He beamed at being given this "soft job," but his glee did not survive many miles, for he found he had to keep at my heels all the time in order to break rocks along the way. He also had a limited vocabulary of pidgin English and could act as a sort of interpreter. I always felt a little dubious about his ability as a translator, from the curious answers he often translated back to me.

Lamina, the cook, reported that he felt ill, so I had to tell him to stay behind, giving orders for him to follow us when he had recovered. I could get on somehow.

When all sixteen carriers, Momo Beer, Amadu and his "learner" or own "small boy," Chaka, were ready, the word "Help 'em up" was called. With many grunts, groans, and adjusting of old towels, grass, and other cushionlike protectors, which each boy carried on his head to help balance his load according to his individual taste, they were off, single file, singing and yelling to the onlookers, for they felt quite superior at being chosen to go out into the world with the Gold Missus and leave the drudgery of the twelve-hour day at the mine. Trekking to new places meant something to talk about for the rest of their days. They would make new friends and perhaps get free chop from tribal brothers whom they met. As I watched the last boy pull out, a motley line of half a dozen women, carrying baskets well heaped with pots and pans, straggled by from the boys' compound. They were clothed in vari-colored cloths, several layers of different colors flaunting conspicuously. Two of them carried "pickins" jogging up and down on their backs, bound tightly in the outer cloth. This constituted the female side of the retinue, not encouraged, but not forbidden, as it meant that the boys would have someone to cook for them on trek. When we returned to camp at the end of our trek, this retinue had been doubled. Some new wives were bought en route; others were followers, but came just the same, and no questions were asked.

A line of unemployed still stood at attention. Turning to the men, Babcock counted out twenty, assigned them a headman, took their names, and told them to relieve my boys at a halfway mark so that I could make better time that first day. They were to return the following day with some machinery now in Matotaka. This seemed a final act of generosity; but, needless to say, these boys evaporated completely and never caught up with my own crew. A chance to earn money for just walking twenty miles was too good to be true. Not to be outdone, the accountant insisted upon my taking his hammock to use in the flat country near the end of the first day's trek, when the heat would be intense. I accepted his offer, saying that I would send the four hammock boys back the next day, as after that time I would be on bush paths where a hammock could not be used. This offer turned out to be a streak of luck, for when I reached the first village, I found my loads dumped about and the boys in utter confusion. The headman came to me talking wildly. Finally, I made out that three of the carriers had "gone for bush," dumping their loads at the edge of the village. The village held no recruits. All the husky-looking men developed complaints when asked to volunteer to carry a load. There was nothing to do but to use three of the hammock boys and send the hammock back to camp by the fourth, with a note of thanks.

As soon as order was restored, I pushed on with my dog and the grunting Momo the First at my heels. Soon even his grunts stopped; it took too much energy to keep up the pace. I was anxious to cover ground while it was still early, then I could loaf over lunch and arrive fairly fresh for my interview with Bai Kaferi.

I saw some monkeys peering down at me. "They be your brother," I said turning to Momo. He looked startled and somewhat annoyed, although he laughed, as if enjoying the joke. Then, becoming serious, he replied, "Oh! No, sah! They no be brudder. They be monkey. I be blackman. I no be monkey."

Of course, he could not know how amusing I found the idea, for Momo was so monkeylike himself. His black face and beady eyes were topped by a striped red and black wool toboggan cap; his prognathous jaw was set grimly, as his long, powerful arms grasped the handle bars of my cyclometer wheel; he wore his newly acquired shorts and the shirt which he had not learned to tuck in, and which hung down ridiculously. The final touch to his masquerade costume was a towel around his neck. He had bought sneakers from a trader at the mine, but these were generally tied around his neck or turned over to his wife to carry proudly on her head, atop a large bundle of kitchen utensils. Momo, with all his laziness, was one of my favorites, partly because I could always smile to myself whenever I looked at him. He did seem as if he had just come out of a tree and should be riding on an organ grinder's shoulder. Perhaps he was the cousin of a serious-faced organ grinder's monkey to whom I used to give pennies as a child.

There was little enough to laugh at in this world of trekking day after day, and there was no one to whom I could really talk. So Momo saved the day many a time, when I was feeling dragged out and depressed. Just a facial expression of his or a gorillalike movement would make me think of myself as an ape among apes, and I would smile instead of scolding the boys for some utterly idiotic mistake they had made. Momo always reveled in his "superior" job of trailing me about with the cyclometer wheel. Many a time I felt sadly out of patience with him as he blinked stupidly while I tried to adjust the cyclometer, which had been bent by some momentary carelessness on his part. But his utter stupidity, as well as his doglike eyes and wrinkled forehead, saved him; after all, he was little more than an animal. He never exasperated me the way his namesake, Momo Beer, the headman, did. Momo Beer was too full of "savvy," or cunning. If anything went wrong and he was near, he was full of suggestions, witticisms, and his own importance pervaded all his suggestions, right or wrong. Stupid Momo the First was a perfect antidote—until he took to smoking a pipe, vile with the smell of native tobacco. Then we parted company, and he got a good hard job for a change.

Noon that first day found us on the banks of a river, big with swollen waters. Although this was supposedly the dry season, an unprecedented number of thunderstorms had kept the water high. We hallooed the opposite side, until finally a few naked children and half-clad natives appeared. One of them got into a

A stage in the construction of a hut. The roof supports are made of bamboo to which the thatch is bound.

Paramount Chief Alimami Souri, Bai Kaferi's rival, with his interpreter (right) and his bodyguard. To the left is his musician playing a guitar-like instrument made out of a gourd.

low-swung canoe, made from a hollowed-out tree trunk with a slight natural curve in the middle. He poled, then paddled across to us, landing downstream in the current. By means of low branches and creepers along the water's edge, he pulled the canoe up to the place where we stood. We piled in, trying to keep our balance in the precarious craft. I had Momo tell him that "Plenty loads come for behind," at which he grinned, for this meant I would give him a big dash. I had heard nothing of the carriers for an hour or more, so I decided to push on and let the loads cross as best they could without my supervision; that was the headman's job, anyway.

Already the cool greenness of the leaves had taken on a yellower, drier tone. The dank smell of the path had gone; it seemed dry. The monkeys were no longer in evidence, and even the few birds seemed to be resting. Only the frogs in occasional pools still lifted their voices. The winged insects took on more life as the day became hotter. Flies swarmed about us as we passed through the village. The most vicious was the tsetse, a variety of black fly with yellow striped wings, which attacked us silently but forcibly. As walking kept them away, we kept going, though more and more slowly.

My eye no longer saw the beauty of the jungle. Everything seemed drab and oppressive. It took a great deal of will power to force myself to examine the rocks we found. I even hoped that there might not be an outcrop for some time. The effort of stopping, examining the rock, noting down the mileage on the cyclometer, describing the rock in a notebook whose paper stuck to my hand, seemed almost too great. Automatically, things were jotted down, but mentally very little was recorded. The sheer effort of thinking in the heavy-laden air was agonizing. Again and again the words "Mad dogs and Englishmen go out in the noonday sun" rang through my head. How right it was! If only I could stop! Nothing, save the fact that it was hot and I was soaking with perspiration, mattered. I dragged myself along, not conscious of how one foot followed the other.

Suddenly I noticed that the rocks on one side of a stream were granite and those on the other side were schist. I stopped and recorded this in my notebook with a careful description of the rocks, the nature of the soil, the size of the stream where the contact of the two kinds of rock was found. This was the hoped-for change in rock types for which I had been searching all day. I sat down wearily on the granite, and ate a banana, then another, then a third. Revived, I ate two oranges. I was feeling strangely cheerful. Even the swarms of black flies could not worry me, for was I not sitting on the key to my future work? A careful examination of the schist indicated in what direction I should turn to prospect. I had not dared hope to have the answer to my problem so soon.

First, however, I must make my visit to Bai Kaferi and follow his clues. I had a topographic map of a sort. It showed the main paths and the main mountain masses, but beyond that it was not much help.

It was much too hot to sit and study the map. Besides, the flies were enjoying the moisture from the corners of my eyes, making me wholly miserable. So I dragged myself up and on.

A little after three, after several miles of dragging along a thick, monotonous, sandy trail, lined with palm trees, the path suddenly widened. Pointed thatched huts came into view through the perpetual green, and we saw several native women bathing in a stream along the path. They shrieked when they saw us appear and, grabbing a pickaninny under each arm and clutching a bundle of clothes to their heads, ran for the village. By the time we reached the first hut, curious natives were already lining the path, the small children, most of them naked, jumping up and down, clapping their hands, and the men and women uttering many ums and ahs as I passed, too hot to do more than grin faintly. These people knew the Gold Missus, and I seemed to sense in their welcome a delight at seeing me again. Sometimes I wondered whether they were laughing at me and my costume, as I was laughing at them, but probably they thought these were the regular costume and habits of white women. My clothes and the strange wheel never failed to arouse the natives' interest. They acted like children being shown the clown at the circus—and many times I felt like one, for I know they expected me to act queerly and even perhaps to do a little magic on the side. Finding gold was magic, of course, but no more strange than why I should want it. Momo used to explain me and my hammer, as I investigated a stone in their front yards, as "missus go look—him money rock," or "missus be Gold Missus." Then my antics would be watched with more ums and ahs, um-ums, and widened eyes and open mouths. Indeed, I discovered later that there was some doubt in their minds as to my identity. I was known to them on account of my appearance and actions as "the man with the woman's voice."

These villagers were accustomed to prospectors, but most prospectors had not had so many jujus—compass, cyclometer wheel, maps, and even the paper bags in which I wrapped my specimens of rock after carefully labeling them. I was worth watching. The white men who came to the village never made such slow progress; they just strode through. It was no use trying to keep the crowd away. They will soon tire of watching me, I thought, little knowing that a native's time is as nothing and his powers of watching something he does not understand, unlimited.

Having finished hammering all the outcrops in sight, I was ready to hunt for Bai Kaferi, for I knew that I would be given a chair in the shade. Moreover, it seemed a better policy to "present my compliments" to the chief as soon as possible. Bai Kaferi might have a real secret to divulge as to mineral localities on his own land; some native, long ago, might have really found gold in the chief's domain, and this knowledge might have been kept a close secret from generation to generation. Greed or jealousy of the prestige of his rival chief would be the only motives which would bring out the secret. Bai Kaferi had learned a bitter lesson the year before, when he drove the prospectors from his land by unreasonable demands for "rent," refusing to let his boys work for the miners for the usual shilling a day, and overcharging for the local food upon which labor was dependent. The real reason for the prospectors' departure from his land was the finding of high-grade gold at Makong; they were glad to leave poorer ground and a troublesome, crafty chief. Perhaps Bai Kaferi would now be ready to help in the development of his land. By a little tact, I hoped to make him want me to come to hunt for gold, and thus help, rather than hinder me. The geology of the land made me hopeful of finding gold.

Accompanied by a motley crowd of dirty naked children and some of the idle men who had been watching me from the shade of their mud verandas, we moved toward the chief's compound, a unit of buildings set apart from the rest of the village. A fairly imposing mud gateway led into the main courtyard, which was encircled by neat, newly plastered houses, probably belonging to the chief's wives. A large bari, with no sides except low mud walls with rough mud ornamentation, stood in the middle of the central space. Supposing that Bai Kaferi would meet me there, I walked over to the shade. Someone produced a low reed stool, and I sat down. After a long wait, one of the chief's messengers came back to say that Bai Kaferi was ready to see me in his house, for he was too ill to come out to "greet me proper fashion."

I was ushered by the messenger, who drove everyone out of the compound except Momo the First. Then we were taken through small alleys until I wondered where I could be going. I seemed to be in a city within a city and felt almost a prisoner. Occasionally a woman glanced up from her pots as if I were an everyday passer-by. Finally we stopped before an old wooden door in the side of a larger mud house. An old woman came forward and said a few low words as she opened the door and bade me enter. For a minute, I could see nothing in the dark cell, into which the bright sun scarcely penetrated. There were no windows; all the light came through the door behind me. Gradually I saw that I stood in an eight-by-ten-foot space. A raised mud bed extended along one side, and on it a figure lifted itself. I recognized the gray-bearded chief, with his gold nose ring, much like a dog license in shape. A dirty dark blue turban was wound around his head; he was clothed in many layers of dark blue robes. Obviously, he was a sick man, but his beady eyes still had a sparkle and withal a kindly look. We touched hands, as I moved to the space by his couch. This was not a formal visit—the only others present being the dirty old woman, the messenger, and my boy—so he spoke directly to me when I inquired concerning his health. If it had been a state visit, he would have felt bound to use an interpreter. First, he asked if I had any medicine for his chest, which bothered him. I immediately replied in the negative, for the old man was so shaky that I would not have dared to offer him quinine or any other medicine, for fear he might pass out during the next few days and I be held responsible for having poisoned him. I carefully explained that I had plenty of medicines for cuts or outside ailments, but none for inside ills. I told him that he should sit on his chair in the sun and let some air into his room. The dampness and airlessness of his hovel were enough to make anyone ill. Poor old Bai Kaferi was actually in the early stages of pneumonia, and narrowly escaped death. He had been taken sick suddenly and could not be secreted into the hills, but had been hidden in this hovel where no one but his one messenger and this old wife had access to him.

According to the tradition of Bai Kaferi's chiefdom, before the breath left him, his head must be severed from his body and transported to a high, bare granite hill, a day's march away. Here, on Gbotto Hill, the head of the former chief of the Matotaka Province lay buried. It would then be disinterred and brought back to the valley to fit on the headless body, and Bai Kaferi's head would lie on the hill waiting, in turn, for the death of the next chief. Because of this custom, each chief always feared that someone who wished to get rid of him would dismember him before he really was ready to die; hence, extraordinary precaution was necessary whenever he became ill. He must never see this sacred hill after being made chief. Nor had he ever seen his gold nose ring, which, I gathered, was some peculiar barbaric mark of the Matotaka paramount chief, fastened to his nose when he took the "stool." Bai Kaferi's body was to be buried at Mamaya in an especially sacred burial grove, several days' rough march away. The whole of the next week, as I was camped at various points along the very route which was to be Bai Kaferi's last journey, my boys, hearing daily by secret tomtom signals about his struggle between life and death, were constantly on the alert, listening for drums to announce his departure. Fortunately, the old man pulled through, with the aid of a black doctor who had been trained in England, and who arrived shortly after I left. Old Bai Kaferi had had enough education to know the value of white man's learning and did not trust his pagan medicine men. Or possibly, the Commissioner at Makeni rushed this black doctor down at Bai Kaferi's request, so that the old soldier—he had formerly served in the native regiment in Freetown—would not be murdered.

Despite a hacking cough, the chief seemed pleased to see me. I explained that I hoped to find gold on his land and, if I did, it would make him rich—rich like his neighbor, the much envied paramount chief of Makali. Perhaps he could help me? Possibly he knew of some place on his land? Our company had started to work some of his land near Matunkara, two years ago, and perhaps he remembered unpleasant palavers over destruction of rice by pitting? If I found gold, would he promise that these unpleasantnesses would not be repeated? Most decidedly, he declared that he would faithfully promise that there would be no palavers, if I would only find gold. He must give me every bit of help, I told him, and I, in my turn, would help him. I had come to help him. I wanted him to have mines on his land. He must order all his people to let me buy food for my boys and help in every other way possible. Thus, everything was arranged.

Then, Bai Kaferi told me he was sure that I would find some gold on his own farm up in the hills. He would send a messenger with me the next day, and for as long as I was there, to show me the way. Having gained my point, I left him, saying he must sit in the sun as much as possible. In parting, I presented him with a shiny Woolworth knife, which he fondled lovingly. I also gave him two shillings to pay for my lodging in his resthouse. These, after a thorough scrutiny, he put into a little square leather bag, which was tied around his neck with strong black cord. He seemed as delighted as a child and touched my hands three times.

I had not realized how weary I was until I started back. The village street and the straight, shadeless path to the resthouse seemed endless. Would I never get past all those thatched houses, past the whitewashed, corrugated iron roofs of the Syrian traders, who stared at me? Mr. Nicols, a black friend of my previous visit, came running after me, holding his immaculate white helmet, and saying "Greetings, missus, greetings. Welcome. I come to see you later in the evening." "Yes!" I feebly said, knowing he was after funds for his pathetic Baptist mission, and I knew I should not have the heart to refuse. At the moment, it just took all my courage to pretend I was not about ready to collapse after nineteen and a half miles in the heat, with all the worries of the first day out of camp—carrier troubles, as well as everything going wrong with Momo the First, who had to be watched with the wheel, and the hammer boy, who had been hopeless. So I set my face into as painless an expression as possible and dragged my feet up the gentle rise to the resthouse, hoping that all the loads were there and that someone had done something about them.

I finally reached the resthouse, only to find boxes scattered in the utmost confusion. Amadu was still in the village, probably imbibing palm wine. There was nothing to greet me but perspiring carriers lying about and looking as exhausted as I felt. I sat down heavily on the cold mud wall of the veranda and, holding my temper in check by a supreme effort, called to Momo Beer, "Send a boy to village to bring Amadu."

Off went a carrier on the run, and in about ten minutes Amadu came trotting up the hill, looking wild-eyed, for he knew he was in for a good scolding. Everyone, even the most truculent carrier, sensed the tension in the air and had collected in a forlorn group. Rumor must have told them I was a hard master, and they all expected the worst, down to a thrashing, perhaps, or a heavy fine.

"Amadu, tell the headman to line up the boys."

They lined up, rather more quickly than I believed it possible for natives to move.

"Now, headman, you tell these boys I fine Amadu two shillings for stopping for village and not coming right to resthouse to fix missus' things."

I saw that the boys were duly impressed and Amadu duly cowed—in fact, almost in tears.

"Now then, five boys go get firewood, five boys go get water, other boys stay here and help fix loads. Any boy who goes to the village before camp is finished, I will fine one day's pay. You savvy?"

"Yes, sah! All boys they savvy proper," said the headman, even before translating my ultimatum.

In another minute, everything was bustle. Thoroughly frightened, they went off on their respective jobs. Amadu moved more quickly than usual, and as a peace offering produced my deck chair from the debris of boxes. There was something almost stimulating in being able to take off my helmet and lean back without hitting its stiff brim, and slowly feel my hair dry. In fact, getting into camp, relaxing in a chair, without any fear of the sun, and having my bare feet up on the footrest was as near bliss as I ever got, except the moment after a bath when all the dirt of the day had gone and I stepped into a pair of dry pajamas. However, it took a resthouse to offer these ideal conditions. A tent was quite another proposition. Such carefree moments of complete physical bliss were rare. Slowly my feet stopped throbbing, and as I lay relaxed, without the binding drag of a helmet on my head, I became interested in watching this crew manage a first camp.

Chaka, in Lamina's absence, had been promoted to "acting" cook. He must have departed with his pots and pans, for a commotion with much jabbering was going on in the direction of the cookhouse, a small mud hut adjoining the resthouse. For once, I felt too peaceful to interfere and left him to settle his own palavers.

A group of boys struggling with that most remarkable of contrivances, the "ruckee" chair, amused me greatly. A crowd of villagers had collected to offer advice and express innumerable ums and ahs. One leg of the chair would be made to stand up; a stick would be pushed in; then the whole contraption would collapse. This task, I felt, was a sort of intelligence test for the native. The manipulation of the chair was a puzzle to even a white man; his poor black brother studied and struggled in vain. The trial-and-error method failed completely. Four legs, two sidepieces, connected by a canvas which was the seat, a front bar, two pointed, badly weighed backpieces, which swiveled unmercifully instead of standing still, waiting for the back to be dropped on, and two straps—no native mind, given a whole day, could solve the mystery. Two boys who had seen it go together, before, were helpless. First, Amadu would have a glint in his eye and tackle it with many directions given to six helpers, as they started all over again. Failing, he would stand back, push his hat back, and scratch his head, puzzled. My rating of a boy's intelligence was the speed with which he could finally, after repeated demonstrations, put it together. Some would have to be shown only half a dozen times. Then with a struggle and several failures to put the chair together, they would eventually succeed. Others never could reason it out, and it ended by my doing it myself. This time I prolonged the test partly because it amused me and partly because I hated to move. Finally, however, I forced myself into my shoes and strolled over. I think my reputation in that village went up a hundred per cent as I flipped this and that, and a chair resulted.

The glee, the wonder, the shouts and hand clapping, the ums and ahs were like those of a group of children when the magician produces a rabbit out of a hat. My rabbit was this chair, when all the boys had failed. Anyone could see that my juju was strong.

The camp bed, with its X pattern, was not nearly as exciting to the audience. They had seen those before. However, when Amadu appeared with my brightly colored tea set, showing his usual native delight in color contrast—setting out a red cup, a yellow plate, and a blue saucer, and finally producing a variegated green-yellow-black teapot—I was firmly established in the eyes of the villagers as a big chief.

Slowly the wood gatherers and the water carriers filed in from an extended trip, looking thoroughly pleased with themselves, shiny and clean. No doubt they had bathed where they had pailed out the water. I hoped the headman was telling the truth when he vowed they had collected the water first. It was a matter of a few minutes before the kettle was boiling and Chaka came with some tea. On a plate was an orange with the skin carefully cut away, then dissected so it opened on the plate like some blossoming flower. I slowly sucked each segment, trying to pretend it had just come off the ice, almost fooling myself, so great was my thirst. The illusion was complete, when I sipped the hot tea. This was the nearest approach to bliss that bush life offered. Relaxed on a deck chair, with legs outstretched, a cup of hot tea to make me cool by contrast, an orange, a roof over my head, and all the loads in—what more could I desire? The boys were actually busy for once, knowing that the sooner their tasks were done, the sooner they could "go for village." Even the villagers themselves had had their fill of gaping at the strange white missus and were strolling off, having been informed that "missus no want man lookum while um chop."

The native mind appreciated this last, for they always ate in seclusion themselves and did not tolerate a hungry crowd of bystanders around their own particular family group—which was composed of men only. The women never seemed to eat. They just scavenged out of the pots after their menfolks had eaten. Or perhaps they slunk away out of sight, on the quiet, if there was food enough to have a real meal. I do not remember ever seeing a woman eating, although the men were always at it.

My peace of mind did not last long. Huddles of carriers squatting on their haunches, casting furtive glances my way, meant something was in the air. Presently Momo Beer came slinking up, pulling off his orange and black wool toboggan cap and scratching his head. His eyes shifted so that the whites showed unnecessarily. This always meant trouble.

"Sah. Boys want chop money. Plenty advances. No get proper place for sleep. Villagers no 'gree for place for sleep."

I might have known the rascals would want to bleed me the first evening; and what guarantee had I that the whole lot would not walk out during the night? Still they must eat.

"All things finish, Momo Beer?"

"Yas, sah."

"You catch plenty wood for cook? Plenty wood for watch-man? Plenty water? Bed all finish?"

"Yas, sah."

A kerosene lantern burned dimly, revealing the white mosquito net carefully tucked into the neatly made army cot. Chained to a leg of the bed was the black tin trunk containing about five hundred dollars of cash in pennies, threepenny bits, sixpence, and shillings. Taking out the small cashbox and locking the trunk again, I found the boys lined up in front of my cleared tea table. One by one they filed by, holding both hands together, palm up, for their precious "coppa." As I called a boy's name, I passed threepence to the headman, who slapped it into the outstretched hands. Threepence was entered in a column of the roll call book headed "Advances." With a deep bow, each boy stared hard at the money, and, gathering up a dirty-looking bundle which contained all his possessions, went down the path fingering it tenderly first in one hand and then in the other, obviously ruminating upon the great problem of how to spend this large sum of money. I noticed a few boys still waiting around the already lighted watchman's fire, when I handed out the last threepence.

"They want medicine," Momo Beer informed me.

"Tell them they can wait small. What advance you want?"

"Five shillings."

"What! You buy new wife for village?"

"No, sah. I go buy clothes. Amadu and Chaka, they want five shillings."

I knew this meant a drunken night and more troubles in the morning. I finally compromised with three shillings' advance apiece and the stipulation that the clothes be shown to me the next morning. Like three bad boys, they counted and recounted their change, slyly figuring how they could pay their debts, do a bit of gambling and drinking, and still buy that shirt or gaily colored hankerchief they had seen at the Syrian's store.

Now for the sick boys, and then my duties for the day would be over. Four boys silently filed up, with Momo Beer as interpreter. The first one had cut his foot badly and had to be sent over to the fire with a pan of hot water, potassium permanganate, and a cloth to bathe the cut before being bandaged. The other three complained of "belly palaver," so a good dose of castor oil was ladled out and cheerfully gobbled down. Momo then announced that he had a head palaver, thereby winning five grains of quinine, for this symptom probably meant a malarial attack, although he had had enough worries that day to merit a dozen headaches. I felt one coming on myself and hoped the five grains of quinine, which I promptly took, would check it.

"Before you go to the village, Momo, tell me, who is to be watchman?"

"This resthouse he catch one fine watchman. He lib for kitchen."

"Go bring him from kitchen. You savvy, I no 'gree for any boy to stay for kitchen. If I catch any boy for kitchen who is not kitchen boy or Amadu, I'll fine him threepence."

"Yas, sah. I go bring um."

A sorry sight in filthy rags was brought before me. I chuckled inwardly when I contemplated to what I was entrusting my life and all my worldly goods that night.

"Hold the lamp to his face so I look at him properly."

Ye gods! He had only one eye and that was as shifty as a leopard's. He looked vaguely familiar. Then it dawned on me where I had seen him before. He had been discharged from the Makong camp for going to sleep on duty when he substituted for the sick watchman. Various small articles had been found missing during the few days following his dismissal, and we had all suspected this man. Here he was, with all his cunning, having me at his mercy for this night. Well, he was a Temne, so perhaps I could fix him.

"Momo, this man is a Temne. He is your brudder?"

"Yas, sah."

"Well, Momo, you tell your brudder I savvy he got one eye. This is your palaver. If he goes to sleep for other eye, I'll fine you three shillings and I'll have Bai Kaferi send your brudder to jail. You tell him I savvy plenty the palaver for Makong. If he goes to sleep, or if anything is stolen tonight, I'll ask the witch doctor to have one big leopard come to eat this man up. You savvy?"

The threat had the desired effect. We were in the heart of the Leopard Society country, and both knew that an invitation to have a leopard remove any objectionable person would be accepted with alacrity, especially if the white man's juju could be used as an excuse. The one eye gleamed with fear as the full weight of my threat sunk into his feeble brain. I knew then that I could sleep in peace and that for this night a big fire would be kept going.

The night chill, now that the sun had vanished, made me shiver in my damp clothes, so I called Amadu to bring my bath. The temperature had dropped only a few degrees, but this change was dangerous to one who had been perspiring all day. I threw my kimono over my shoulders while I rummaged around in my box for my pajamas and toilet kit. The mosquitoes and flies were gathering around the lamp, so I put it in the corner farthest away from the square canvas tub, shut the door of my mud room, and as quickly as possible sponged myself. Then I put on my pajamas and mosquito boots and finally my khaki shirt and jacket as extra protection against being bitten and infected. Once more, relaxed and rested by the change, but feeling decidedly limp and let down, I reclined in my deck chair, and called to the boy to "bring chop one-time!"

I could have predicted my meal weeks ahead, I thought in disgust, as I drank the flavorless, slightly greasy chicken broth. My thoughts were interrupted by the appearance of a shadow at my side and the announcement, "Dog's chop, sah," at which Balto aroused himself from his seeming unconsciousness. To the cook boy's consternation, I dumped my half-finished soup on the dog's chop—it would save my having to push down any more of the greasy fluid—and told him that it was fit only for a dog. The next course was boiled chicken, rice, and a tasteless green, which Chaka had undoubtedly stolen from the tops of the sweet potato plants on the outskirts of the village, charging me a penny for them. Sandwich spread, generously spooned out, was the only thing that helped me to down these greens. For dessert, I had cut-up bananas and oranges. Chaka certainly did not have Lamina's knack for flavoring.

After supper I called for my knapsack, took out various notebooks, jotted down a few things in my diary, checked over my accounts, and glanced at my geological notes of the day, filling in more detail. Even this slight effort got me into a perspiration, and clouds of flies, which hovered around the lamp and kept lighting on the white paper, did not add to my comfort.

As I finished my work, Amadu and Chaka came from the kitchen with their bundles, and I said good night to them. Absolute silence in camp at last. I stood for a moment on the porch of the resthouse, looking up at the brilliant stars and the extra-white Milky Way. Below the horizon was blackness. Only faint lights in the distance marked where the village lay. I was too far away to hear whether the villagers were all in bed. My eye rested for a moment on the crouched figure of the watchman, wrapped in a striped cloth, the fire lighting up his black face, his one eye staring into the fire as he leaned forward. His pointed wool stocking cap made him look like a gnome, as he held one skinny hand out toward the flame. He never glanced my way when I wandered about the compound with my flashlight, followed by the trusty Balto. Everything seemed in order, so I turned the lantern low, placing it in the doorway where the light would not reflect on my bed. I then pointed out a mat for Balto's bed and he immediately collapsed on it. Removing my skirt, jacket, and mosquito boots, I crawled under the net, my flashlight firmly clenched in my hand. After tucking in the net where I had pulled it apart, I flashed the light on, scrutinizing every nook and corner for a possible mosquito or a fly which might have entered with me. Then, putting my keys and the flashlight under my pillow, I stretched out and pulled the edge of a light-weight blanket across me (I never used sheets). Soon I was oblivious to everything, save as I became half-conscious whenever the watchman coughed or a stick snapped as he stoked the fire. At first the incessant ring of crickets sounded in my head like a bad dream, but gradually even these faded.

Suddenly padded feet and the sound of rummaging near my bed brought me to life with a start. A thief-man, I thought as I opened my eyes, and a cold sweat came over me. Then I relaxed. It was only Amadu, hunting for breakfast things. I felt as if I had been asleep only about ten minutes, but my flashlight showed my watch at 5:05. I must get up. Breakfast at 5:30 was my order. Everything felt damp—my blankets, my net, even my hair. The early morning mists saturated the air to such an extent that I felt as if I must push the atmosphere aside in order to get out of my net. Luckily, I had covered all my clothes with a tarpaulin the night before and had locked all my boxes. Otherwise, all my belongings would have been dripping, like my soggy-looking mosquito boots. Before getting up, I reconnoitered with a flashlight, partly to discover whether any stray snakes were snuggling up against my boots. I never found any, but I was always on the watch. It was fun to watch Balto come to life gradually, from the tail up, finally emitting a yawn, as he arched and slunk over just in time to give my feet a lick when I stuck them out from under the net.

Peering out of my shelter, all I could distinguish was the squatting watchman huddled over his dimly burning fire, motionless, as if he had not stirred since the night began. Amadu shuffled back and forth, a shadowy form. He looked so much like a scared animal as he moved about in the dawn, that he gave me the creeps.

"Chop, leddy."

"All right, Amadu."

That was the extent of our early morning talk. Bananas and oranges were swallowed in haste. Then Wheatena was gulped down with a little sugar and canned milk, followed by the inevitable egg, poached by preference, for only a reasonably good egg could stand up in boiling water. Tea was the only part of the meal that I really enjoyed.

While I was eating, dark shadows had come up from the village, one by one, crouching in turn around the fire. I had been conscious of a bustle in my bedroom for some time. It was Momo getting on with the business of taking down my bed and packing various boxes. Light was coming, and almost without warning it was broad daylight; but there was no sign of the sun through the mist. I went to oversee the final packing of the boxes.

Everything was ready at last. Noses were counted, and each carrier wound up country cloths for his head cushion. In some remarkable fashion, it appeared that I had boys enough for all the loads except for my personal extras—ruckee chair, lunchbox, and small suitcase. Just as I was about to tell the headman to have the boys hoist up the loads, Amadu pointed out a great delegation from the village coming up the trail. A visit from the headman, he said. So wait I must. A few drums pounded erratically. Arrayed in their best clean clothes, one layer of cloth showing beneath another, the elders, with canes and neatly embroidered turbans, swarmed around me. Bai Kaferi's chief clerk then presented himself with a flourish, doffing his felt hat as if he were in the prologue of a play.

"Bai Kaferi presents his compliments. He wishes you good health and happiness. Will you be pleased to accept these presents his headman brings to you as a dash. I am your humble servant."

Another flourish and a broad grin as three little boys, two of them stark naked, trudged fearfully toward me, bearing calabashes on their heads. The first contained three chickens, with feet tightly bound, thrown over one and a half dozen eggs, which were carefully counted by Amadu, who had suddenly come to life and was moving with unprecedented rapidity. The next calabash was piled high with nice pink rice; the third contained some sweet potatoes, okra, some tiny red tomatoes, a bundle of greens, about a dozen oranges, and a bunch of twelve bananas. Amadu or Momo must have had some say about this magnificent dash, or else Bai Kaferi was particularly anxious for me to find gold on his land. Here was almost a week's supply of food and all the things I particularly wanted. I took six shillings out of my pocket and gave them to the clerk "for a dash for Bai Kaferi." This was sufficient payment for all this food. The money was handled and passed around among two or three of the chief elders, whose eyes grew big as they touched it. The grunts of contentment were apparent. No doubt they bought a cow and had a celebration that night on the proceeds. My status as a big chief was secure.

I expressed the desire to have my compliments sent back to Bai Kaferi with the hope for his speedy recovery; then I asked about the guide that had been promised. The crowds parted and from the background came forward two fine-looking types. They were to go with me wherever I went while I was in Bai Kaferi's territory.

"They are not fit to go into the bush in those clothes!" I said in consternation, knowing that their nice gowns would be in shreds if they followed me. So they were sent back to the village to change into bush regalia.

The next request was for one boy to carry my leftovers.

"He does not need to be a big boy," I said, "but I want a good boy."

This request was met with silence. Time was passing, and the mist was beginning to burn away. I had the dashes distributed among the loads as well as possible, amid the grunts and remonstrances of the carriers, had their loads hoisted on their heads, and sent them off. The headman put a local boy in front who knew the trail to the village where we were to camp that night. The clerk then came to me with a small fine-faced chap, somewhat of the build of Amadu.

"This boy will go with you. He speaks English."

"But I don't want an interpreter. I want a boy to carry that load."

"I be fit, missus. I go carry that load." His smile won me.

"What is your name?"

"James Conte."

"Are you Temne?"

"Yes, missus."

"For whom have you worked?"

"One white man. One missionary. He teach me English. I can cook; I can do anything. I want to work for you."

I hesitated just a second. He did not look strong, but he had a clear, quick eye and was clean. It would be an asset to have with me a boy who could interpret.

"All right. One shilling a day, and carry that load."

If he were above the job, the price would fix him. But no, James was desperately in need of money and was determined to go with me, so he nodded assent and took up the load.

CHAPTER THIRTEEN

FALSE LEADS

AT LAST I was off to start real exploration in unprospected territory, with the lure of possibly finding gold always before me. It was something of a thrill to think that I was again hitting into the unknown, with no one to turn to for advice. I felt like a true forty-niner, heading westward with no greater aim than a shiny yellow metal dug from the depths of the soil. All my thoughts were to be wrapped up in this goal for months to come. The chance of finding the hidden treasure carried me through the heat, one day after another. Perhaps it was the wanderlust inherited from my hardy ancestors that pushed me forward, or perhaps it was just my own cussedness. Whatever it was, the explorer's delight in not knowing what is coming day by day, or even minute by minute, the unexpected at every turn, the new things never seen before by white man—all these counteracted the actual drudgery and hardship, so that I kept on, as have the hundreds of other explorers and prospectors. A few months back in civilization, and the old routine and the unpleasantnesses of jungle life are dimmed and even hard to recall. Only the happier aspects are remembered—the exciting moments of a trip, the natives and their curious ways and customs. Seeing the new, thinking the new, and hunting for the new has ever been man's greatest delight.

As I went on, the elders, headmen, children, and even the usually absent women thronged the village where my path turned off. Some looked serious; the women clapped their hands; all looked at me with sparkling eyes, with many ahs and ums, and a few "Hello, missus." The children parted like magic as I approached, then fell in line in swarms behind me. I was a real curiosity. Most missuses they had seen were either accompanied by a "master," or were going to or from a master. A missus who wandered about alone must be a big chief. Gradually the children tired of following us or had their fill of staring, and we were alone.

The trail followed the flats of a river most of the way, so the going was easy; there had been no rain the day before, and the path was packed hard. Tall elephant grass, which seemed to thrive in the sandy soil, bordered the path. The sun beat down through it without mercy, shriveling the stalks so that they rattled and shed dust on me from head to foot as I pushed through. I missed the high jungles with their shade and was glad when I had been carried across the last stream and was told, "This be Masaka." Fortunately, there had been no rocks to examine along the way, for I was too hot to want to bother about geology.

When I reached the village, I found that nothing had been done about looking for a camp site, for the boys, too, were apparently feeling tired out or lazier than usual. We were at an elevation of only three hundred and fifty feet and so could expect no breezes, day or night. I sat down on the mud veranda of one of the houses, in a courteously offered chair. For a few minutes I was too hot to notice the filth and flies, as I mopped my head, but finally I got up energy to go and look for a camp site. As I was to be here for several days, I might just as well get as cool a place as possible.

Paths radiated from the village into the surrounding bush, some of them leading to farms and some to the "kitchens," generally in some shady spot near-by. Some places were more of a refuse dump than others, and smellier, usually marked by lines of driver ants passing in and out of the vicinity. Many times a nice cool-looking region of virgin forest would turn out to be the Poro or the Bundu Bush, sacred land, at which I longingly looked; but if I had as much as put my foot into this bush, "something dreadful would happen." This was a deeply ingrained superstition among the natives, and sacred this inviting territory must remain. Other plots of green virgin forest near the villages were cemeteries. Many a time have I camped beside the cool-looking mounds with a few stones or broken pottery marking the heads of the graves. The best thing to do was to go at least a quarter of a mile away from the village to get quiet, clean, and unused ground.

Masaka was on the Song River, and as I meant to test the gravels of this stream for gold, I decided to wander upstream from the polluted waters of the village and put my camp near a place where I could watch the boys dig in the afternoon. Four boys and the headman came with me and chopped a "beef-hole" for me through the underbrush. Not far above the village, but far enough, we came to a meander in the river, where the undergrowth was slightly thinner and where a tributary joined the Song and there were distinct terraces. We looked for a place which could be cleared of brush and yet a spot where no big trees would be liable to fall on my tent if a thunderstorm (or so-called tornado) came up. We picked a good place, a little too low in case of a sudden rise of the river, but one that was worth the risk, as a better spot could not be found. The ground was sandy and would drain rapidly. It was shady and reasonably cool.

Three of the boys went right to work clearing trees and bush with their cutlasses, while the headman and the fourth boy returned to the village for the rest of my retinue. Balto seemed to know this was "home," for he burrowed under a log, where it was cool, and curled up. I took a canvas specimen bag from my knapsack for use as a fly-swatter, but the faster I swatted, the more I perspired, and the more flies delighted in annoying me. It was a vicious circle, but I swatted anyhow, wondering what had induced me to come to Africa.

I always marveled at the speed with which the boys could clear the bush when they wanted to work. They sang in a sort of monotone, which became intensified as they swung their arms back for a hard blow at a larger tree, ending with a grunt or groan when the blow really required force. Their bodies gleamed with a melted-chocolate glow, as they bent to the work. The rhythm was catching, and one by one, as the other boys appeared with their loads, they joined the outward-moving semicircle with a shrill cry. That day they had only carried their loads a short distance and were apparently urging each other to cut as quickly as possible. Gradually their enthusiasm lagged, and there was a definite slacking of blows as the space grew larger.

Amadu finally appeared with Chaka, looking thoroughly refreshed. Probably he had met some brothers—this was Temne country—and had been treated to palm wine. They pulled at the various loads, resurrecting my deck chair, which they set up near my log. Gratefully, I slumped into it and got out my map and notebook in order to decide where, and in what rivers, I would have the boys start pitting. I picked out three near-by tributaries which I thought should be investigated, as they drained across what was probably the granite and schist contact. I would wander up these streams in the afternoon to make sure.

The sun was getting almost overhead; I judged it was about noon. To check myself, I asked the headman what time it was. He looked asquint at the sun and said, "Twelve o'clock, sah." So his guess was as good as mine. If I remonstrated, he would have changed the time to eleven o'clock, or two o'clock, depending upon which time he thought I would prefer it to be.

"All right, you give me ten boys who are good to dig pit. Each two boys are to take a shovel, a pick, a bucket, or head pan."

These were doled out to the boys selected.

"Now, you finish making camp with the boys who are left. I am going to show these boys where to dig pit."

I set two boys to work on the left bank of the Song River, below camp, on the lower terrace, and two boys on the right bank, just in case one could not "bottom" his pit. The next two I ordered to cut a small trail up the tributary near camp until they were well above the floodplain region of the main river where I had them clear a place to dig a pit on the inside curve of a meander, on the upstream side; for if gold had been brought down by the stream, this was the most likely place for it to be deposited. There were four boys left, and with them I set off, up a small farm trail, to find the two tributaries which were on the map. The first, about half a mile away, was small and sluggish, but boulders showed that it could be a torrent at times. Another quarter of a mile upstream we came to the east tributary. Leaving the boys there, I sauntered back to camp alone, slowly, looking carefully at every twig in the path and noticing every rustle. I realized suddenly how nervous I had become at being entirely alone. When with the boys, perhaps I was putting on a bold face, or their company and the knowledge of their quick eyes made me feel at ease. I resolved to manage somehow to have the headman or some boy along when going so far again. Subconsciously, I had learned to watch for snakes, and when one crossed my path I recoiled by instinct even before becoming aware of it. Now I jumped at a snapping twig, and once my heart fairly stopped as Balto came bounding back into the path, after a hunting expedition of his own. Foolish of me to be so on edge! I fought the feeling of wishing to rush madly back to camp in a panic. I stopped short before a line of driver ants, just as I was about to put my foot into them. Funny, how my instinct for these black pests had developed. A few mistakes of stumbling across their line of march had taught me exactly how vicious these hordes were. I stepped over them and turned to see Balto leap wide. One experience with them as a pup had made him run at the sight of them, remembering the hot stings he had received when he had broken their march. Now, one bite from an ant, and he was off, tail down, yelping and madly running in circles with the dread of repeating the performance.

A creeper brushed against my face, and I recoiled. A lizard rustled in the leaves, eying me with surprise. Then, a mad chattering and swinging of the branches above and I caught a glimpse of peering eyes, as some red monkeys spied me. After staring for a moment, they swung gracefully upward, hand over hand, until they were lost to my view in the foliage. Then there was silence the rest of the way, except for the buzzing or droning of the myriads of unseen insects.

Camp was like a big room chopped out of the jungle. The foliage arched over the cleared space like a lattice. Every leaf had been brushed away, and the ground looked black and cool. Momo had spread out the tent loads and was down on all fours, struggling to fit the tent poles under the tent and the fly into the proper sockets, while his helpers stood hopelessly around, and Amadu, fluent with wrong directions and a manner of "I savvy all," stood by. A few orders from me resulted in three boys standing at the base of the three poles and three more holding the guy ropes. With a "one, two, three," the tent was erect, Momo dashing around with sledge hammer and large pegs, thumping them in where I directed him. I hoped, soon, he would remember how to do this without supervision. With much palaver and talk on all sides, the last rope was finally in place, ready for the flaps to be tied back and the ground sheet spread on the inside.

In the meantime, Amadu and Chaka had, with the assistance of James Conte—who turned out to know as much about camp life as any of them—set up the bed, my washbasin and table, and unpacked the cook's various culinary supplies, depositing the latter away from the camp in a small clearing which was henceforth to be known as the kitchen. An extra tarpaulin was stretched over a pole and tied to the bushes to serve as protection for the fire in case of a thunderstorm. Two boys were put to work making a table out of four sticks driven in the ground, three or four feet apart, to form a square. Then a series of parallel sticks was tied across these with "tie-tie," or conveniently gathered creepers, making a nice, flat table for the dishes and pots and pans. Other sticks were cut for raising my boxes above ground, even though they were placed under the edges of the tent fly; otherwise, the damp earth would soon rot the bottoms off the boxes.

My bed was put inside the tent, my bell-shaped net fixed to the roof, and my two personal tin trunks brought in and chained together, as well as to the bed, to prevent theft. This precaution seemed less necessary than at places near the road, but one never knew when a boy might turn thief-man, or when a thief might follow me around, hoping for spoils.

Tea suddenly appeared in a miraculous fashion, borne on a tray by the perspiring Amadu. I made myself a jam sandwich and finished off with three bananas. The flies continued to bite; my clothes felt clammier than ever. How I longed to be able to take my helmet off! The tent was too hot to sit under, so I returned, with map and notebook, to my original place on the log, while the final chores around camp were done. Gutters must be dug entirely around the tent so that the ground would drain, and a latrine had to be constructed.

James Conte cut long sticks which he planted for a clothes-line; this was immediately filled with my yesterday's clothes, already rinsed out in the kitchen in a kerosene tin by Amadu.

As the sun lost its ferocity, I called Momo to collect a dozen head pans, gold-washing pans, a small ground sheet, and a tape measure. Then, having carefully noted the position of camp on the map, I set the cyclometer wheel at zero and went out to see what progress had been made by the pitting boys. Those just below camp had dug down about five feet, but they had not yet reached the coarse gravels where the gold would be found. I knew that they would be digging for another day, for after getting down five feet it was necessary to haul up every bit of dirt in a petrol tin, and it would mean constant bailing of water when they reached the porous sands below. Large boulders would undoubtedly cause further delay. Perhaps they would not be able to reach bottom, but I did not suggest that. I merely told them to go on digging and had Momo Beer explain that they "get plenty more for to dig."

We found the two boys at the pit in the tributary stream above sitting down under a tree fern, chewing kola nuts. They had finished their pit and were just waiting for developments. One showed me the bottom clay, a white sticky mass—the kind that would make good porcelain—with a few shiny white mica flakes which flashed as I kneaded the clay. Yes, this was the granite rock at the bottom of the pit, but it was thoroughly decomposed. If it had been green puttylike clay, showing that a schist rock was underneath, I might have been more hopeful of finding gold. I must have a sample to find out whether or not we were in good territory. The boys bailed out the pit with pans and buckets, the ground sheet was spread down, and as soon as I saw the white granite clay of the bedrock we were ready to cut the sample. Momo Beer had already removed his toboggan cap and jumped to the bottom of the pit with a head pan and cutlass. On the surface above the place where he had smoothed off the wall of the pit, I marked a square foot, so that he could cut a column of dirt straight down to the bottom, just exactly one foot wide and one foot across. In this way the correct number of cubic feet in the sample I was taking could be figured out, for I had already measured the depth of the pit.

The top foot was nothing but "overburden"—the fine, light silts of the river—and would not carry any of the heavy minerals or the valuable metals. All these, if any, would be in the bottom two feet of coarse gravel made up largely of pebbles and boulders. In fact, most of the gold would be found at the very bottom, right on top of the clay; for gold is such a heavy metal that the stream carrying the sands and gravels would act as sorter of the materials, as they rolled over and over, the heavy gold and iron minerals sifting down below the light sands. In the churning process, which results in the laying down of these river gravels, some of the gold might have been stirred up and not have had a chance to sink. To be sure of finding all the gold possible, every bit of gravel collected in the sample was panned.[1]

Momo Beer threw the top silt aside as he sliced down his foot column. As soon as he reached the gravel, every bit of it was carefully collected in the head pan, then dumped on the ground sheet so that none would be lost. Finally the sample taking was finished, and Momo Beer carefully took a few inches of the bottom clay just in case a flake of gold had settled into the spongy mass. Out he jumped. We filled the head pans with the sample gravel, and the boys took them over to the stream, submerged them, and began washing. With seriously set faces, they moved their hands about in the pans, a cloud of yellowish mud pouring out of each pan as they stirred the material. If their hands encountered a larger boulder, this was taken up, held over the head pan, and carefully scrubbed before throwing it out. This allowed any heavy materials to fall back into the pan, while the light material floated away in the current. The pans gradually lost their cloud and finally were only about a quarter full. This was the sign that the boys could take the pans by the handles and swish them about, half under water, using a circular motion and tipping them forward so that the lighter material would gradually spill out, leaving the heavier material in the bottom. When they had only a few inches of shiny black or gray-looking concentrate left in the bottom, they stopped. Momo Beer and I carefully collected the residue in two gold pans, which were much smaller than the head pans and were very shiny and black, the rust having been cleaned off by burning them over a hot fire. Momo Beer took one pan and I the other, while the boys stared, motionless. This was the crucial moment. Was there, or was there not, gold in that pit?

[1] For a diagram showing a typical cross section of pits in gold-bearing river gravels, turn to page 138.

Momo Beer swished his pan and sifted out the lighter material until only a spoonful of concentrate was left; he then examined this last bit, shaking his head mournfully and murmuring, as he turned to me, "He no deh, sah." There was great disappointment. I think the boys felt that it was their fault that there was no gold, or felt that their work had all gone for naught. I swished my pan, then, standing up, turned the residue to the light and carefully worked it around the pan until the "tail" finally showed the gleam of two tiny flakes of gold, mixed with some grains of pink zircon. I showed the boys these specks. A childish glee spread through the group. They seemed so delighted that I did not enlighten them or explain that that much gold was as good as nothing. I just showed it to them and let them go, happy in the thought that they had done something worth while that day.

To Momo Beer, however, I was more explicit, as I jotted down in my notebook the position of the pit, its depth, the depth of the gravel, the character of the soil, and what minerals I had been able to discover in the concentrates, with the aid of my hand lens.

"There is not enough here; we'll try the other pits."

The paraphernalia were collected by the boys, and we moved on. Already the pit was filling, the sides caving in as the water rose higher and higher. The boys at the other pits on the tributaries upstream had met with somewhat the same conditions and with as little luck.

We filed back to our camp home, with a feeling of relief and of accomplishment, for three pits had been completed and sampled. I knew that many a day I would return to camp with much less accomplished. Before dismissing the boys, I made each bring two logs of wood for the campfire. There were no laggards today, no demands for chop money, or medicine, for they were going to be here several days and were too hungry to remember their illnesses.

I told Momo Beer to report with the village headman and the two guides after supper and to ask the chief for a good watchman. The guides had gracefully disappeared on arrival at Masaka, and I really did not care if they never showed up again, as they seemed thoroughly stupid.

As I dropped into my deck chair, which had been put in the open space in front of the tent, Amadu appeared, immaculately clad in long white duck trousers, spick and span white sneakers, a white shirt neatly tucked inside a gorgeous leather belt. My stained khaki seemed the more dirty beside his cleanliness. A pot of tea made me quickly forget the unfavorable comparison, and I handed him my heavy helmet, glad at last to dare to go bareheaded. A bath and clean clothes completed my feeling of well-being, as I came out to the cool damp of the evening.

How different from last night! Then the cool of the forest had not penetrated the sun-baked mud of the compound. Here the damp ground, the high trees, the moss-covered logs, and the gradually collecting river mist were a delightful contrast. I loved the forest camps—homes of my own making. Isolation, peace, and quiet, and yet, when I stopped to listen, or when I became conscious of them, the forest sounds were almost deafening. I could hear the tree bear, shrilly calling to its mate, with a maddening regularity, piercing right through my head, as I became conscious of it. If I was tired, the shrill whistling of bullfrogs cut through my brain like so many blades. But tonight these sounds were peace. There was no one to whom I could talk, just boys to whom orders could be given, and a dog at my side who was just there, a shadow, never requiring speech. Yes, this was peace.

Bringing back the honey obtained by chopping down a tree, and smoking out the bees. The boy on the left is my headman wearing the clothes given to him by his former master.

My boys with a native chief. The boy on the left holds the cyclometer wheel. Note the native chair constructed from a three-limbed tree with a bar for a seat.

In the midst of these reveries, the rain came without warning. I knew night had toppled down, but in the forest one cannot see; one just notices the difference between night and day. First, there was a gentle rustling of the leaves in the treetops. Then silence—a sudden quieting of the animal noises, save for one cricket. Then a twisting of the treetops, leaves and branches dropping on the carefully brushed ground. A frightened Amadu scurried out of the kitchen, dishcloth on his arm. Balto made for the tent, slinking, with his tail curled under his stomach. There were large hot raindrops as I extricated myself from the deck chair, which Amadu almost pulled from under me. Chaka grabbed the table with its plates. Amadu rushed back for the knapsack. Covers were hastily put down on the chop boxes under the tent fly. Tent flaps were closed. A pelting on the tent roof, and Chaka tore off to the kitchen, returning with arms full of odds and ends, clothes plastered to him, raindrops creeping down his oily face. The lamp flickered, but was saved as Amadu built up a barrier around it. I stood helpless, wincing at the continuous flashes of lightning and the frequent thunderbooms. The rain sifted through the dry fly in a fine mist, gusts blowing the rain right under the fly itself. Amadu stood leaning against the tentpost, trembling, never speaking, his clean white shirt soggy, his white sneakers mud-spattered. Near-by trees crashed. The camp site was well chosen, safely away from half-dead trees. The gutters were like young rivers, but were keeping the water away from the tent floor. The nicely cleared ground showed like a small lake as the lightning flashed.

Fifteen minutes of fury and then it was over. Dead silence for a minute, then a million insects burst into song simultaneously, all in a different key. Fireflies lighted the ground. The damp was oppressive. I pulled my khaki jacket out of the tin trunk, for I was shivering. Supper! Goodness knows whether that was saved. Amadu came to life. He placed a box near the already set table, put the lamp on it and said, "I go bring chop." What an anticlimax! But one must eat. Chop appeared—lukewarm soup on a plate that glistened with the raindrops, soggy bread, half-cooked chicken, stringy sweet potato, slimy pawpaw, and well-watered fruit salad. I ate. Then I crawled into bed even before Amadu came to say good night. I knew that no visit would be paid me by any chief that night. Natives do not get their best clothes wet. Amadu's head stuck in the doorway.

"We no get watchman, sah."

I could not be bothered. My head ached. Probably a touch of malaria from the damp.

"We don't need a watchman tonight. No thief-man will come; it's too wet."

"But wild beef, sah."

"I no fear um," I said, lying, for I was afraid of the leopards. Anything to go to sleep. I would run any risk when I felt like this.

"Take the chickens to the village," I told Amadu. "No leopard will come to a new camp if there are no chickens."

Looking a bit dubious, but satisfied, Amadu withdrew, and I saw his flickering light casting weird shadows along the trail. He had left a lamp burning low under the fly. I could not sleep. It seemed to me that the noises in the forest were as loud as those in a city, and much shriller. The back flap of the tent was still closed. I closed the half by my bed to keep out the light, squirming under the net without getting up. Then I fell into a fitful sleep, thinking over and over, "I like being alone; I like being alone," trying to dispel the growing feeling of fear but too tired to care.

I did not move until I gradually became conscious that it was getting light. I could hear Chaka breaking firewood. Relief spread over me. I had slept the sleep of utter exhaustion and here I was snug in my net and not devoured by any wild beast. I peered out and saw Balto's form beside my tin trunk. So the leopard had not come, and this was just another day.

Breakfast was ready under the fly when I came out in the semilight and saw a mob of natives jabbering near the kitchen. It was the local chief and his villagers, come to bring me a dash. After hurriedly breakfasting, I had Amadu usher the visitors forward; my two guides accompanied him, the rest bringing up the rear, anxious to get a good look at me. I accepted the calabash of rice and a chicken, eggs, cassava, and some oranges, and then inquired about the trails in the vicinity, for I had picked out various villages on my map, which I wished to visit in the course of testing the near-by streams for gold. Our conference having got down to an awkward interpreting of words back and forth, I suggested that the chief come to see me that evening, if he wished. He took the hint and departed with his villagers.

Finally I lined up the boys, and after roll call I said, "I am going to take eight boys with me. They are to bring cutlasses, picks, shovels, sledge hammers, and head pans. The rest can go sit in the village. I am going to give each boy threepence chop money when I have no work for him." If I hadn't given them the money, they would have deserted.

Then I singled out the most intelligent looking, taking Momo the First, James Conte, and a powerful-looking boy named Basi, for my special, personal retinue. This was my chance to pick out a permanent watchman. The first boy I chose refused. So did the second.

"They fear too much. They no fit for stay awake."

Finally Momo Beer singled out the most decrepit of the lot, an emaciated boy clad in filthy rags, and announced that "he 'gree." So I told Momo Beer to tell him to "go for village to sleep" and to come back at night, that he was to be watchman from now on. When we moved camp, he was to carry a light load and be relieved from any duties of making camp. He seemed quite pleased. I wondered just how much protection he would be. He looked as if he would run at the sight of a toad.

I gave James Conte the cyclometer wheel and my knapsack, and off we started, the guides leading toward the mountain. James Conte soon showed his intelligence in managing the wheel. He even grasped the fact that the turning of the wheel changed the numbers. The third time I stopped to record some observation in my notebook, he said, "One point two," which was the mileage shown on the wheel. Surprised and delighted to have acquired a boy who could read, I foresaw many ways in which he could be of use. Thereafter I had only to tell James to let me know when the wheel reached so and so.

We made quick time at first, then we began to climb; I puffed and panted and perspired. This hill, just under a thousand-foot elevation, would have been nothing to climb in a cooler region, but it took every bit of energy I possessed to lift one foot after the other in this oppressive atmosphere, which clogged the lungs and did not satisfy the desire for breath. I thought of all the stories white persons told of being pulled up hills with a bath towel around the waist, two boys pulling on the ends and two boys pushing from behind. I had laughed, thinking them fantastic, until I tried climbing mountains in the hot humid tropics myself. I could feel my heart thumping, as if it had decided it would refuse to try to get air out of this humidity. I wondered how many months I could stand it, before having to be pushed. Frequent rests made me feel better; the boys did not seem to puff and showed no change of color.

Here, much of the bush was scrubby stuff, only a few years old, about on a level with my head, thus allowing the sun to strike us with full force. The natives farmed these hills in ruthless fashion. They chopped down virgin forests, let it dry a few months, then fired it so that the ashes might give some strength to the poor red lateritic soil. Then, having raised one year's crop of hill rice, they passed on to another plot, repeating the procedure and leaving the abandoned area to sprout a mass of secondary bush, for eight or ten years. This ruined the forests, spoiled the soil, gradually depleted the streams in the dry season and allowed torrential floods to course down, unchecked, in the wet. The government was just beginning to make forest reserves on the higher lands and thus protect the country from the destructive soil erosion resulting from the indiscriminate cutting of the forests. The natives grumbled at the interfering government, which refused to let them destroy the forests wherever they wished.

After an hour's steady climb, we reached an uncut section of large mahogany trees at the divide. Here we were heralded by loud screams and a pounding, as of drums. I caught a glimpse of a troupe of chimpanzees scampering away, running along the ground with a sort of side gallop, then swinging upward, hand over hand through the creepers until they were out of sight in the high trees. Chimpanzees were fairly common in these parts, but generally they saw you first and escaped without being seen, despite the terrific racket they made.

The upland we had reached was hilly, cut by streams draining down the slope opposite the one we had climbed. The trail followed the main stream for some distance, branching off over a series of ridges after a mile or so. Then we came to open land with half-grown rice waving over many acres. This was Bai Kaferi's farm, I was informed. It was a messy-looking bit of land, the great, partially burned logs lying hit or miss just as they had been felled, giving an unkempt appearance to the necessary lack of symmetry of the rows of rice. Cotton, some okra, and a few tomato plants were scattered about. I spied a yellow gourdlike affair, which Momo said was a pumpkin. He promptly picked it for me, taking it for granted that I would relish the tasteless vegetable. In the middle of the main rice field stood a raised dais, roofed over, but with open sides, just big enough for a man. This was where a watchman sat at night to drum and frighten away monkeys, chimpanzees, and other animals.

We made for a tiny thatched roof, which marked the farmhouse, its temporary walls built of still green banana leaves and palms instead of the customary mud. Various boxlike structures with nicely thatched lids stood on stilts near-by. These were the storehouses for the rice. A miniature one belonged to the chickens, so that they would be out of reach of any night prowlers.

The guides pushed back the mat of the farm hut, and we peered into the blackness. All I could make out was a poorly burning fire on the floor and an iron pot steaming above it. But one by one, out came a man, a woman carrying a suckling pickaninny, another woman, and then six youngsters of various sizes, naked but cleaner looking than their elders, who had on dirty brown rags, made of bark and not the usual native cloth.

The head of the household was presented by my guides, who told him that he was to show me around Bai Kaferi's farm, wherever I desired to go. The guides then promptly retired into the bare room and sat on the raised mud bed, dipping their hands into the pot in front of them. Their duties were done, I could see that. I looked at my map, then at the farmed area, and inquired about any available trails. I was informed that there were plenty.

The best procedure seemed to start two boys digging a pit in the stream by the farm. I then sent two more sets of boys up near-by tributaries to pit at spots which I pointed out. Seeing nothing but the ever-present laterite soil, which told me nothing at all, I asked my guide to take me up a path which would lead me to the nearest ridge behind the farm. There I was lucky enough to find some rock outcrops. Then with three boys with cutlasses in front, cutting the thorny twigs and creepers in the way, we went up and down every footpath in the vicinity, so that I could map any rocks and get an idea of what to expect in the way of possible mineral wealth on this side of the mountain.

Finally I decided to spend the rest of the day exploring the largest tributary, as the boys had not finished their pits. The farmer remonstrated.

"It be far too much," was what Momo Beer interpreted. "It no be fit for white man."

I told Momo to tell the guide that if he feared to go with me, I would report him to Bai Kaferi. That made him change his mind, and we set out. Over boulders, around boulders, hacking "beef-lines" (openings wide enough to squeeze through), through the matted creepers at the edge of the stream, into the water, on and on, always fighting the black flies. On a nice flat boulder surrounded by water, I had a lunch consisting of a chicken leg, a hunk of bread, two bananas, and an orange. I washed this down with lukewarm boiled water from my thermos.

As we pushed on, it seemed to me as if we were the only living things for miles; everything else knew better than to be abroad at that hour in the broiling sun. A black flash off to the right caused the boys to freeze in their tracks, and I knew that we were not the only animal life abroad. I seemed to feel snakes all around me the rest of the day, and the boys were more wary. We reached the source of the stream in an hour, but without seeing anything of interest except large boulders of high-grade iron ore lying in the stream. As we progressed, these boulders became much larger. With the sledge hammer, Momo Beer broke one after another. They were all hematite (iron ore) of unusual richness. We were surrounded by huge boulders of hematite at the head of the stream, so I knew we must be near the place whence they had come. A little scrambling, a few more gashes on my bare knees, and lo and behold, there was a ledge of solid iron ore, thirty to forty feet wide, and running parallel to the ridge as far as we could see. This *was* a find! Even if Bai Kaferi had no gold on his land, here was iron enough to keep him and his people in tools for eternity. Or perhaps some concern might make a mine here some day. The spot was only a hundred miles from the coast. I felt the day had been far from wasted. But there was no time now to stop; we would have to hurry in order to get down to camp before dark.

At the farm I collected the guides and the pitting boys, who said, "Gold no be deh," to my inquiry. I would have to check up on them myself the next day.

Going back took a quarter of the time of coming up. It was cooler, too. I took my hat off, passing it back to Momo Beer to carry. The sun was just setting as we went down the mountainside, and to my joy we could actually see the sunset. It was a mass of flame, reflecting great thunder caps, which were collecting on the horizon. We hurried to beat the light as well as the rain, but even so, big drops were coming down when we came into Masaka. I ran for camp, getting fairly wet but arriving before the rain descended in full force.

The rain stopped before I had finished supper. The watchman came up, saluted, grinned, and departed to a smoldering campfire. Apparently he had been busy that afternoon, for I noticed two great poles with a hammock slung between them beside the fire. He was not going to take any chances but was going to have all the comforts of home. I hoped it was not so comfortable that he would sleep at his post. But I was too tired to think about it and fell asleep at once.

The next four days were spent going up and down that now hated trail over the mountain to Bai Kaferi's farm. If I had realized how far it was, I think I would have tried to have my boys set up my camp there, even though the path was narrow and steep for boys with sixty pounds on their heads. The pits in the streams on Bai Kaferi's farm yielded only a speck or so of gold; wherever I pitted outside his farm, I invariably found more gold. But there was only one place that showed any particular promise. As for those pits in the vicinity of Masaka, only tiny flakes of the yellow metal showed, the only sample of possible value proving very light when weighed.

At last, I felt we could move on to the next camp—Masankoro.

CHAPTER FOURTEEN

BLACK DEVIL CAMP

BREAKING CAMP WAS a joy, everything collapsing in the open camp space in record time, until my erstwhile home was again nothing but a little hole in a vast forest—a forest which, in a few months, would creep in, destroying every trace of my occupation. Bundles were tied and laid out in neat rows. The boys fought for loads that had been theirs before, even if it were the heaviest load of the lot. What they had had, they wanted again. The watchman was given an odd assortment of lamps, pots, and pans, with the chickens, legs tied together, perched on top. "All ready! Up!" and a mad scramble to be first on the way, as their neck muscles became taut, the loads settling down on the round grass cushions on their heads.

All the village turned out to see us depart. The chief and my two guides, who were returning to Matotaka, came forward for dashes. I had to shake hands with these three, or rather, touch palms, as a token of good will. Then James Conte, who had the cyclometer wheel, pushed a path through the gawking children, and we were on the move again. I was well pleased with the growth of my map and the work accomplished during my stay at Masaka. A red line marked the position of the large iron ore deposit, and dots showed pits dug, numbers indicating the specks of gold in the samples taken. These finds were not of much importance, but even the finding of a speck of gold showed I was on the right track and gave me a feeling of satisfaction. I had dreaded the thought of going out prospecting and having to return to report not one speck of gold. Now I would have at least something worth while to report.

Masankoro was a messy little village, the walls of the dwellings broken down, dirty thatched roofs half gone, and an air of general slovenliness. After finding the chief, I was told that he had a nice house for me in his new village near-by. I wondered what he meant, for no resthouse was marked on the map, and the tumble-down aspect of the village was not encouraging. I looked askance at these people, who had great leopard traps at the entrance and exit of their village. I knew I was in the country of the Leopard Society, about which James Conte had become quite confiding one day and told me tall tales of its activities in these parts.

Makrugbe, the nearest big village, was powerful in the Leopard Society, and I had heard of former arrests from this village, for the government was trying to stamp out cannibalism, which was what the Leopard Society really represented. A drive had recently been made to kill all the real leopards in the vicinity and give the people confidence. Several persons had been killed within the past year, the numbers varying according to the chief I questioned. A woman and a child, so James said, had disappeared from this very village fairly recently. Hence, the large oblong cages, with new ropes and heavy weights behind the doors, waiting at the entrance of the village to catch marauding leopards. However, everyone knew the disappearances had been the work of human leopards. These traps were mere ornaments to persuade the people that something was being done about trying to catch the leopards.

The primary object of the Leopard Society was to obtain human blood and fat to anoint the "Borfima," or medicine charm, which was considered to make all-powerful the witch doctor who possessed it. The charm contained white of egg, blood of a cock, a few grains of rice, blood and fat and other parts of a human being.[1] The members of the Society met in great secrecy only when the Borfima needed feeding. Then someone was chosen, often a chief, or someone who had made some real advancement, to supply a victim for the Society. He was threatened with death if he did not suggest or present a victim. Usually he picked some relative, possibly one he disliked or considered imbued with a bad devil. A group was chosen to do the killing; the time was set; and some woman or child disappeared, carried away by the killers. They were dressed up in leopardskins and claws, to give the impression to anyone who witnessed their act that it was a leopard that entered the hut or jumped out of the bush at the victim.

The body was taken to the men's sacred grove, the Poro Bush, and the Borfima was "blooded." Then the body of the victim was divided among the members. The flesh was either eaten raw on the spot or taken away and cooked. "Some like it raw, some roast, some prefer it boiled with rice."[2]

Knowing all this, I did not feel particularly happy to be with these people, who more or less openly admitted that "leopards" were about, killing people. Later, after I had become friendly with them, I asked one vicious-looking old man, who became very confidential when I was questioning him about the Leopard Society, whether he thought my dog would make good chop. He eyed my plump dog. His mouth began watering and

[1] Facts about the Leopard Society are based on *Human Leopards,* by K. J. Beatty, Hugh Rees, Ltd., London, 1915.
[2] *Ibid.*

his eyes sparkled. He remarked, "He make fine chop. Missus gib him me when she no want!"

Perhaps he had heard me remark what a useless cur he was. No doubt, several had had their eyes on Balto, hoping he might stray some day. But Balto knew better.

I asked the old chap whether he ever "chop plenty dog." He said he had, "plenty!" Then I asked him if he thought *I* would be "fit for chop." He gave me a scornful look and answered, without a second's hesitation, "Missus no get plenty fat. She no be fit."

I felt slightly relieved, and then asked if "man taste good past beef?"

"Man be plenty sweet past beef," and his eyes rolled and his tongue touched his lips.

Here was admission of cannibalism. These remarks satisfied me that there were those who had eaten human flesh and were proud of it. Usually they were guarded in their replies, having been persecuted for their acts, but my friend had had just too much palm wine to make him cautious. Besides, the natives knew that I was no prying government official, seeking to arrest them or collect taxes. I was just the "Gold Missus," trying to help them by finding gold on their land.

The Poro Society, the secret society for men, had been the chief power in the interior of Sierra Leone before the British government took over the country as a protectorate in 1896. The secret Poro Bush was holy ground, and a terrible punishment was meted out to any uninitiated person who encroached upon it. The Society goes back into very ancient times, its origin being uncertain. The heads of the Poro Society hold supreme power, being above the chiefs. They live in the woods and exist by making raids on the village for clothes, goats, rice, and other necessities. They are never interfered with in this. They, not the chief, have the final word in case of criminal punishment.

During the dry season, boys between the ages of seven and twenty are taken into the Poro Bush and taught to dance and sing, are circumcised without the use of anesthetics, and are generally initiated into the secrets of their elders. They are then assigned to three classes of native social order—(1) the chief's class; (2) the messenger, or servant, class; (3) the Mohammedan class—and their education is then carried on in these groups. Since the Leopard Society had been suppressed, it was suspected that the activities of this Society went on under cover of the Poro Society, for all the men belong to the Poro Society.

Native punishment for cannibalism is death by burning. In 1891 the natives burned eighty persons for cannibalism, a group called the Tongo Players acting as judges of a man's guilt in a human leopard killing. The Tongo Players, who lived in the north, were called to a village where a disappearance had occurred. They employed spies to find out who were the suspected ones, and when they had found out all they needed to know they called the whole village together and had huge fires built. Any suspected individual was called forward and made to dip his hands in boiling oil and pull out a piece of hot iron. If his hand was burned, this proved his guilt. During the great dance that followed, the headman dealt a blow on the heads of the accused and their bodies were thrown on the fire.

The government drove out the Tongo Players in 1892, because of their illegal burning. This resulted immediately in a new outbreak of cannibalism, because the people no longer feared being denounced. The government next passed laws against the Leopard Society and the possession of leopardskins, claws, or any charms that might be connected with the Society. Heavy fines were imposed upon the chief, whenever any of these goods were discovered. Laws against the possession of alligator skins were also imposed when it was discovered that there was a Human Alligator Society, with aims similar to those of the Leopard Society. With the government in control, eighty-seven persons were sentenced to death for taking part in human leopard and alligator deaths. In 1912 it was actually proved in different law cases brought before the D.C. that twenty murders were carried out by the societies in that one year alone. Finally things became so bad that it was made an offense against the country for anyone to sleep in an open place exposed to danger. A bari was taboo. For this reason, my boys would walk miles in order to sleep in a village, rather than sleep in the open near my camp. Also, it was the reason why it was difficult to get a watchman to stay out all night, and why the chief of Masankoro was so anxious to give me a house and was horrified when I said I preferred the bush. He was so urgent that I finally decided to look at his house.

The new village was about an eighth of a mile away from the old. A huge tract of bush had been cleared on a rise in the land, and several new huts were grouped about a large central one. Many were still merely a fragile network of sticks bound together, waiting for the thatched roofs to be tied onto the steeply dipping skeleton. Women were moving back and forth from the houses to a clay pit in the stream bank, bringing calabashes loaded with dripping clay on their heads. Other women rolled the clay and laid it out in rows between the sticks, as in brick-laying. A substantial wall, held together by tied twigs, was rapidly growing as the clay rolls were piled up. Other women were smearing more clay over the completed work, giving a beautifully smooth finish to the sides of the houses. In time, the sun would dry the clay and make a good firm makeshift cement.

I was shown the central house, which seemed more of a meeting place or central bari. Possibly it was to be the chief's future home. It was much larger than the other huts and contained openings for windows—a thing never found in most huts—and had a large central porch. As we went in, I was told over and over that the chief thought this a suitable place for the missus, for no one had ever lived in it. But the stench that greeted me as I entered was overpowering. Several goats were hastily shooed away from their meal of a few bundles of thatch which had been left lying about. Great gobs of mud were heaped up on one side, waiting to be rolled out into a smooth floor. The dampness of the undried clay made me shiver, and the fact that this seemed to be the temporary dwelling place of all the goats and chickens of the village made me decide immediately not to subject myself to the dangers of infection from animal filth and the possible insect life associated with them. The prominence of the situation, with every window a barricade of curious black faces, was too much for me. I preferred the cleanliness, quiet, and privacy of the forest. Though the old chief tried to argue with my boys, I was adamant and demanded to be removed far from any source of pollution. So, crestfallen, the villagers and the boys followed me, doubtless marveling at the asininity of a missus who refused a perfectly good, brand-new house and, in leopard country, preferred the bush.

It proved harder than usual to find a suitable spot to pitch camp. All the nice places were part of the juju bush, and strictly forbidden. Finally, in desperation I pointed out a cool-looking spot just beside the trail, but at the edge of the Poro Bush. I explained that I would not really be inside the sacred territory, for the place I had chosen could be seen from the path. A hurried consultation of my headman with the chief and his elders resulted in my being allowed to make a camp site there, to the accompaniment of the excited chattering of a troupe of monkeys.

Obviously, this was their happy hunting ground too, for one by one, as things quieted down in camp, after the ground had been cleared and the tent had been pitched, I was visited by these curious fellows. There was a swaying in the treetops, a noisy crashing, then silence, a slight rustle, and, peering over a limb, I saw two beady eyes, with a dazzling white spot between. I could not decide for a long time whether this spot was on Mr. Monkey's nose, between his eyes, or on his head; it made my vision wander—a true camouflage. Finally, one came near enough for me to see that it was on the nose. This same fellow was grayish around his face and had a long streak, or bar, of gray on each shoulder. Bending forward, intently, he stared at me and I returned the stare until a twig snapped. My friend was off like streaked lightning, jumping from limb to limb in great swings or leaps, a black tail twice his length weaving frantically or standing at right angles to his body; motionless, gripping the limb with all fours, he finally stopped to give me one last look.

Red monkeys and all-gray monkeys made their call. That evening I saw a gentle swaying of the branches on the highest, flattest-topped tree, then a jerking of the berries that grew on the tips, far out from the tree trunk, and then a flash of white. It was the colobus monkey, a rare animal except in these remote valleys in the hinterland of Sierra Leone. I looked closely and saw a long rope of white hanging limply down, then another, and another. At this moment, the colobus highest up must have seen me, for there was a shrill whistle, white tails up on end, a flashing of bodies, and they played follow-the-leader, leaping from tree to tree until they were quite near. A row of wise faces stared down at me, their blackness set off by a frill of white, making them look like old grandfathers. These beasts were much bigger than the common monkeys and, somehow, seemed more human, with their beards, and the way they spanked their children, and picked the berries from the trees with their black hands. There were several frisky youngsters dashing around. At first they cuddled up against their parents, as they looked down at me. Finally, the elders had had enough of staring and swung off through the branches calling the children to come. Only one obeyed, grasping its mother across her white breast, and clinging there as she ran off. The leader, who was bigger than the others and seemed very much of a bully, went hand over hand up some treacherous-looking creepers, followed in every move by the rest. Then they sat down on a huge limb, a line of black backs turned to me, great long tails hanging motionless. The youngsters could not make the creepers and jumped from limb to limb, trying to reach their parents. Finally one bright fellow got within reach of a tempting tail and without any hesitation scampered up, hand over hand, to be soundly spanked when he reached the top. Darkness came only too soon, and cut short their amusing performance.

Camp having been cut out of the jungle—and a really cool, quiet camp it seemed to be, but without the margin of space around the guy ropes that I really liked as a protection against marauding beasts or attacks of driver ants—I went off with a group of pitting boys to start work in the vicinity. There were plenty of flats along the network of streams within reach of camp. Soon the boys were set to digging in various gravels that seemed likely places to find gold, if there were any in this vicinity. I found that some of the pits, which I had reached by a long roundabout way, were only a short distance above camp, so I had a couple of the boys hack me a "beef-path," or short cut, by which I could go back and forth to camp, instead of waiting at the pits.

When I was sure everyone was working, I left all the boys to help with the pits and strolled back to camp. The quiet of the path, the hugeness of the tree trunks, and the shimmer of light that managed to sift through from the height of the forest made me forget that this was Africa. It was like any deep forest on a hot day. I could not blame the natives for keeping their beautiful forest for themselves and their own superstitions. Everything was so serene and lovely—the forest and just myself—when something made my heart jump a beat, and I stopped, frozen in my tracks. My mouth opened, but the cords of my throat were paralyzed. A half-formed exclamation or cry could not escape. Fascinated, my legs refusing to budge, I saw a great black shadow noiselessly unfold, moving across the trail with a slight swinging motion, the large raised head somehow keeping two blinkless, beady eyes fixed on mine, hypnotizing me. Eight feet of graceful movement slowly glided over the top of a large rotten log in the trail, the leading part pausing a moment in the shimmering sunlight at the top long enough for me to see a blood-red streak as the sun lighted up the underside of the raised hood of the serpent's head, which turned toward me, hesitating a minute as the hood was spread and a long thin forked flash of lightning pointed my way. I was transfixed, powerless to do anything but wait for that hideous triangular-shaped jaw to be raised and a thin spray of deadly venom directed at me, powerless even to blink in time. I knew instantly that this was the black mamba. For a moment that seemed eternity, the snake poised, then the head turned, the hood collapsed, and foot by foot the black form slid over the log, gaining speed as it rushed off into the woods, seeming scarcely to touch the ground as it went its noiseless way. My motionlessness must have saved me.

I drew a deep breath and felt my eyes stinging, as I called shrilly from my cracked throat, "Boy, machete! Boy, machete," then turned and ran back along the trail. James Conte, working at the nearest pit, had heard me, and came at a run, wild-eyed. My voice had been enough to warn him that something was wrong. I turned back and pointed at the rotten log and the woods beyond. He was off, gliding like a watchful cat, black eyes alert, prying into the depths of the forest. In about five minutes, he returned wider-eyed than before.

"I see him," he said. "He go far for river. He be bad past all snake. He be big too much. I no be fit to kill him." So that was it. We went back to camp, single file, James leading, I dreading to have that creature still alive so near camp.

At camp I was greeted by flat-faced Loya, who came up with a deep bow, holding the canvas mailbag in both hands. Loya had been away five days, getting the mail and taking a few of my specimens back to the mine. A note from the accountant explained that the boat train was late and mail had been delayed two days. Also he had waited still another day in order to bring my cook's things, Lamina having recovered sufficiently to travel again. This was the best news yet, for greasy, badly cooked food was making my temper thin and I was eating less and less every day. Lamina heard my voice and came forward out of the kitchen, smiling, glad to be back.

Mail day was always a pleasure. I had my deck chair put out in the shade of the mammoth tree at the side of the tent and settled down to letter after letter, telling of the affairs of a world which seemed even more remote than my world must have seemed to the writers. I did not care whether a new governor had been elected, and the idea of cold weather and snow seemed only another weird fancy. Most of the news was so old that I felt as if I were reading a history book. I was so out of touch with the world with all its complicated social demands, machinery, worries, and excitements, that I felt almost dizzy when visualizing the giddy life of others. I felt tired when I put down the last letter. I would not change; I was content with the quietness of my world, my mind completely absorbed in hunting for gold and in mapping the rocks and having their secrets gradually unfold.

Putting my personal letters aside, and not even bothering to open my business letters—they could wait—I took up *Time,* glanced through it, and cast it aside to finish later, some day when I had less to do. I put the *Reader's Digest* in my knapsack —that would be fun to read while waiting for the boys to finish pitting—and tore open the *Saturday Evening Post,* fingering it from cover to cover. It was the ads which really fascinated me —advertisements of electrical equipment that seemed to belong to another age, food which made my mouth water, salads of which I would dream at night. The headman coming up interrupted my contemplations.

"All pits be deep too much. Boys no reach bottom nowhere. We go finish next today. All boys beg missus give um chop money soon. Boys go look for house in village."

Oh, yes, it was payday, and what was more, the end of the month.

"Yes, Momo, go tell all boys to come here."

Off he went at a trot, beaming from ear to ear. It was amazing, the speed with which the boys showed up. Probably they had been waiting quietly, just out of sight, having sent Momo ahead as emissary. They did not have to be told twice to form in line, and I noticed an amazing advance in their intellect—or possibly it was the headman's idea—they appeared in line according to the order of their names in the book. Momo the First, Abou, Loya, Chaka One, Salifu, Yunka, Alimami, Kalfalla, Santigi, Basi, Kamara, Sedu, Sixpence, Abduli, Pretty, James Conte, Lamina, Temne, Susu—each answered with a snappy "yes, sah" to their names, then came up, both palms held together for their savings. A grin, a careful fingering of the money, and they walked away, their voices joined in much argument as they wandered off, settling a complicated system of debts which they had incurred with each other. Next, the higher-paid boys drew up and "borrowed" only what they wished, for they preferred me to be their banker rather than run the risk of being robbed at night by their brothers. Momo Beer decided that all he wanted was one shilling. I suspected then that he fined the boys on his own, keeping his living expenses down to less than nothing. Bribery by a headman was common. I became serious and asked Momo if his belly troubled him.

"No, sah—I mean yes, sah."

"You no fit to chop for one whole week?"

"Oh, no sah—I mean yes, sah." Light was beginning to dawn that perhaps there was something behind my seriousness. I finally explained that I did not consider one shilling sufficient to nourish such a fine headman as he was for one whole week. The sarcasm struck home, and, hanging his head and shifting his eyes, he decided he had better have two shillings. Amadu, Lamina, and Chaka, whom I now graduated to the name of "Lemon" to avoid confusion with Chaka One, one of the laborers, each took two shillings apiece, probably to allay suspicion.

Payday finished, I had chop and spent a restful, undisturbed night. The next day being Sunday, I decided to give the boys a day off to recover from the probable spree they had had that night with "too plenty copper." I spent the day getting my monthly report written, catching up on my correspondence, and weighing the paltry samples I had collected—a hair-raising job, for the weights had to be handled with tweezers and every drop of moisture from my hands would throw things off balance.

Gold specimens from the pits, at least anything which looked at all possible, were kept in bottles; the gold was collected in a little ball of mercury, which had to be dissolved in nitric acid, and the gold annealed and brushed onto the tiny tray of my miniature prospector's weighing scales. The lengthy procedure turned out to be most discouraging. Calculations of the weights of the gold I had struggled so hard to procure showed that the amounts were so small that the valleys where they had been collected were valueless. So my first monthly report from the field was mostly geology and very little gold.

In the evening I sent for Loya and gave him my letters and the report, with instructions to go back to Makong "one-time" and give them to the paymaster. I noticed James Conte hanging around the kitchen. Somewhat annoyed, I called to him. He had been hanging around, apparently, bursting to tell me what he had gleaned from the villagers. Before I could reprimand him, he began:

"The people for village tell me that big snake live for Poro Bush for ten years, maybe. They call him Black Devil. He no be real snake. He be some big chief that go die before ten year. Them women who go wash last night for river near them big pit see him go look all three pit. They no wait to see if he 'gree for gold work. They run for village and leave them clothes for river. All men fear for go back."

This was a predicament, because I might be forbidden to continue with my prospecting here. The only thing to do was to summon the headman of the village and his elders and with much argument persuade them that the "Black Devil" was merely looking to see if we had found gold and that the very fact that he had harmed no one showed that he " 'gree for missus to find gold." The elders solemnly nodded their heads, following my argument, and finally agreed that it would be all right to continue the work.

CHAPTER FIFTEEN

SNAKES AND MORE SNAKES

S NAKES WERE a real worry. Almost every day, after leaving the "Black Devil Camp," we met one kind or another—in camp, by pits, on the trails, and especially when bushwhacking along the watercourses, as we cut our way through the rank vegetation along some tributary stream. All of them were poisonous. Life became a veritable nightmare to me, for I dread snakes of any variety. Nowhere before nor since have I so consistently met snakes of so many kinds day after day. The valley we were now in must have been ideal breeding grounds, or traps, for these snakes—with too sparse a native population to keep them in check.

One day when making a trek to the south from "Black Devil Camp," we followed a stream up to a flat, partly open spot—broiling hot, of course, but quite a change from the dark green of the forest. As we came out into the sunlight, a mass of red and white flowers, feathery ferns, and green creepers sprawling all over palm trees spread out before us in a beautiful, luxuriant tangle. A sticky mist clung to the foliage as if held down by the blazing sunlight, almost suffocating me. Swarms of flies lazily collected around me, making life still more miserable. But this was the place to dig for gold—plenty of gravels brought here from the hills above, and the right kind of rocks in the stream. So here we stopped, and I set boys to work in various places, while the headman hacked out a little clearing big enough for me to sit in and enjoy comparative shade. Amadu brought my lunchbox, but I was too exhausted to eat more than a few bananas and oranges; perspiring profusely, I swatted the incessant flies. I tried unsuccessfully to satisfy my thirst with the lukewarm boiled water from the thermos flask.

I must have dozed—at least, my mind must have been blank for an interminably long time. During the heat of the day I could shut off my thinking powers for hours at a time while waiting for the boys to finish their work. Suddenly I realized that the sun had shifted considerably, and, instead of being in the shade, it was beating down on me. I had a splitting head— my eyes saw black and red spots from the intenseness of the light. I pulled myself up and stepped into the shadow of the palm. Then my heart missed a beat. I was staring down into the eyes of a creature whose head looked like a miniature dinosaur with blinkless eyes.

Once before, on the Gold Coast the previous year, I had met this type of demon, the horned cerastes. I had been stepping off a log, when the boy behind paralyzed me with an unusual sort of grunt. I stopped motionless, one foot ready to reach for the ground. A machete was thrust beneath my leg, severing the hideous head of the great fat snake just beneath my foot. It had been crawling by the log. It was a fat, sluggish snake, peculiar to the West Coast, with a diamond-shaped pattern of dark browns and black on its hideously long fat body. I had had seven boys with me that day, cutting a straight traverse line through virgin bush, and each one of them, after first politely offering me a share, had marched home with one-seventh of the white fishlike flesh for his evening chop. A large ground squirrel, as big as one of our gray squirrels, had been found inside the beast, and this, the boys said, had made an excellent stew! The cerastes had a pair of recurved teeth an inch long, through which a fine spray of venom had been injected into the ground squirrel as it passed over the log, the snake just grazing it with its fangs. So powerful was the venom that it had undoubtedly been a matter of seconds before the poor beast had succumbed. His lazy antagonist had swallowed him at his leisure, being in the process of digesting his prey when I had chanced along. The skin of the creature I later had made into a pocketbook.

And here I was again, face to face with a five-foot horned cerastes. Stepping back, I called in a voice that I tried to make calm, "Boy—machete! One-time!" Two boys ran up, dripping with mud from their pitting, and cut off the sluggish creature's head. Balto would not even sniff at the corpse, but the boys shouted and jumped about like so many children, carefully wrapping the meat up in large leaves to take home for supper.

Pits dug, samples carefully taken and washed, a few specks of gold carefully collected in mercury and sealed in a bottle, and we returned to Masankoro and home, for every camp seemed like home. Once the boys had learned my wants, they never failed to do exactly the same next time, regardless of whether or not I might have changed my mind. Often when I failed to be consistent, Amadu would remind me that "missus always want it so and so," and I would succumb to the line of least resistance and let routine rule me. The tempers of the boys were much better that way.

Camp life was going well except for a slight uneasiness I felt about the watchman, whom I now called "Aladdin," a name to which he answered with alacrity. One night I vowed I would stay awake a long time and see what he did, ensconced in his comfortable-looking hammock. After the boys had departed and I was tucked into my mosquito net, Aladdin stretched, put a few sticks on the fire, and sauntered into the kitchen, taking a long look around, after the manner of a scavenger dog; then, apparently certain that there were no scraps left, he began wandering around the enclosure, holding his lantern low so that every bit of ground was examined. After looking long and suspiciously at one spot, he put his lantern down, took a shovel, and went to the fire and dug into the ashes. These he scattered near the lamp; he must have spotted some marauding ants. Next, he scattered hot ashes completely around the camp as an extra precaution, hoping to smother and force back the driver ants if they decided to come that way. I was getting tired of waiting for him to quiet down and had almost decided to turn over and forget him, when he made for his hammock, pushed the logs a little farther into the center of the fire, placed some banana leaves on one side of the lamp to reflect the light over the camp ground and to protect the globe from cracking in case of rain, then climbed into his hammock.

The flickering light of the fire shone in bronzed patches on Aladdin's dark skin, as he stripped to his waist. His shirt was his only apparel aside from his loincloth, so his idea of retiring for the night had been to strip. The shirt was placed under him, probably because the native rope of the handmade hammock was not particularly comfortable. Still he did not settle down. After tossing a bit, he got up and went to the kitchen, returning presently with my nice clean dish towels. To my horror, he climbed into the hammock and stuck the towels under him, carefully trying not to fold them. I boiled inwardly, but remembered that I could not explain anything to him, as he did not understand one word of English; I decided to let his punishment wait until morning, the harm having already been done. I should have to have every cloth in camp boiled anyway—and it would take Amadu to explain to him the full enormity of his wrongdoing. Usually, such things would not have struck me as humorous, but for the first time in weeks, it seemed, I kept myself from laughing out loud only with the greatest difficulty.

I thought of the tale, told me by one of the miners, of the cook that some white lady in one of the coast towns had had, who was noted for his marvelous croquettes, which she always had on special occasions. A friend, who was anxious to learn the art of making these croquettes, asked if she might come up to the house the next time the cook was preparing a dinner and see how they were made, for a verbal attempt to describe the ingredients proved futile. A few days later the lady was entertaining a particularly prominent guest and told her friend to come to tea and see the secret of the cook's art. When they went into the kitchen the great fat cook, stripped to his waist, was caught in the act of rolling two croquettes at a time up and down his fat abdomen!

Finally I went to sleep, thinking this was a suitable time to have one of my weekly attempts to drill sanitation into the boys. Everything in the camp would be boiled—and not half-boiled, either—and I would personally inspect the boiling of the water.

Camp life continued fairly smoothly, after the cleanup. A contrite Aladdin spread ashes around the next night and walked round and round my tent with his padded footsteps, while the flash of his lantern disturbed my sleep. All my attempts to try to make him return to his hammock and leave me in peace were unavailing; my sign language just did not work. So I had to issue a new set of orders the next day—that the watchman was to wander to the back of my tent and not pass it. He was not to let the light be seen. Peace was at last obtained, as Aladdin fathomed the strange wishes of his missus.

Gold prospecting was yielding no results at all; but I found that the iron ore on Bai Kaferi's farm was part of a continuous bed and not just a small local deposit. I had hopes, as I worked north, of tracing the ore to connect with the rich deposits I had mapped the previous year. Some gold had been found in the pits to the east and below the iron ore, and, although the iron ore had nothing to do with the gold, it was proving a marker of gold sources. Anything that was a clue to the structure of the region was of help, ultimately, in the unraveling of the perplexing problem I was facing. The contact between the granite and the schist seemed to be the place where the gold was to be found, so I was carefully mapping these two rocks. But the reefs, or gold-bearing quartz veins, might easily have an affinity for one particular rock, or the gold itself might saturate some special formation in the schist belt. If this iron ore, which was so outstanding and resistant to erosion, were a marker, it would at least give me the relative position of the gold-bearing rocks, of which I kept finding small outcrops but which I had been unable to trace. Then, regions likely to produce gold could be plotted as I worked north, until I almost knew where I would, and where I would not, find gold.

The excitement of following out these theories made me forget the days slipping by; I followed stream after stream to its source, boys hacking the way, foot by foot, flies biting, sweat pouring off my brow. The boys themselves got the fever of the chase and worked fairly well, looking carefully at the various rocks broken along the route, grinning with pleasure when a few specks of gold turned up in a pan. We never exchanged ideas on the work. They followed my instructions, trusting in my juju. I never asked for their advice, feeling that this would cause me to drop in their estimation. If the headman asked me a question, I always had some sort of answer at the tip of my tongue, so that he was satisfied.

We had been working in the drainage area of the Tebenko River, following up its headwaters. The streams in this water-soaked region formed an intricate network; yet we owed it to the streams that we could even hunt for gold. Each stream we reached emptied into the Tebenko, and eventually the Pampana.

After combing the hills within a radius of Masankoro, we moved to Makena. Camp was made in a humid, low place beside the Kote River, which empties into the Tebenko. All possible sites were turned down for this dank spot, partly because the sun was affecting me after the days of trailing about in the open, protected only by a sun helmet and spine pad. I craved the cool offered by this evil-smelling spot, away from the village. I should have known better than to let the boys pitch camp under the huge half-rotten trees with their great radiating roots, but the women washing their clothes in the stream looked so cool and happy. I had forgotten that we were getting longer showers every day and that places like this reeked with mold. I was so cross to the headman, when he remonstrated, that the word must have been passed around, for a clearing was hacked out without the usual singing to the swing of the machetes.

My head felt better in the shade, and I began to feel slightly amused as I watched the pickins bobbing up and down on their mothers' backs as they rhythmically pounded their clothes on the rocks at the water's edge. How both the pickins and the clothes survived this strenuous treatment, I could not quite figure out. Each woman had brought her livestock along for fear a neighbor would run off with it in her absence. The poor, skinny fowls, secured by one leg, hungrily snatched at the various beetles and ants within reach, for this might be their only chance of getting sustenance that day. One or two mangy, pointed-eared, hyenalike curs curled their lips at me, periodically, or were kicked aside as a mammy found them in her way. One by one, the women finished their work, and clothed themselves by tying a great strip of cloth around their hips. They apparently had no idea of how to make a knot, for they twisted the cloth into a great wad which looked terribly insecure and shoved it into the waistline. The pickins were scrubbed, to which indignity they retaliated by screaming, and then were tied inside a strip of cloth, which was wound across the mother's breasts to secure the child in place. Then, with much ado, the clean clothes were piled in a large calabash, which was placed on the woman's head, and some kind friend hoisted a great bundle of firewood, gathered earlier in the day, on the very top. Off they went, single file, pickins happy again, the chickens in their coops balanced on top of the wood or carried by the legs upside down, squawking. They took one last look my way, for they had shyly watched our preparations, as much interested in me as I was in them.

After the women had gone, I turned to watch the boys. While supervising a boy who was hacking away some of the roots, I was sure I saw a black tail slip into a hole. Digging failed to bring out anything, and I decided that my imagination was playing tricks with me.

I had just chosen a few places where pits were to be dug, and some of the boys had already started to dig, when the clouds burst. The rain ceased quickly, but the incessant drip-drip from the leaves went on the rest of that day and night. The ground steamed.

Lanterns had to be lighted early in this dark place, and my persistent struggles with the petrol lamp failed to have any

The village barber at work.

A mother and child. The mother probably has a headache because she has tied a bandanna around her head to drive away the bad devil.

effect. I put in two new generators, in an attempt to get the thing going, and Amadu pumped and pumped. We pricked the generator with wires, but all to no avail. The damp had got the thing, so we had to make the best of the situation with the kerosene hurricane lamps. Then I found I should have to send Loya out to Magburaka the next day to buy more kerosene. There was a leak somewhere. I vowed that hereafter I would supervise the filling of the lamps myself and keep the key in the box. Kerosene was at a premium in these parts, and it was easy enough to overfill a lamp and sell a cupful or two to the villagers or to the carriers. Henceforth, Amadu and Lamina would have to resort to using lighted brands to get them back to the village after supper.

With the hurricane lamp perched on the end of the table, turned low so that it would not attract too many insects into my soup, I began a soggy meal—sour bread made with palm wine and baking powder instead of yeast; rancid canned butter; chicken "cut-legs" (cutlets) thoroughly greasy with moldy lard; tasteless sweet potatoes—the cook was getting back at me for my economies by omitting salt entirely—cooked yellow pawpaw that might have been mistaken for squash if there had been a trace of any sort of taste in it; and fruit salad, made up mostly of overripe bananas, oranges being very scarce.

I was sitting in my deck chair, like the good old Romans, feet up on the footrest, trying to pretend I was at a real banquet, and was just finishing the fruit salad, when suddenly two small eyes flashed in the dull shaft of light beyond the table, and a sinuous form became visible. It slowly advanced toward the table. Suddenly I found my voice and, leaping bolt upright in my chair, let out a piercing shriek. The object of my fear was as scared as I by my actions, and made for the nearest thing, which was the table leg, winding to the top like greased lightning. Baffled, as its chance of escape came to an end, and dazzled by the light, we eyed each other; just then Aladdin slithered up, machete in hand, and made a clean cut through the snake's neck with a twist of his wrist, as it stood facing me, poised, its triangular-shaped jaw just ready to open.

Inwardly, I was as near being hysterical as I have ever been, but outwardly I was calm. Amadu was at my side by now. To him I said, "He is to burn *that* in the fire—*now!*" I sat down, trembling, absolutely unnerved, and watched the reluctant Aladdin burn the body—a native hates to burn anything. He had to be told three times. The head was buried at the edge of the camp in a hole dug with a machete; otherwise, the poison fangs of this deadly green mamba might be stepped on by some native.

I put off getting up out of my chair for a long time. I felt snakes all around me; I jumped at the sound of a twig. A rhinoceros beetle, hitting against my face, made me wince, and I even called the watchman to push him off the table. A praying mantis was no longer an object of sheer delight; its absurd antics and distorted legs made me shiver. Finally I forced myself to get up, but not until, with the aid of my flashlight, I had scrutinized every inch of my surroundings about the tent. I even closed the back flaps—a thing I never did, unless it was actually raining. Then, using my small hammer—I would not touch anything with my hands—I pried all around the edge of the net and the mattress and explored behind the boxes. I even dreaded putting my hand into the tent pockets to pull out my toothbrush and face cloth and towel. I had heard of snakes getting into the basin water, so that was examined with the flash. After I finally got into bed and turned off the light I could see green heads and lidless eyes poised on all sides, whether I opened or shut my eyes.

For hours I lay rigid, not moving a muscle. I imagined myself going insane, bit by bit, as the tropics and snakes got me. Whether or not I slept, I never knew. I heard the watchman pushing up the logs every half hour or so. The night noises were terrifying. They hummed and shrieked in my ears. Drops of moisture from the leaves above sounded like rocks being dropped on the tent. When Amadu finally appeared, with a lantern, to get the food out of the boxes for breakfast, I was still in the same tense position, hair and face damp. It took all my nerve to get out of bed. The forest was still dark, although I could see gray sky above.

I dressed and had breakfast, and by the time the watchman came up and stood beside me, obviously trying to get me to come and look at something, I was almost my usual self, although feeling a little watery-eyed and weak. Calling Amadu, I asked him to find out what the watchman wanted.

"He go show you something. I no savvy him."

So over to the fire I went, and, with a proud flourish and a grin a mile wide, as if he were showing me a work of art, Aladdin pointed to three long, thin, green bodies, neatly laid in a line beside the fire. So that was how he had spent the night! Obviously wide awake! And thoroughly proud of his night's work. After praising him for his vigilance, I told him to burn the trophies, and feeling queer inside and weak-kneed, I returned to my chair and called to the carriers to line up.

After looking at the map, I assigned several boys to the pits already begun, and then set off with a few laborers to a point far away from Makena, feeling safer at a distance from that snake-infested spot. Walking in the early morning coolness restored my equilibrium, and I was almost cheerful by the time we reached some open farm fields and the brilliant sunshine. The starting of more pits and the plotting of streams which were not on the map kept us busy all day. Several good shows of gold were found in various samples washed before we returned that evening, tired and feeling as if we had accomplished something. I never again felt safe in the camp at Makena; my one object was to work like mad and move on as quickly as possible.

But the mountains were high, the rivers long and tortuous, and the bush thick, so it took almost a week of hectic sampling and bushwhacking, traversing up and down streams or ridges, before I was satisfied that the country had been even moderately well combed. The surveyors who had mapped this country had done a very poor job—nor was that entirely their fault, for it was almost impossible country in which to get around. They had not been able to follow all the tributaries, so had "sketched" them, when money gave out or work pressed. Hence, the streams we followed did not arrive where expected, and hills did not stop where the contours indicated. In order to plot the position of pitting operations or to place the rock structures correctly, it was necessary for me to correct the map, no easy matter in country where a far view was rare.

CHAPTER SIXTEEN

FINDING GOLD

AGAIN WE STRUCK camp and moved on into even more remote country, where crossing streams was difficult and villages were far apart. The village of Makele, our next stopping place, consisted of only one or two families, the more up-and-coming natives having moved out to the larger towns on the roads or railroads, after the manner of farmers elsewhere. Here the boys were forced to build shelters for themselves, for there was not enough room in the two dilapidated huts which were all that was left of the formerly large village. In a remote place such as this, I kept two or three boys always on the trail buying food.

From Makena to Makele the trail had been narrow, little trodden, for few used it, and full of fallen trees and bushes. The weaker boys had a hard time of it; lifting themselves and the sixty pounds on their heads over a log was difficult enough, but when the tree trunk was four feet thick it required a half hour's delay to see them all over. Sometimes a side trail had to be cut before the boys could find a way to get their loads past an obstruction. The rivers were high, owing to daily downpours, so that fording became a real adventure, full of thrills, or, rather, anxiety for the safety of the loads. Twice we had to cross the raging Tebenko where there were no helpful villagers and their canoes. Momo Beer bravely stripped at the first ford, and halfway across was completely swept off his feet and carried, struggling, a hundred yards downstream before making the bank. Obviously we could not ford. James Conte called from farther downstream and announced that he had found a raft, which had been tied to a large tree trunk, half submerged in the water. It was made of several large logs lashed together with tie-tie, and proved so unsteady, half sinking with two boys on it, that it was necessary to chop down several trees and lash them as a second layer on top of the first. One load at a time was taken over, two boys cautiously paddling with sticks, and several carriers swimming alongside to help propel the raft. When it was my turn, I fully expected to be dumped into the water, but somehow we arrived dry. Balto, who refused to come aboard, finally leaped in after the raft and swam behind it.

It was pitch dark when we finally brought the stragglers into the village of Makele and hastily cut a small camp site on the edge of a stream. I wondered how the boys would manage to get any chop that night, at that desolate, almost deserted village; but as all returned at dawn the next day, cheerfully smiling, I asked no questions. The best policy was always to let them shift for themselves until they came forward with their demands, which was generally all too frequent.

The spot where we had settled for the night was such an evil-smelling, reeking-hot hole—I lay all night perspiring on top of my cot, without a breath of air stirring—that the first thing I did the next morning was to announce that we would move camp somewhere else, as soon as I had reconnoitered.

Study of the map seemed to show that the best place for camp would be the other side of the Tebenko, up in the hills, away from the village and the flatter country. We looked over the possibilities of a ford beyond the village and found a place where the footing was poor, but the water came only to the boys' armpits. Getting me across took the combined force of all my followers, four perching me on their shoulders, where I held on for dear life, fingers clutching kinky hair. The rest of the boys acted as props to my bearers so that they would not slip downstream. Two boys had the job of holding my feet out of the water, but managed to submerge them thoroughly when one slipped. It was much like riding on a camel, for the boys did not move in unison. Once I was almost dropped right in the middle between the four boys, much to everyone's consternation.

Balto had made two attempts to swim across, and the current had all but drowned him; now, he stood on the opposite bank, shivering and looking thoroughly disconsolate. Momo Beer had the bright idea of bringing him over in a head pan, and the boys cheered with glee when Balto arrived on his high perch, looking pleased with the world. In fact, he enjoyed his unusual place so much that he refused to get out of the head pan until shoved.

About a mile up a hunter's trail, we reached some rice farms, and I found a fine place for a camp on top of a knoll, or divide, at the junction of two streams. The place had been farmed within two years, so that the growth was not great.

The sides of the stream valleys rose fairly steeply for a hundred feet, but it seemed like five hundred as we struggled up, pushing through sword grass and itchy, catchy, stringlike creepers, beautiful to look at but dreadful on clothes and knees. Great logs lay rotting, mute testimony that here had once been a big forest.

At the top of the knoll, in the blazing sun, I wondered if I were wise to have a camp where the sun beat down with such terrific force. Then I remembered my snaky, shady camp and my clothes and tent beginning to rot for lack of direct sun, so I decided to stay. Besides, I would be away during the heat of the day, and the view down the valley—for I could see out— was worth any amount of effort. This was the first chance I had had for weeks to see any distance, and it made me feel free again. I would get away from the oppressive shut-in-ness, which I suddenly realized had been weighing on my nerves. So the whole gang was set to work—and how grudgingly! "Missus must be mad," I could see reflected in their looks and in the sullen way they gingerly chopped back the mat of thorny creeping vines. The site was a mile and a half from the nearest hut, and many more from a real village, but I saw smoke from a farm hut in the field below, so I knew someone was there, guarding this year's crops. This meant that my personal boys could stay near-by, unless they preferred to build shelters below my lookout hill.

The surrounding country was deserted and uncut, save for the few patches which had been farmed. There would be unlimited opportunity for exploration in the hills, which rose fifteen hundred feet high behind the camp. I could trace the indentations in the solid dark green slope that marked the streams up which I would soon be gasping. The heavy misty atmosphere of the Tebenko stretched away in front. A great hawk lazily floated over the mist, peering down, as if the effort of dropping down on some spotted prey was too much. Everything seemed in a stupor, except my sweating boys. They were fighting against nature—just a warning of the change and movement which was to come. That oppressive dead spot would see life appear, men come and go, a mine grow up, gold pour down toward the Tebenko, and then, before many years, after man had all this wealth that he wanted, peace perhaps would again come and the forest gradually destroy all signs of occupancy. The futility of it all struck me for the first time —perhaps because I could, literally, see beyond my nose for the first time in days; and this was only a small section of the valley laid out before me. I realized that all this effort was to line someone else's pockets with silk.

I was brought back to earth from my mental lapse by the perspiring face of Momo Beer, announcing that the camp site was cleared. I divided the party, keeping a small group to go up a branch of the near-by stream and sending the others back to Makele to move camp. Momo Beer could be trusted to do that much, after I had carefully marked the place for my tent veranda, the rear of the tent, and pointed out where they must build me a shimbek.

When we entered the forest and started up the rocky stream, I decided I liked the place—the cool air about the stream channel, the high trees, the reaches of swift water, the chutes where beautiful potholes had been developed in the hard granite gleaming with mica, and finally a waterfall, tumbling down in a twenty-foot cataract.

My enthusiasm for living returned—real rocks to map, plenty of them, easy to study where the river had cut a deep gorge through the old granite; many contacts of the granite with the green schists; a white quartz reef, cutting an intricate pattern, which suggested possible gold. The first shallow pit we attempted caved in, but a shovelful of the coarse gravel from the bottom was rescued and, when washed, revealed many sizable nuggets of gold, larger than pinheads. The boys were as excited as I. Previously, we had found only tiny flakes; here we could even pick up pieces. How much brighter and yellower they seemed, surrounded by the heavy black iron grains, than a gold piece which has been rolled smooth and blended until it has lost its true character. Every piece had a different shape —one, like a tiny complex leaf, rough and irregular; another, rounded and smoothed or flattened, showing that it had traveled some distance and been rolled and crushed.

We dug another pit and cut a routine sample, a sample which, when washed, amazed me by the amount of its gold content; it seemed too big to be true. Then one of the boys was told to scoop up what gravel he could from one of the potholes in the river. He submerged completely in his effort to please, filling his gold pan and washing it breathlessly. The number of tiny nuggets of gold rolling in the pan after the final washing fairly made me gasp. I tried not to show my surprise and delight for fear the boys would spread tales and someone would come in to peg a claim before I could communicate with my headquarters. This stream was far off the beaten track, but it wouldn't do to spread word that might bring other white men.

Back at camp, I wrote two letters—one to the manager at Makong to tell him about my finds and the other to Mr. Babcock, who was up north making the rounds of some of the company's mines, asking him whether I should peg any land and advising him to stake a claim on this region just as soon as he could. Two messengers were sent off with these notes and some samples.

I worked feverishly the next few days, clambering up every stream bed, collecting the samples, many of which contained large amounts of gold—one sample, when weighed and recalculated by a formula corrected for the current price of gold, showed that particular place to be worth a dollar for every cubic yard of gravel.

The river along which I worked most of the time, and on which my camp was pitched, was not named on the map, but

Salifu, my local guide, said it was the Mapoko. We followed up every tributary of this widely branching river to its source, scrambling over waterfalls and up great rocky channels carved out of the dark green schist, carefully pitting in every patch of gravel, and sometimes digging a few shovelfuls from the channel. Gold, in varying quantities, seemed to be everywhere we turned. Rock outcrops were so numerous that before long I had a fairly good geological map of the region, right up to the top of the hills.

Not far above the place where we first found gold, we came to an even more magnificent waterfall than any we had seen before. The water cascaded down over the grayish-pink granite, sparkling in the sunlight, a rainbow arching the spray. At the base of the forty-foot fall, great angular boulders were piled hit or miss, some of the largest forming natural caves. We wandered into one, to be met by a terrific outrush of flapping wings and weird cries, as the large bat inhabitants tried to escape. Soon the whole chamber was a seething mass of these shadows, frantically beating from side to side. The boys shrieked with glee, and those who had hats or caps scooped bat after bat from the air, promptly snapped their necks, and piled them up to take home for evening chop. I named the place "Bat-cave Falls," for it had no name and was not on the map.

No one had explored all these streams, partly because of their inaccessibility and partly because of a superstitious fear of the unknown virgin forest and the darkness of the gorges. Salifu proved hopeless when it came to finding short cuts, his knowledge of the vicinity being limited to an acquaintance with the few places that had been brushed for farms. He was worth his weight in gold as a bushwhacker; he was the first native I had in my ever-changing retinue who was not afraid of work. His arms were a bulging mass of muscles, and it was a delight to see him wield a machete, slashing from side to side almost as fast as I could walk. He immediately grasped the fact that we had long distances to go and that all I wanted was a passable way through the creepers. A real bush-boy, he instinctively recognized the most painful ferns and became genuinely concerned if he failed to cut some thorny twig which made me wince as it gashed my knees. He was proud of his strength, and especially proud the second day when I allowed him to lead. There were so many places to pit in this region that eventually I put Momo Beer in charge of the various pitting gangs, while Salifu and Basi, who, although still a willing worker, was much put out that he had fallen from first place among my bush cutters, James, and one carrier for the load of pans, picks, and shovels, accompanied me, as I made a general survey of the hills and carefully marked places where pitting was to be done.

One morning, as we followed a hunter's trail, Balto gave us a good scare. Parallel to the trail, hunters had built a rough barrier with only a few openings, in each of which a trap was set. Chasing along this barrier following a scent, Balto reached an opening and thrust his head through. Instantly, the noose encircling the opening tightened, releasing a stick which had held down a great bough. Balto shot up into the air. Two boys jumped for the noose and hacked away until a much frightened, but fortunately uninjured, Balto lay gasping on the ground. The previous year, Buster had walked into the same kind of trap, but because she did not struggle, and stood quietly at attention for what must have been more than an hour, the noose was not sprung, and the boys finally found and released her.

That day we found a large boulder which, when cracked,

revealed steely-gray splotches of a metallic substance which made a silvery streak when rubbed across a piece of porcelain. Looking carefully around, I saw more boulders and bigger ones containing this mineral. It contained the rare metal, molybdenum, an alloy used in the manufacture of high-tensile steels, a new find for West Africa. Greatly excited, I collected some large samples to take back to England for analysis.

As I was eating lunch, a strange boy sauntered up, saluted, took a letter out of his pocket, and handed it to me. Opening it, I found a brief note from Mr. Babcock, saying he was pleased with my Mapoko findings and was making arrangements to have the whole area turned over to the company for a year, as an "exclusive prospecting lease." Before going further, however, I was to pack and trek to Nerekoro, two days north, in order to investigate some property where prospecting rights had been allowed to lapse. It was urgent that I hurry, as rumor had reported other prospectors in the vicinity. If I found anything of value, I was to peg the place for the company. I would find further instructions at Nerekoro.

I hated to leave the Mapoko job, but I must obey orders. Back to camp we hurried to make all necessary preparations for an early start the next morning.

I spent the rest of the day finishing a hasty report of the Mapoko district and working over my maps and samples. The boys were delighted to leave this isolated district, where food was hard to get and distances to villages great. The idea of sleeping in a village that night, instead of in makeshift shimbeks, caused them to work fast; camp was struck just as the sun sent its beams over the hill to dissipate the heavy morning mist, stretching like a white blanket in the valley below. Singing and shouting, they set off at a dogtrot.

Recrossing the Tebenko was like saying good-by to a friend.

I was not even annoyed when my feet got wet, as Salifu, who had been delegated the job of carrying me across, slipped on a boulder, almost pitching me over his shoulder.

Before noon we came to Mamaya, a village of many huts, which seemed like a veritable city after the tiny villages we had seen. This was James Conte's country, and he entertained me with stories of his own farm and of Bai Kaferi, his chief. He showed me the graveyard where Bai Kaferi would be buried. A few heaped-up mounds with small cairns of stones at the head and broken pieces of pottery marked the graves.

As we came to the village, James suddenly put down the wheel and leaped on Balto, who was eating some rice cooked in orange-colored palm oil with a few opened raw eggs on top. Balto was eating the devil's food, he explained. It had been put at the entrance to the village to propitiate any bad devil who came along the path.

"So his belly no be empty so he no steal from women." I remarked that Balto had a bad devil in him which was now propitiated, but James looked dubious. Anyhow, I began to understand why village dogs did not actually starve. James insisted that the food was taken at night by the bad devil and that the dogs never touched it.

"They savvy it be devil-food."

I wondered if leopards ate rice and whether they were not really the bad devils in need of propitiation.

At the edge of the village we passed the Poro Bush, an arbor of green fronds and palms marking the entrance. James told me that at the moment he had a small brother in the Poro Bush, being circumcised; this was the season of the year for the initiation of young boys.

I rested at the chief's house, for I owed him a dash in payment for a large but exceedingly tough duck, some delicious squashes, a dozen rotten eggs, and rice. Also, my cook had apparently obtained many things from the chief without paying for them. The chief, young and powerful, offered me profuse thanks for coming into his land and finding gold there.

James had wandered away, but he soon appeared with a tale of needing three shillings to pay the man who cared for the boys in the Poro Bush. I wondered, but feeling lenient, handed over the money.

The next few hours, we followed the banks of the Pampana, a large river, full of rapids at this point, where it cut through the range I had been following from the south.

We passed through several large villages. At one point James suggested a short cut to a ford of the Pampana that could be reached by a small trail through his father's farm. Anxious to cut down our mileage, we hit out across rice fields, where the sun beat down with horrible intensity. Beyond, the shore of the Pampana came in sight with its little sandy beach, high trees, and cool breeze, offering a delightful contrast. In this thoroughly enjoyable, flyless spot I ate lunch, and waited as the carriers came in, one by one, soaking with perspiration. They helped each other down with their loads, and stretched out in the shade.

James had again disappeared, but returned shortly with a toothless old man and several intensely shy, pretty women, who, he said, were relatives. On their heads they carried great calabashes of cassava. James evidently told everyone to help themselves, for the boys grabbed great roots, tore the brown skin off with their teeth, and gnawed at the white pulp. I could not suppress a grin at the lordly way James presided over the distribution of cassava, hacking off chunks for new arrivals, jabbering excitedly with his family, tipping his chin constantly in my direction.

Momo Beer finally came up with the stragglers, and with an air of importance began reconnoitering the ford. Suddenly he missed his footing and fell headlong into the current. For a moment he floundered helplessly about, but finally gained the opposite bank amid loud shrieks from our side. Amadu also added to the general amusement; he slipped at the very start, and then dog-paddled across, enjoying his swim to the utmost, but coming out a sorry sight in dripping khaki shorts and shirt, hat lost, but with a wide grin. Then to complete the picture, my bearer slipped, dumping me into the water. No one laughed, fearing my wrath, until they saw that I took it as a good joke.

Late in the afternoon we passed through the large town of Masumbiri with its great open, central square, well swept, and bordered with freshly thatched houses. Traders had their wares spread out on their porches, and the market place was still crowded with bargainers. Masumbiri lacked the signs of shiftlessness so evident in more remote places; evidently the influence of the Provincial Commissioner had been felt. My own carriers dallied here, spending their hoarded earnings on food and clothing. They begged me to spend the night in Masumbiri, for they hated to move on. Only after repeated threats and whacks from Momo Beer's cane were they persuaded to go on. I knew we must not linger, for the nearer Nerekoro we slept that night, the sooner we could get started to work the next day.

We reached our goal, Kpfafaia (pronounced Bafia), at suppertime, after crossing the first real road which I had seen for weeks. It gave me a bit of a thrill to know that I was near civilization. I had no desire to see other white persons, but it was nice to know they were at near-by Maranda. I camped in a clean, open grove of coco trees beside a cemetery, wondering

A village store.

A ferryboat made of a hollowed-out tree trunk. Note the ferry-man's lunch of two plantains, his shoes (pieces of automobile tires with rope lacings), and my sledge hammer for breaking rocks.

how deep the natives buried their dead. The tired boys made camp as quickly as possible, not bothering to make more than a small clearing.

After supper I had the usual chief's visit with a sumptuous dash of rice and two fowl. I thought from the size of the dashes that these people must be particularly rich, here on the highway. Amadu explained later that the people were poor, but that they considered me a big chief, for they remembered the time last year when I had stopped the Ramadan feast dance. That incident was made even more vivid by the chief's decisive announcement that a dance, scheduled for that evening, would be postponed until my departure. The arrival of several natives from Maranda, with presents and their chief's greetings, showed that Amadu spoke truly. Several laborers from the mine at Maranda also came to ask to be transferred to my employ. They seemed thoroughly crestfallen when I told them I could not take them away from their present masters. One man in particular was especially persistent. He told me that the mine was always having trouble; that they had only a few hours' work a day.

"They done work for months and months to put up a big machine. Then a few days past, fire done come and go spoil em all."

He meant lightning, I gathered. He looked hurt, but I had to turn him down, too.

CHAPTER SEVENTEEN

CLAIM JUMPING

DAWN SAW US once more on the trail, all in high spirits. We had only five miles to go, but those miles meant climbing steadily on a trail that was steep and narrow.

I reached Nerekoro ahead of the carriers, only to discover that neither James nor Salifu, who were with me, could speak Limba, the speech of these villagers. I looked around for a familiar face, for I had camped here the previous year. I recognized none. No interpreter, nor anyone who spoke a word of English, could be found in the whole village, so we stupidly stared at each other, grinning and nodding, like children at a children's party.

Finally Momo Beer and the carriers arrived, and I found that none of them could speak Limba either. It dawned on me that Momo Beer had had me pay off various boys the previous payday, and that by this gradual process of paying boys off, all the races except the Temnes had been eliminated from my retinue until only a crew of "brothers" remained. I had heard of this trick, and now I realized just how difficult such a situation could be. I spoke sternly to Momo, telling him to find two Limbas who could speak a little Temne or English, and that I would discharge some of the lazy Temnes next payday. Furthermore, I wanted two Karankas and two Mendes, as well as any Konnos who came around, so that I would have many tribes represented in this group. Thoroughly cowed, Momo promised immediate compliance.

Beyond the village we found a possible place for camp. To be sure, the tent would slope about fifteen degrees, but I was in a hurry, and hunting for a good camp site would waste valuable time. I realized how fortunate it was that I had visited the old prospector and his workings the year before, for I had a definite idea of where I should look for the gold. I sent Momo off with eight of the best pitting boys to a spot in the gorge of the Tonkolili River, five hundred feet below, which I felt was the crucial point in the mining prospect. If this point did not give payable ore, it would be useless to work the lease.

I waited to "boss up" camp, intending to join him later, but Momo came panting up as I finished lunch, excitement gleaming in his eye. He blurted out:

"One white master he go walk the river. I no savvy him. He be old man. Get fat belly. He no look plenty for gold. His boys, they no savvy nothing. They no be our company. I tell him I work for one white missus. He say, 'Tell your master I go lookum next tomorrow.'"

So other white persons also wanted to find gold here! Mr. Babcock had had good reason for sending me to Nerekoro. Thank goodness I had come immediately! I hoped that this man was really a stranger and would waste his time fruitlessly, giving me time to prove the land.

I sent Loya off with a note to Mr. Babcock, telling him that I had arrived, that my boys had started pitting, and that a strange white man had appeared. What should I do? I explained that from my previous knowledge of the ground, I thought it impossible to bottom the broader flats of the Tonkolili, where most of the gravels had been dumped by the river. I did not want to peg the claim for the company without really proving the ground. Nor did I have a copy of the mining laws with me. Would he please send me one as soon as possible, if he thought it desirable for me to "jump" the claim, provided I found only fair indications of gold after working a few days.

I set out with the rest of the boys and spent a feverish afternoon trying to get samples up and down the river from the most likely places. I saw no sign of the strange white man that day nor the next. My boys outdid themselves in their efforts to make speed in sinking pits, sensing the tension under which I labored. Gold there was, but in places where the river currents ran strongest. There were few patches of gravel. Pits were started at various points in the floodplain of the stream, but all caved in after being dug about eight feet. The bottom gold-bearing gravels were probably at much greater depth. In desperation, I decided we must do something on a larger scale.

I marked out a square in the flat, thirteen feet by thirteen feet, and set the whole crew to work, some digging, and, as the hole became deeper, others carrying buckets or head pans of gravel out of the pit. Progress was quick that day, for no water came through the silt, but the next morning the hole was a lake and bailing had to be started immediately. The sides were caving slightly, so I decided to barricade the whole pit with logs which could be forced down as the pit became deeper. Each boy cut down three or four saplings, at least ten feet high and three or four inches in diameter, trimmed them, and dragged them to the pit, where they were placed on end and fastened with tie-tie, top and bottom, until the pit was encased like a small fortress. The energy with which the boys attacked this work was contagious. They sang, yelled, and laughed, thoroughly happy with their new toy. Rumor had it that the white man was working downstream somewhere, and the thrill of seeing a white face again, no matter if it were that of a rival prospector, kept me excited. Darkness came before I was aware that the day had gone.

The boys had shifted my camp from the original site to a plateaulike shoulder, high above the spot where the pit was being dug. Here, a grass-grown bit of land—coarse twelve-foot-high elephant grass—was cut away, so that I had a wide view of the mountains to the west. Returning at night to this ideal camp ground, I watched the clouds which now gathered earlier every day, for it was March, and the rainy season was drawing near. As the sun sank, there was a brilliant sunset, followed without warning by a severe "tornado." I felt secure inside my flapping canvas walls. These storms were becoming a regular part of the day's program.

The third day, when I had almost completely forgotten my white competitor, the boys suddenly stopped their digging and stared. There, looking through the top of the barricade, was a red, almost apoplectic countenance, streaming perspiration, gray hairs showing under his sun helmet. Panting and puffing, he came up to me, introduced himself, shook hands, and asked me how I was making out. He seemed to think I was undertaking rather a large project in trying to bottom by hand labor. I realized this, having had nothing but trouble. He said he was using a drill to get to the bottom. I was even more skeptical as to the success of this method, but I did not say so. The experience of my company had been that the drill invariably encountered large boulders, putting a stop to the drilling without reaching the bottom gold-bearing layer, thereby giving poor and untrue results. My visitor said he had found great difficulty in climbing the hills and so had had to send his boys up the bad places. His obvious lack of experience in this part of Africa made me doubt the results of his findings. Even so, I kept wondering if he would jump the claim, just to annoy my company, and prevent our doing so.

I ordered some logs to be placed in the shade for us, and we sat, chatting, consuming lunch, bitten by black flies, and swallowing them along with our jam and bread, trying to be pleasant to each other. It was fun to be talking to a white man. I hadn't seen one since early January, when I left the mine, two and a half months before.

We parted late that afternoon, both of us having abandoned our boys to their own resources, each secretly trying to prevent the other's finding out what he was up to.

It was late, so I climbed the five hundred feet to camp. There I found Loya waiting with a large packet of mail, including a letter from Mr. Babcock, telling me to peg, by all means, if I found any gold, and enclosing blanks for pegging mining rights, together with a book on the mining laws of Sierra Leone, over which I puzzled until late that night. I decided that I had enough evidence of gold to stake a claim; but first I knew I must make a map of the mining right, plot the location according to directions in the book, set up posts, marking the claim to be held by the company, fill out endless forms, and send them straight off to Freetown to the Mines Department. This was a case of "first come, first served," and if my map were wrong in some slight way, or if I made other mistakes, my claim might be pushed aside in favor of that of my rival. All that night I had bad dreams about forty-niners jumping claims in Arizona, sheriffs chasing claim jumpers, and Westerners shooting. I woke up relieved to find that everything was peaceful and that I was not surrounded by white men with their hands on their holsters.

All morning I remained at my table, drafting maps, swatting flies, and mixing perspiration with ink, as I tried to compose an official request for privileges of mining. Finally, at four, just as the day's thunderstorm arrived earlier than usual, I finished the documents, sealed them with red sealing wax, stamped them with my thumbprint, as well as with an "L"— an extra precaution in case of tampering—and called Basi, who knew the country well. He could go as fast as any boy, and knew more English than Loya. I started him off with orders to run all the way, so that he could send the letter down on the morning's mail train. Loya was sent northward with a note to Mr. Babcock, telling him what I had done.

I had carefully painted two signs to mark the claim. Just as the storm broke, amid the blackness, torrents, and thunder-clashes, we slipped down to the Tonkolili, Momo carrying the signs and some nails. We crossed the river on a fallen tree, nailed one of the signboards to a log I had previously cached, dug a hole, set the post up, and piled a great heap of rocks around it, in order to keep it in place. Then we scrambled along the banks to a point about a quarter of a mile farther up the stream. We had hard work to keep from slipping into the swollen river, for the banks were steep and wet. When the upper marker was in place, I had a sudden feeling of relief, for I knew that this stretch of river was ours to mine. No longer any need to worry about the other fellow. I could take as much time as I wished to bottom that pit, I thought, as we slopped back to camp by the light of a lantern.

I slept late the next day and woke with a sense of security. I hoped that my rival would arrive before I did at the claim marker, and that the shock of the claim being jumped would have passed before I put in an appearance. When we met, I found him cheerful about it all, saying that he really had no intentions of doing any pegging this trip, and that he was interested only in the land where he was drilling below my lower beacon. He guessed he would head back toward Freetown the next day anyhow, and hoped I would succeed in bottoming. We parted on friendly terms.

That day the boys got down about fourteen feet in the pit. Suddenly a pick hit some sand and, like an artesian well, water poured in; the bailing crew had to be doubled immediately. Work as hard as they could, the water line gradually rose and then, slosh, slop, a whole section of the wall collapsed behind the logs. For a few moments the bailing boys kept up with the water, then the digging boys worked like mad until they were almost submerged. It was no use, Momo declared; we must have pumps. In desperation, we obtained a few shovelfuls of gravel from a depth of about fifteen feet and let the water come in for the night. We panned this gravel, but only found several specks of gold. We couldn't tell anything about what was on the very bottom. Another boy had to be sent off to Mr. Babcock, explaining my predicament, and asking if he could send me a spare pump. I also told him that I would abandon work in the pit until further instructions, and would now devote my time to exploring the endless possibilities in the vicinity of Nerekoro.

The country was fairly high and rugged, and the beauty of numerous waterfalls interrupted the usual monotony in following stream channels. I found gold in several places. Gradually, I was able to determine the probable source of gold in the Tonkolili channel I had pegged. A letter from Mr. Babcock said he was coming down to look the place over, and that he and his wife would arrive in three days. This was news. Thank goodness, he would take the responsibility off my shoulders about how to reach the bottom gravels in the Tonkolili. He asked that my boys build a large shimbek, about fourteen by fourteen feet, and clear ground for their tent.

That night Basi came in, just at dark, looking wild and with his shirt half torn off him. At first I thought he had been drinking. He handed me a large envelope, covered with red government stamps, and with the wide lettering "On His Majesty's Service" across the top. Telling Basi to wait and that I would hear his story later, I tore the letter open and found that the Mines Department had accepted my application for lease.

Then I called Basi, who went into an eloquent tirade about how he had been attacked a few miles back by a man with a knife. He had struggled, got hold of the man's wrist, and forced him to give up the knife. His shirt, his filthy muddy state, and a few cuts showed that he was not lying. "He no savvy" why he was attacked, so I sent him back to the village, thankful that I had my registered letter intact.

The next morning, as I was finishing breakfast, a long procession appeared from the direction of the village. The chief, dressed in his official crown (an especially vividly embroidered three-cornered cap), an umbrella held over his head as a mark of royalty, despite the misty state of this time of day and the lack of sun, was approaching. Momo Beer came forward and said that the chief had come for a palaver. The array of men convinced me that something was wrong; obviously, they had a prisoner.

The chief, the elders, Momo Beer, and an interpreter stepped forward. Bit by bit, I gathered that the prisoner, Bangba Bita, a cook for Schumann, a Syrian trader in Magburaka, had tried to set fire to the village of Nerekoro early that morning. This was a serious offense, for the thatched roofs burned like tinder. When I asked why he should do such a thing no one seemed to know. The prisoner was brought forward. He sulkily told me that he had come into one of the huts at one o'clock in the morning (I never could find out how he knew the exact time) and found his wife sleeping with a man. This man, he said, was Basi. Basi was then produced; he denied the charge. I asked them to send for the woman. Basi would undoubtedly lie. I decided that without doubt the prisoner's wife had proved unfaithful, to put Bangba Bita in such a furor. Still, he looked like such a desperate character, I certainly did not want him burning up the village, much less my camp.

Seriousness marked everyone's face, as they turned to give way to the chocolate-colored woman who shyly came before me, accompanied by two other women. She must have come from the north, and had an Arabic strain in her, for she was taller and thinner, with higher cheekbones, than the women of the village. Her hair, save for two little pigtails which stuck out about an inch in front of her ears, was hidden under a gaily colored striped silk bandanna. I wondered if she had much white blood in her, for she was fair, and, although obviously not a young girl, she was fresher in appearance and less wrinkled than her companions. She answered the interpreter without any hesitancy, her white teeth flashing, but her eyes were lowered as if she dared not look at the white missus who was questioning her.

She said her name was Abatu, and that she had known the prisoner, Bangba Bita, for several years. No, she was not married to him; he had never asked her to marry him, but he had given her parents several cloths. Bangba Bita nodded affirmation, declaring that he was going to pay her parents for her in time. Yes, they had lived together, off and on. No, she had not run away; she had only come up north from the railroad with some fish to sell. She had met our people and followed the trail with them in the hopes of selling all her fish. Yes, she had sold the fish and had collected three shillings, which she then had. What was she going to do with the money? Give it to Bangba Bita. She had spent the night in the chief's hut. Bangba Bita had arrived early in the morning, found her, beaten her, and cursed her and everyone in the chief's house. Then he had grabbed a firebrand and tried to set fire to the house. The chief had caught him and then had hidden the woman in the hills for the rest of that night. Did she want to go back to live with Bangba Bita? Oh, no! He would kill her. This was probably true, for if she had been unfaithful, native law would not interfere, as far as I could gather.

Basi was defiant. He said that it was this man, Bangba Bita, who had attacked him the previous day, when he was bringing my mail. I wondered what the native law was in such a case, and what a D.C. would do. Here was an offense with which I could charge the man. Attacking a messenger with important government mail would have to be dealt with severely; and it was not a matter with which I could deal.

After questioning various other persons, all of whom confirmed the things said concerning Bangba Bita, I decided that the best thing to do was to have the chief send him under guard to the paramount chief in Mabonto, with a note telling all I knew and saying that I did not dare have Bangba Bita wandering around my camp causing trouble; that he had attacked one of my boys—a *santiggi* (messenger) with important government mail—with a knife, and then had tried to set fire to the village. I hoped he would make further inquiries into the case and punish Bangba Bita suitably. I thought this a good solution, for even Bangba Bita had acknowledged that the woman was not his lawful wife. Woman palaver, if such could be proved, was a minor offense compared to the other accusations. Amadu remarked later that "Missus decide well."

"It no be so bad for these peoples for one woman to sleep with other man. Maybe it no be proper for white man. But black man, he be different."

When we moved from Nerekoro, I noted with amusement that the lady in question had joined the ranks of the woman caravan, which trailed my boys everywhere. As a matter of fact, every time we moved, the retinue held more strange women, with large bundles of pots and pans on their heads, and an occasional pickaninny.

"The laborers, they no get plenty things to buy on payday," Amadu remarked, "so they fit to buy a wife. Woman no cost so much upcountry."

As the women kept out of the way, I said nothing. To have contented carriers was the main thing. By explaining my moves in advance to the headman, the boys knew where to send the women to meet them.

Before leaving, the chief had practically forbidden me to go down one stream near camp. It was a "bad devil" place, he assured me.

"Any white man who go down there, go be very sick. Maybe go die."

Not one of my boys would go with me, nor would anyone in the village, so I had to content myself with pitting above and below the "bad devil" place. Fortunately, these pits did not carry much gold, so I did not mind obeying the orders enforced by native superstition. But in the streams feeding the Tonkolili gorge I found gold and knew that there must be gold at the bottom of the abandoned pit. The government map of the region was sketchy; tributaries had been plotted by joining them by guesswork, according to the contour of the land.

The day after the palaver the boys whom I did not take exploring with me were left, with Momo Beer in charge, to build a shimbek for Mr. and Mrs. Babcock. I had carefully gone over the ground and chosen an ideal site for their camp. I gave orders to Amadu to be sure and give the visitors boiled water, or tea, if they wished, when they arrived, and to invite them to supper. Then I planned as good a menu as possible, digging out some of my carefully hoarded reserves for a special treat to supplement the inevitable chicken.

When I returned, after a particularly trying day, I found Mr. and Mrs. Babcock in camp. They had arrived quite early, having come in hammocks carried over "hammock trails." I was later than usual, for everything had gone wrong. The boys would not dig their pits quickly in the tributary I followed. Standing over them, watching them struggle with a boulder, and urging them on was slow work. Then it showered, and even in the shelter of a root of a huge tree I was thoroughly soaked. This did not improve my temper; but the more I scolded the boys, the more obstinate and slow they became. Then I, in turn, became obstinate and refused to budge until they reached the bottom of the pits. Hours went by, but finally they reached clay.

It was so dark in that part of the forest that I had no idea of the time when, samples taken at last, I turned down the stream. The going was slippery and treacherous; I could move only by feeling cautiously with each foot. Finally we reached the trail, which was easier going. It seemed very dark, even here. I knew it must be later than I had realized, and I fairly ran along the pathway back to camp. I saw strange boys about the place, and Amadu came to meet me announcing, "They done come."

I found Mr. and Mrs. Babcock ensconced in deck chairs, dressed in clean clothes, coolly sipping whisky and soda. Their tent was such a palatial affair that mine seemed like a tiny hovel; their boys had built additions to the shimbek I had had built. They had accepted my invitation to dine and said they would come over in twenty minutes.

I changed quickly, and my guests and I had no sooner started on some particularly greasy soup, than the threatening storm arrived with a puff which almost upset the table. A few flashes, a few drops, and we huddled under my tiny fly, while the boys rescued the table. It was hopeless to eat there, so we decided to go over to their camp. With raincoats over our heads, we ran, the blackness lighted by flashes of lightning so that we never noticed the watchman and his feeble lantern trying to show us the way.

The Babcocks' tent was nice and snug inside. Soon the boys arrived, soaking, and served us with the soggy remnants of a lukewarm meal. I hope the Babcocks had enough to eat, I thought, as, waking in the middle of the night, I wished I had a cookie jar by my pillow.

Mrs. Babcock stayed in camp when Mr. Babcock and I started forth at a late hour the next morning to look at the pitting in the Tonkolili, leaving word that we would return for lunch. The flies were bad, the heat sultry, and it was late when we finally had inspected the limits of the mining right. The abandoned pit was filled to the brim with water, and no amount of bailing had any effect. Mr. Babcock decided that he would send an engineer with a couple of pumps to do the job; I had done all that was possible without machinery.

The climb back to camp was sufficient to make Mr. Babcock decide not to go anywhere else that day. It seemed delightful just to sit idly and sip drinks all afternoon, and know that I did not have to walk miles before reaching bed. Mrs. Babcock, frantic with the flies, had finally arranged her net so that she could have her table and chair under its cover, despite the lack of air. I had never before been in this camp in the daytime and had not known that the tsetses invaded the place by day. I decided that I preferred the black fly to the tsetse; its bite doesn't hurt so much.

That night I was invited to dine with the Babcocks and was put to shame by my feeble effort of the night before. Everything went like clockwork. I could easily imagine I was at a private home in the city, for we had candles, with lamp shades, on the table. A real Indian curry, groundnuts grated over the rice, fried oranges, eggplant, some Bombay duck, bits of savory, and other things I had forgotten existed, were served.

The Babcocks stayed two more days—days spent showing Mr. Babcock the country. It was a most pleasant vacation for me. The day before they left, the Mines Inspector and his still rosy-cheeked English bride came through camp on the way to inspect the new mining right, the work I had done, and then to visit the mines in the north. They traveled in hammocks, their route being by wide trails. We all gathered inside my tiny cleared space, cut out of the bush, and surprised we were to find less flies here than near the tents. Even the breeze was cooler than under the canvas. I felt as if I were back in civilization again with so much polite talking, discussion of world affairs and topics I had not thought about for months.

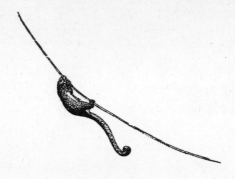

CHAPTER EIGHTEEN

ARCHIE

SUNDAY MORNING as I was eating breakfast, before Mr. and Mrs. Babcock left, Amadu, a sparkle in his eye, appeared with a ragged hunter, whose Dane gun, carelessly swung over his shoulder, terrified me for fear it would explode. The hunter had a dash for me. I had made a practice of turning down animal dashes, which were any wild thing a native thought the white missus might adopt. Once it had been a half-grown wild pig, tied round and round with raffia binding so that the poor thing could only squeal. Sometimes it had been a small baby buck or a mangy monkey, and more rarely a mongoose. This time, a peculiar scaly ball was produced from the triangular leather pouch at the boy's chest. The ball was set down before me; then I noticed a slightly protruding wicked eye gazing at me. Gradually the ball unwound until a tapering tail, about a foot long, appeared, then an armored back, a tiny pointed head, and four clawlike feet supporting this dinosaur structure. In amazement, I watched this foot and a half of queerness waddle awkwardly along, front feet bent back, one finger representing all that remained of what had once been, generations before, a five-fingered foot; the back feet were flat,

Chief of Nerekoro with some of his wives and pickaninnies.

The village kitchen: rice steams on the fire, while the chickens pick up insects and scraps. The five-gallon gasoline can in the foreground is used for carrying water.

Curious native women.

A coastal village near Freetown. Picture taken at low tide.

five-toed like a bear's. When I touched the amazing creature, it coiled instantly and rolled over, looking like nothing so much as an artichoke. I must adopt this weird animal—"Archie" it would be from now on.

The boy looked thoroughly pleased at the two shillings I offered him. He told Amadu that he had found the animal on a palm tree and that it ate palm kernels. I dispatched a boy to a palm tree for supplies, but Archie would not even look at palm kernels. When some water was presented in a tin can, Archie sniffed with his little snout, threw back his head, and a great dartlike tongue flashed out—three inches or more of it—into the water and back again. Amadu then brought a large piece of an anthill and placed it before Archie; his tongue flashed down into the long thin mud cells, coming out coated with white grubs, disdaining the swarming ants which crawled all over him. In his desire for more grubs, he climbed up on the broken anthill and pulled chunks off with his front paws until he had the hill demolished.

A box became Archie's home, but he often escaped, having an uncanny way of being able to squeeze through much too small cracks by a process of flattening out. When he became used to the smell of my hand, as he did in a few days, he no longer coiled when I touched him, but let me handle him as much as I wished. I found to my great surprise that Archie had a hairy tummy. Somehow scales and hair on the same animal did not agree with my memory of biology. Another strange thing about him was the hole he had for an ear. Later I found that Archie was known as the hairy anteater, an animal like the Mexican armadillo, but different from the armadillo in possessing hair. Though Archie traveled several weeks with us he did not live to reach Freetown. I felt a semi-attachment for him and would not let the boys skin him, but had him buried off in the bush. Possibly he was resurrected and eaten, but I never inquired. Only Balto seemed pleased at the departure, for Archie had put his nose out of joint. He never really appreciated this strange pet, which coiled into a scaly mass when investigated.

I was both sorry and glad to leave Nerekoro. I liked this community. The chief had been a real friend; in parting, he even allowed me to take a picture of him and some of his family, the women having refused to be taken when I first came. I would miss his daily visits and his cheery smile, for none of the other chiefs had seemed so friendly and unsuspicious, or so thoroughly interested in my progress in their territory. He complimented me by saying that I knew more about his country than he, which was true, because I had thoroughly explored it.

To the north lay the area closed to prospecting, the very region I had tramped through on the previous tour, mapping the iron ores. The government was still deciding whether to let one or many companies mine the rich iron ores there. I had mapped those deposits, but now I could not enter the limits of the area, as it was still forbidden ground. I decided to strike due east and cross the mountain range, heading back toward Makong, and mapping the eastern boundary of the granite and schist, while looking for gold.

Apparently the boys had a final debauch, their last night in Nerekoro, for a sorry-looking lot appeared in the morning for their loads. James Conte came and pathetically showed me his swollen arms, covered with a vile green mash. I was most solicitous until I found that some medicine man had been cutting an intricate pattern on one arm and the word "James" on the other. The poison to keep the cuts from healing had penetrated even his shoulders. Would I give him medicine? Certainly not! I was afraid of blood poisoning and, thinking that these witch doctors would have the best remedy, sent him back to the village for medicine. He returned with a white puttylike substance smeared over him, covering the purple gashes. Various other boys had been ornamented during the palm wine feast, but none suffered as did James. Perhaps the others had had less money, and therefore had not been able to afford such extravagant designs. I had to leave James to join us later. The rest of the boys shouldered their loads in a semi-grumpy fashion.

What a day we had—climbing two thousand feet, resting every few minutes! I sat under one of the low-spreading acacias on the divide, for we had reached orchard-bush country, and watched the slow procession trudge up, their loads hiding their heads and walking sticks steadying their wobbly pace. I liked climbing to heights in this country, for I could see for miles at this time of year, row after row of blue ranges stretching off into the distance, wave after wave of dark green treetops below. Even Bintimani—the highest point in Sierra Leone—was visible, fifty miles away. To the east rose great domed mountains of granite, sticking up out of the lowlands. I was glad of the long wait for the carriers. It gave me a chance to survey the country that had been hidden from me when I was in the lower forests.

The strength of the sun finally drove me down the other side of the mountain into the forest belt to Karandugu, twelve miles from Nerekoro. There were grass stretches along the side of the path, and the village lay across the river, just in sight. I decided to make my camp in the grass near the path, knowing that after the two-thousand-foot vertical climb the boys would not have much energy left for bush clearing.

Just across the path from the spot I selected was the Bundu Bush, the sacred bush of the women. I was promptly forbidden to enter that place or to construct a tiny shelter from the sun. I sat by the trail, hot and cross. Various kinds of monkeys came to look at Balto and me. It was late when the boys finally dragged in, and later still by the time camp was organized; the evening thunderstorm kindly waited until I was almost through supper.

The Karandugu people were shy, and a visit from a white person was a rarity. The next morning a steady procession of women and children strolled innocently up the path past my tent and then back again, pretending they were out on business; but I recognized the faces as they returned, and knew they had only gone just around the bend out of sight before returning. I called some especially pretty girls, clad only in dark blue-and-white-striped skirts and red beads, to my tent, as I sat eating breakfast. Shyly they stood before me, giggling like school children. I had nothing to give them except a handful of groundnuts, which apparently pleased them, for they got down on their knees and touched their heads to the ground by way of thanking me.

Much searching of the country failed to reveal gold in any quantity. The Mawuru River flats, which interested me especially because they drained the closed area, were impossible to bottom, much labor revealing only a few miserable flecks of gold. We moved camp southward, at the rate of about twelve miles a day; the climate became gradually hotter and wetter, for the dry season was nearly over. There were frequent downpours. As the rivers rose and the flats became wetter, it grew increasingly difficult to reach the bottom clay.

It seemed advisable to move toward Makong, forty miles away, as speedily as possible. I was feeling tired and touchy—"irritable" was too mild a word—and so were the boys. We had been three months on trek and needed a change. In fact, at the monthly payday which came when I was at Karandugu, half of my original carriers asked for all their savings and departed, leaving me without steady workers. The Limbas I was able to recruit from the town never did anything right, and I was exhausted at the end of the day from trying to force them to work. They even had to be shown how to dig. Momo Beer was as worn out as I.

At Basaya, our next camp to the south of Karandugu, we had luck in finding gold up in the hills. But even the sight of gold was not enough to restore my spirit. Enthusiasm had waned. Walking up the hills was hard work. I had to rest frequently and would flop on any log, careless of whether or not I might pick up hookworm or some disease caught from the ground. I was content to sit for hours idly doing nothing, while the boys dug their pits near by with an equal lack of enthusiasm. Breathing was harder than ever, especially when climbing. My appetite was gone; probably I was anemic. I was fighting against the malarial germs too, for I had had a light dose of fever. I had been out in the bush almost six months, and I realized that when I returned to camp I should be quite ready to sail for England. Still, I conscientiously covered the ground—everything became like a bad dream. I think if I had had any liquor with me, I should have taken to drink. Writing a letter was painful; the monthly report was a nightmare.

The day I reached Magboloka and found a real mud resthouse stands out as a red-letter day. As I slumped on the mud wall of the piazza in the shade, waiting for my deck chair to arrive, I suddenly realized that what I wanted most of all, and was suffering for lack of, was a thick roof over my head. Having the sun cut off by a heavy two-foot thatch felt like heaven. For months I had not been able to remove my helmet during the day, while the sun was beating down through the trees.

This was the first time that my forehead had been dry and my sticky hair could dry out during the day. Slowly, I came to life again under a roof. The boys were as glad as I, for all they had to do was to dump their loads on the veranda and depart. I sent word that the chief was not to call on me until night; after a hasty lunch of left-over chicken and a piece of sour palm wine bread, I stretched out on my cot, dozing contentedly the rest of the afternoon.

A large compound, scraped clean of every blade of grass, surrounded the resthouse, and a rough, tightly woven wooden fence, to keep out the wild beasts, shut in the compound. The resthouse was isolated on the highest hill, a hundred feet above the village. The three of us—Archie, Balto, and myself—dozed, relaxed, as the shadows grew. Not a boy was in sight. Even the watchman had not come forth from the kitchen quarters at the rear to light his waiting fire. Night was coming swiftly. I was appreciating the beauty of the silhouetted palm trees and my isolation in these clean, unspoiled surroundings with nothing to worry about or disturb me, content in the realization that I had a waterproof house and everything under cover for once.

Suddenly Balto stiffened, pointed, and let out a barely audible snarl, as he rose quivering, facing the trail. I looked hard into the shadow of the path until I thought I saw something move. Then I caught a yellow flash of two eyes as they moved, catching the light from the lantern which Amadu had hung from the gatepost. A great black form moved, slinking, across the path, thirty paces away, passing out of sight in the bushes.

I screamed to Amadu, the watchman, Lamina, Chaka, anyone, and they all came running, eyes bulging. I pointed and gesticulated, showing with my hands the size of the "beef" as I recovered the use of my tongue. Amadu volunteered the information that it must have been a leopard trying to smell Balto or Archie, and promptly set the watchman to work building a large fire.

Leopards were frequent prowlers around this village, the chief told me later, so I got out my automatic, polished it, and put it under my pillow. But the beast did not return. Next morning, the boys found his tracks in the bushes where I had seen him disappear. The watchman was so terrified that he kept a large fire going all night. Whenever I peered out of the door, I could see him crouched before the fire, his machete thrust in the ground in front of him, nervously peering about. Balto had been so thoroughly scared that he insisted upon sleeping underneath my bed, waking me every time he scratched.

Magboloko was just a stopping place. We moved on the next day. In the early morning we had the good fortune to come unexpectedly upon a large waterbuck, drinking near a grassy opening. I was leading, and came around a bend to see the beautiful beast standing looking at me, head thrown high, ears forward, his great curving antlers bending back like two long horns. After several seconds, he bounded away, slowly and gracefully.

Seldom did I see real game, for game must be tracked down in these forest regions, and I was out for rocks, and nothing else. Occasionally a hunter would come to camp with some sort of buck and I would buy the meat. However, these occasions were rare, and usually the hunters had only a guinea fowl or some sort of bush fowl, like our partridge, which were fairly common in the grass regions to the north or on cut-over farm lands. They made a pleasant change from the perpetual chicken, and I often wished I had the time or energy to hunt.

After the day and night in the resthouse, I felt much more energetic. In fact, we all became mildly enthusiastic over a rich gold find, having spent most of our time recently in discovering nothing. Also, being nearer Makong, I spent a few last days combing the hills, this burst of energy inspired by the knowledge that I could soon have a real rest. I had covered almost all the territory I had originally planned to prospect; only a few more days of getting soaked, struggling with wet things, and endlessly following up streams, pitting in every available place —then Makong and civilization.

Leaving Mamusa, our next camp, and struggling across the range of mountains and back again into the Pampana Valley was an unforgettable experience, for we found ourselves in clouds most of the way. We climbed up into a wet, soggy blanket and felt our way through the tall trees, relying entirely upon the tiny, poorly worn footpath. Not a song from the boys. Just sloshing, slipping along, with the peculiar spinal twist of the back that always developed when the going was on slippery ground. The head loads did not move in unison with the rest of the body. Down, down, we went, finally out of the clouds. An even filthier village and more decrepit-looking villagers than any we had seen received us for the next few nights' stay.

Then the final trek into Makong—just trekking, with no work to do along the trail. This made the boys happy, for after pitching camp they could count on having the rest of the day in the village, to strut around in their best clothes and be admired by the flirtatious young girls. They were men of the world now, with plenty of money, and the villagers were just ignorant bush people. The crossing of the Pampana in a canoe ferry was easy and not such a lark as the last time, far below here, when we were bound for Nerekoro.

Up and down, on, on—monotonously dragging one foot after the other, subconsciously studying all the little streams and their flats. It was second nature to me, by now, to pick out a likely place to pit and to note whether we were on granite or on schist.

A rest in the little village of Mabobo was delightful because of the orange trees. Oranges could be had for the asking, and we were all thirsty and hungry, too. We bought bananas at the unheard-of rate of about eighteen for a penny. That night we camped at a village called Petifu—this was the third village of this name that I had been in. Here it poured and poured, starting soon after we arrived, and letting up only at daybreak.

Then on to Makong from here, over a rough narrow unfrequented trail, wet and slippery. I swung along briskly in the early morning, James trotting behind with the wheel. We had seen no sign of life, not even a bird, for several hours, when, rounding a bend in the dead silence of the thick jungle, two young girls came toward us, balancing loaded calabashes on their heads. The moment they saw me, both screamed, dropped their head loads and bolted into the forest, a pile of rice, bananas, cassava, and palm kernels being the only trace of their flight. James Conte called to them in several languages, but they would not reappear. I sauntered on, hoping that the white devil had not scared them so that they would not return to gather up their goods.

"They think you be white debil," James volunteered. "They fear too much when they see white man." So that was why youngsters often stared at me with such mixed expressions of curiosity and fear, undoubtedly having been brought up with stories of the "white bogieman," the way we had been taught to fear the "black bogieman." To those who had never seen a white man in their short lives, I must have appeared as a horrible sight—something to frighten them in their dreams. Or perhaps their mothers had brought them up on stories of how the white man would get them, and meeting the white devil, face to face, was just too much. Or their young minds had been fed with stories of the bad white men who caught little girls and took them far away to be sold as slaves. It was not many years since these back-country villages had been pillaged for slaves.

It bothered me the rest of the day, as we walked on and on, to think how white men had entered the country of these people, semicivilized them, tried to take away their old customs and superstitions, substituting a religion they could not understand, teaching them what they thought they should learn, not what they really needed. White men destroyed the beauties of the land by starting mines and bringing in money, always a trouble-causer. I hated to see this happening to these gentle, primitive people, and to know that I had helped bring the contact with the white man. Africa should be wild and untouched, full of bashful maidens, such as the ones who had fled at my appearance, happy in their primitive state. White men were there only to get the best out of the land and the peoples. All the "conversion of the native" only caused unhappiness, satisfying a certain human ego—that of being able to instill one's own hard-earned knowledge into peoples who were not ready for it and were not in need of change, especially a change which merely brought worries, complications, and unhappiness. One form of slavery was merely being exchanged for a new one. Their own feuds and oppressions were suppressed, but worse evils would follow. Yet, as I walked along, I knew that the benefits of government control were real—a chance for relief from the oppression of bad chiefs, a chance for wiping out disease by new hygienic conditions. The government was doing a fine work. But the miner—and I was guilty, in finding more gold for greedy stockholders—gets what he can from the land, regardless of the native.

I thought these problems over as I shuffled on, not seeing anything but the twisting of the ever-continuing path. Glad I was to have seen the untouched native and to have had him work for me; still gladder that I probably should never see the country when ugly towns had grown up and when the people lived for payday at some underground mine. This part of Africa would always remain in my memory as an endless jungle, inhabited by kindly natives in picturesque, round, thatched mud huts, people with few wants, with beaming faces, always childish—the true African.

This reverie was shattered late in the afternoon, when we came into the great open space, devoid of even a blade of grass, where the rectangular whitewashed mud huts of the Makong compound stretched out in a neat row. In a short time I was sitting down with Mr. and Mrs. Babcock to a daintily served cup of tea; there were even flowers on the table. A dinner with real beef tasted like the meat visualized in my dreams.

I excused myself early in order to pay off my boys; they would be assigned to work in a paddock in the morning. Each boy bowed low as his money was poured into his outstretched hands, seeming to say, "Thank you, and farewell." Mr. Chequers laughed at the strange line of women who brought up the rear as my caravan filed off toward the village. The number of women had at least tripled since my departure, so that my retinue appeared to be of considerable size.

How familiar the five-thirty rising bell sounded the next morning; I had almost forgotten it. I stretched under the clammy dampness of my mosquito net; in another week I should be where I could sleep as late as I wanted. I had decided to catch the next boat for England. I had been out six months, and felt too anemic to risk joining Jock on the Gold Coast this year.

The next few days I spent finishing my reports for the London office, drafting my maps, studying the progress made in the various alluvial diggings at the mine, and talking, talking incessantly. It was fun to be able to speak English once more.

Leaving camp was even sadder than I had anticipated. It was hard to say good-by to people who might be dead in a few months. Eighteen months was too long a time for white men to stay; already they looked yellow and pallid, and they had served only a few months of their "tour." This time I accepted the offer of the hammock for the twenty-mile trek by the hammock trail to Matotaka, but I found jogging along was painful and unpleasant, and I walked most of the way, finding that I was in far better trim than the four sad-looking bearers who had been allotted to carry me.

At Matotaka I found the lorry which was to take me to Magburaka and the railroad. The resthouse at Magburaka was a substantial building, and quiet. I was the only guest.

The train ride, which began at seven the next morning, was the same nightmare as the trip up. The sight of a narrow trail striking off into the forest, a half-naked native struggling along it under a great cigar-shaped bundle of palm kernels, made me homesick for the bush. But not so homesick that I failed to remember that the one thing I was really looking forward to was a full-sized bathtub and water from a faucet from which I could drink at any time of day.

Toward evening, as I sat in my deck chair, covered with a fine sandy grit and with my head throbbing from the heat, I saw the mountains of Freetown as we rounded a bend and knew the journey was almost ended. Real houses, throngs of people, and the familiar sheds of the Freetown station at last appeared. To my joy, I saw the face of Miss Carey among those waiting at the station. She insisted that I stay with her until my boat came. I didn't need much urging, for I had dreaded the thought of the horrible hotel, or the idea of having to move into the old barracks, or resthouse, and carry on my own domestic worries. A waiting lorry received my goods, including Amadu and Lamina, while Balto and I enjoyed the luxury of a real automobile instead of a rattly, springless lorry.

A bath in a white porcelain bathtub was followed by ice-cold orangeade on the little terrace garden with its view of distant peaks. Below, a deep canyon stretched toward the blue sea, and the crimson sun sank into a brilliantly colored horizon. I felt thoroughly relaxed for the first time in months.

The next few days passed pleasantly and quickly—a long siesta in the cool of the house, a swim at the beach in the late afternoon, visits. All too soon, a puff of smoke showed on the horizon; a funnel grew recognizable; and then the boat was waiting to take me back to England. Amid a hustle of boys, loads, farewells, Miss Carey drove me to the dock and went aboard for her monthly haircut.

My tiny cabin looked immaculate. Among the strange faces were a few whom I knew. Faces everywhere—sallow, yellow, sickly, tired; these travelers did not have the same vitality of those outward-bound. I sank down, looking as frail and yellow as the rest—wondering if I should ever again feel full of life and energy.

The trip was uneventful except for an incident as we rounded Cape Verde. Late one afternoon, as the first cool blast from the north blew in our faces, we rounded the point known to West Coasters as the "Boneyard." A figure in a white shroud was quietly slipped overboard. The sea had claimed another victim of the tropics, dead of malaria. West Africa is truly the black man's home; if it has become the "white man's grave," that is largely the white man's fault.

Part III

MAPPING MOLYBDENUM

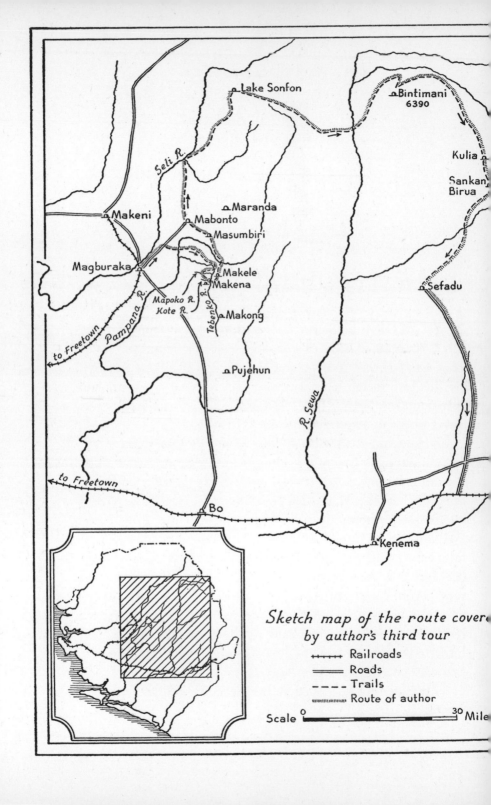

Lake Sonfon

Bintimani
6390

Kulia

Sankan
Birua

Seli R.

Makeni

Maranda

Mabonto

Masumbiri

Magburaka

Makele

Makena

Sefadu

Mapoko R.
Kote R.

Tebenko R.

Makong

to Freetown

Pampana R.

Pujehun

R. Sewa

to Freetown

Bo

Kenema

Sketch map of the route covere
by author's third tour

+++++ Railroads
———— Roads
- - - - Trails
⊙⊙⊙⊙⊙ Route of author

Scale 0 _____ 30 Mile

CHAPTER NINETEEN

MAPPING MOLYBDENUM

M Y WORK in Sierra Leone was not yet done, for the steely blue metal I had found near Makele turned out to carry five per cent molybdenum, a percentage unusually high for this rare metal. This was the first time molybdenum had been found in West Africa, so it was decided that I return to Sierra Leone to investigate the deposit further.

Molybdenum is valuable for use as an alloy in steels, for it can stand terrific heat and pressure. When found in quantities, it is of great value. Ninety per cent of the world's output is mined in Climax, Colorado, so a find in West Africa was of intense interest to the British mining world.

A mining engineer had already been sent out to Makele to follow my gold findings; the company had obtained a large concession as soon as my report had reached them. He was systematically putting down test pits along the river. Mines were also being started in two other places where my prospecting had revealed good gold values. In fact, from a country with hitherto no revenue from mineral export, already mining royalties were pouring into the colony's coffers.

As the landing boat sped across the now familiar harbor of

Freetown, I searched among the shiny black faces on the dock. Sure enough, there was Amadu, waiting for me. Somehow, I had known he would be there; I just couldn't imagine being in Sierra Leone without Amadu.

As we struggled with the customs delays and vexations, Amadu told me the gossip. I was not prepared for his stories of the great changes in mining development that had taken place since I left in the spring. The natives had at last learned something of the value of gold. The craftier Syrians and the shrewder coast natives were stealing at the sluice boxes. There had been riots at Makong. Minor uprisings, palavers, and fights had been successfully coped with up to this time.

A few weeks before I landed the trouble had come to a head at Makong. Mr. Chequers was doling out wages on payday. Several hundred natives had already received their month's pay. Several hundred more stood uneasily in line, four deep. At a prearranged signal there was chaos in the mob. Natives pulled up the picket fence at the edge of the compound and made for the paymaster. Luckily, Mr. Chequers sensed the situation, and slipped the cashbox, containing five hundred pounds sterling, to the orderly who had brought it to the mine and was standing behind him. By the time the onslaught reached the table, the money had been sped quietly away in the six-o'clock dusk. The paymaster edged slowly backward toward the assay hut, facing the angry mob with his gun in his hand.

The other two white men in camp, having heard the commotion, rushed to the paymaster's aid, and the three reached the shelter of the hut amid hurtling rocks and sticks. The mob closed in around the tiny building; the white men were prisoners.

Some of the headmen, whom everyone thought would be faithful to the end, were among the ringleaders, but a few natives stuck by the white men. At the first sign of trouble, a fast messenger had slipped off to warn Alimami Souri, the paramount chief of the region, who lived only five miles away. He came to the aid of the white men, and within a few hours arrested the ringleaders—who, however, promptly gave Alimami the slip in the dark.

Meanwhile, the mine workings had been picketed, and no work was done. The three white men made trench bombs out of tin cans filled with a little powder, nails, and odd scraps, and these were kept as ammunition in case of a new attack. They also laid a powder line in a trench across what would be the line of march, intending to set it off and give the natives a terrible fright. Fortunately, two and a half days later the D.C. from Makeni arrived with some soldiers, after a forced march, and succeeded in arresting the ringleaders again, slipping them off to Makeni by a roundabout way before their friends realized what was happening. Things had apparently quieted down now, the palaver having been settled by the D.C., who meted out jail terms of several years, with heavy fines, for the leaders.

As I listened to Amadu's tale, I was glad I was heading for Makele rather than Makong. I didn't want to go into a camp where the natives would be sure to be restless; I was anxious to get right into the bush, where things like this didn't happen.

After a brief stay in Freetown with Miss Carey, Amadu, my new cook, and I went by train to Magburaka, where we recruited boys for carriers. At Makele I was accorded a royal welcome. The chief dashed me a duck, which is a great honor, indeed, but rather tough eating, I was to learn in due course. The company's new engineer came to see me and learn the news.

Two of my old boys—Mende brothers, whom I had privately dubbed the "Gold Dust Twins" because of their small stature and extreme blackness—appeared the next day. They had deserted their masters in the rival camp of Maranda, when they heard I was back. My last tour's stand-by, James Conte, appeared the same day, from Makong, having taken Dutch leave. I scolded the three runaways, but of course took them on, inwardly touched and not a little flattered by such devotion.

My trusty pup, Balto, had died of snakebite while I was in England; but when the bundles of head pans, picks, and shovels from Makong reached me, there was a new pup, sent by Mr. Chequers. Everything was finally ready; we could start.

I decided to camp far up the Mapoko, on a hill I had noted in my previous explorations as a fine place for a camp. It would be cool at night, even if unbearable by day; but then I would be working during the day. Furthermore, the site had a view, so there would not be the shut-in-ness of a forest camp, which I so much disliked.

This time, the mapping of the rocks must be done in great detail, for I hoped to be able to work out the extent of the molybdenum deposit, and also to collect information of value to the geologist with regard to the method by which it had been formed. Accordingly, we spent days tracing every tributary in the vicinity to its source. The original discovery had been in the stream boulders, about two miles west of Makele, which is on the main branch of the Mapoko River, a tributary of the Tebenko. Therefore, I knew that the source of the boulders must be up the Mapoko or one of its tributaries.

It was hard work following up the tributaries, for the rocks through which the streams had cut were hard granites and schists, with many rapids and waterfalls, the country itself being hilly and covered with dense forest.

The third day out we prospected a divide, more than fifteen hundred feet higher than the camp. We had found nothing of

importance all morning—only a few rocks to plot—so I decided
to head toward camp by following a small tributary which, according to the topographic map, would bring me to it. It was
then about noon, and I judged that at our present rate of travel
—it would be downhill all the way—we could surely reach
camp by teatime, so we set off.

Down and down we slashed, wading one minute, half slid-
ing down small, slippery waterfalls the next, cutting detours
through the bush where the channel was too dangerous a gorge
to risk the slippery rocks. And there we found it—our goal,
molybdenum! During the previous days of exploration we had
found gold and iron; and now, here in this one valley, were all
three—gold, molybdenum and iron! The last-named we found
in steeply dipping rocks, slanting at a high angle right down
to the heart of the mountain, so that, if mined, they would not
be mere surface mines, but deep, long productive horizons. The
iron was another link in the great beds of this ore which extended down the backbone of Sierra Leone for at least sixty
miles.

And here also was gold in quantity and quality to warrant
extensive development. It was in gravel deposits, to be sure, but
with more intensive search perhaps the gold, too, could be
found in the solid rock.

Here was enough iron, enough gold, and enough molybdenum—all in one little area—to repay three years of effort.

My excitement was so intense that I failed to note the passing
time, until a slowly sinking sun recalled me to the immediate
problem of getting back to camp. On and on we struggled, mile
after mile, but I noticed with dismay that we were heading into
the sunset, and not toward camp. On the map, the stream we
were now following had been joined incorrectly to the Mapoko
River. Still, Salifu, my guide, insisted that the stream would

reach camp, and I was willing enough to believe him, for I was tired and the thought of climbing was unbearable; it was hard enough just going downhill.

The pup had ceased his hunting expeditions off into the woods, and stayed close at my heels, as we slipped from rock to rock. At one point, where the waterfall was particularly steep and long, he decided he knew more about stream exploring than we did; nothing would induce him to keep away from the upper cascade. A slip, a frightened clawing, and down he went in a swirl of water, rolling and bumping, feet wildly clawing for a foothold. Down to the bottom whirlpool and out of sight he went, while the boys and I anxiously peered over the edge of the gorge. Then we shouted as a wet head appeared and pointed toward the bank. Quick as a monkey, almost leaping from bush to bush, Salifu slithered down the side of the gorge, lay on his stomach, and, reaching down into the steep-sided stream, grasped the half-drowned dog by the scruff of the neck and hauled him to safety.

A short distance farther on, where the increasing volume of the stream and the steepness of the banks made it impracticable to follow the channel, we were forced into the bush. James, Basi, and Salifu were all ahead, pushing forward at a fast walk-ing pace, and only the pan carrier followed me. I stopped to rest for a moment on a log, and then started to catch up with the trail makers, when a startled exclamation from the pan carrier caused me to stop short. I looked quickly at the boy, and saw that his chin was in the attitude of pointing. His frightened eyes made me turn to follow his gaze upward. I looked intently into the uncut creepers just ahead, but could see nothing except the gentle swaying of the vines and the slow quivering of the leaves. I could fairly feel "snake" from the boy's look, but where was it?

Finally I saw it—gray-green, lying twined with a gray-green creeper, the fore part swaying gently with the movement of the forest, a leaflike head pointed straight at me, on a level with my eyes and only a few feet away. Its protective coloring, grayish on the underside and greener on top, like the vines themselves, was uncanny. Horrified, I moved slowly backward, calling for James. Slowly, the green mamba moved nearer, seemingly not touching the creepers at all, head raised and slightly swaying. I moved back as fast as I dared, but the mamba kept the same pace. Then, beyond the mamba, I saw, to my intense relief, James and Salifu warily approaching, sticks clutched in their right hands, machetes in their left. With one whack and almost without motion, Salifu brought the snake down on the ground with its back broken, and James cut off the head. We continued on our journey, no one making any remark, the pup not even deigning a glance at the still-quivering tail.

On we hurried, anxiously watching the wheel mileage and the compass, which was veering more and more from the direction of camp the farther downstream we progressed. Whenever I rested, which was with increasing frequency, I studied the map, and finally decided that the stream I was following must join the Kote, which would eventually bring me out at Makena. Going back was out of the question, so we slashed forward through the bush or waded in the stream where it was shallow enough. Gradually the grade flattened out, and at last we came to a point where our stream joined another. On the left was a tiny farm, and James immediately recognized twigs cut by the boys the year before and the remains of old pits, where we had tested the gravels of each of these streams during our stay at Makena. Relieved to know where we were, I sat on a boulder in the middle of the stream and ate my last banana, which I had been hoarding in case we were bushed for the night. Then wearily I followed the now silent boys, who picked up the old trail with renewed zest, while I stumbled along behind, unable to make the effort to avoid logs and creepers. My knees were badly scratched, for I could no longer avoid the sword grass and thorns in the half-light of dusk. All I could do was to watch the white shirt in front of me.

After what seemed miles, but which the wheel showed was only three-quarters of a mile, we came to the path into Makena, where we were met by the ums and ahs of the surprised inhabitants, who were lounging on their mud piazzas around small fires that glowed through the increasing darkness.

A threepence caused a couple of dozen bananas to appear with miraculous speed. I told James to take some firebrands, hurry ahead to camp, and have the watchman come to meet us with a lantern. James set off at a lope, clutching the firebrands before him. We took one of the head pans and filled it with firebrands and coals and set out after him, just as the flicker of his brands vanished up the hill.

Along the well-worn trail we toiled, the stars and a lovely half-moon lighting our way in the more open stretches, and the brands, swung back and forth in front of me, giving light enough to show the trail in the darker stretches. But for the most part I kept my eyes fixed on Basi's white shirt, following it implicitly, soon learning which motion meant that there was a log to step across, and which that I must go up or down. This process became a game which became so engrossing that afterward I could remember nothing except the silence, broken only by the occasional snapping of a twig.

We eventually came to the Tebenko, which we crossed on a raft, moored to the bank for that purpose. I wondered vaguely how James had fared, for he had had to swim the river.

For almost two hours we kept on our way, stepping up and

down recklessly, stumbling along, but luckily with no casualties. I was just beginning to think that it really was not half bad to be walking through the tropical night, with a lovely moon overhead and the cool of dark undergrowth to dim the remembrance of the hot day, when a great cloud came between us and the moon, and pitch blackness made us rely entirely upon the firebrands. The cloud did not pass, but suddenly, to our joy, we saw a light. Basi shouted, and we stood still until Momo's perspiring face shone in the light from the lantern. He and Loya had traveled at high speed to meet us as soon as James had arrived.

It took another hour to reach camp, but when at last I dropped into my deck chair I was not half as tired as I had felt when I had reached Makena, three hours before. Amadu was waiting with a pitcher of orange drink to greet me, and announced that supper had been ready for hours. After a big dose of quinine—for I was afraid that, having been exposed to mosquitoes, in my overtired state I would get an attack of malaria— I wrapped myself in a steamer rug, ate heartily of soup and chicken and rice, and crawled into bed.

Thunder was rumbling up the valley, but not even thunder could keep me awake that night, I thought, as I dropped off to sleep. I was wrong.

The storm continued to gather force. Somehow I knew something was wrong, but I was too comfortable to worry about it.

Botheration! I thought. Just turn over and go to sleep again. I tried to obey, but could not; something was holding me. Gradually I grew conscious of terrific clashes of thunder; then I realized that the lightning flashes were almost continuous. Finally I knew that there was a strange dampness on my face. Again I tried to turn over; again that something wouldn't let me. Then I realized that something was lying across my hips. A flash of light showed that the tent had collapsed on and around me, and the ridgepole was lying, partly supported, partly across me. I jerked myself to the upper part of the bed, extricated my legs from canvas and mosquito netting, and grabbed the flashlight to survey the mess, all the time calling for the watchman. This was futile, I knew, for, what with the clashing of thunder, the terrific downpour of rain, and the wind, I could hardly hear my own voice. In vain I blew my whistle for help.

Flashing the light around, I could see that the front part of the tent was completely down, but the back pole was half up, held by some guy ropes. The thought that possibly the wind might lift the whole canvas off from over me, as it rushed right at my little hillock, finally spurred me into action. I scrambled out of bed, got into my mosquito boots and my raincoat, and struggled free of canvas and net, out into the downpour. The pup had crawled under the bed for safety, and had no intention of leaving that comparatively dry spot.

Clutching my flashlight and raincoat, I dashed to the kitchen shelter. There, head buried in one of my precious towels, I found a drenched and terrified watchman. I dragged him through the rain and pointed to my tent. Helplessness showed through the fear of his eyes, and only ahs came from his mouth. A sledge hammer was lying by an uprooted peg, and grabbing it I thrust it into his hands, then rushed to the front pole. He helped me hold it up, but seemed not to have the faintest notion what to do next. Leaving him to hold the pole, I grabbed the hammer and began hammering pegs into place again and pulling the ropes as tautly as my dripping hands would allow. The wind was dying down, but frequent flashes of lightning enabled me to work without a torch.

Having fastened the main ropes in place, I pulled Aladdin from the pole he was still clutching, pushed the hammer into his hand, and made him pound in peg after peg until the tent was firm enough to stand anything but the most vicious sort of blast. The gutters around the tent were clogged, so I thrust a machete into the watchman's hand, pointed to the gutters, and left him working in the rain, while I dug out dry pajamas and a towel. After a good rubdown, I crawled back into bed, grateful at finding that only the top blanket and pillow were wet.

Next morning I waked half cooked by the sun beating down on the canvas, which was steaming like a Turkish bath. The pup had already retreated to the palm shelter, which I had had built near the tent, and I followed him, deciding that I had earned a day of rest. I was not even going to be bothered by going out to inspect pits or take samples.

As I sat in my palm shelter, eating a leisurely breakfast, I looked up and down the valley which I knew so well, letting my eye wander over the green blanket of the treetops, tracing the almost invisible line where each little tributary flowed beneath that great green canopy, reliving the struggle up and down each gully, and mapping in my mind's eye the places where I knew there was mineral wealth waiting development.

Here was everything I had struggled for and searched for during my three treks to Sierra Leone. I had found more than I had even dared to dream of finding in those days, now so long ago, when Jock discovered he was not allowed to take me with him to the Gold Coast, and my thoughts had turned toward Sierra Leone. What matter if I did get no material recompense from all the tremendous mineral wealth which I had helped uncover for industry? I had had that incalculably valuable privilege, which no stroke of fortune could ever take from me— the chance to see primitive land and primitive people, unspoiled by civilization.

CHAPTER TWENTY

HEIGHTS

FREQUENTLY, during the last few weeks, I had caught glimpses of misty, jagged peaks far to the north. Could I possibly scale the highest of these and meet Miss Carey for Christmas, as previously arranged, on the plateau of Sankan Birua? Looking at the map, I found I should have to go northward via Lake Sonfon, in order to reach Bintimani, the sixty-four-hundred-foot peak which looked so tempting. It would mean making a hundred and sixty-five miles in eleven days, with many thousand feet of climbing. It was worth the effort; tropics or no tropics, I felt I could do it.

For this trek I wouldn't need a large retinue—just Amadu, the cook, headman, and eleven carriers. I paid off the rest of my boys, promising to hire them again, whenever I came back to do more exploring in their country.

My first stopping place was Masumbiri, where a young man who had come out on the boat with me was stationed to develop mining in a valley where I had found gold indications. He was having all sorts of difficulties with the natives. Unreasonable demands were being made of him for more pay. Thieving was rampant. There was a general feeling of unrest everywhere, he said.

As I continued northward, I found that the natives were uneasy in all the new mines. Rumor of trouble at Lake Sonfon, which I should reach in a few days, said that Riley, the young white man in charge of the mine there, had had his moneybox, with about five hundred pounds sterling, stolen. A thorough search had revealed no trace of the money. Riley had discharged one or two suspicious characters. One of these was a headman, who, accompanied by a band of followers, had attacked Riley the following day a mile from his camp, demanding that he should reinstate their leader. The white man had fled amid missiles, and finally reached the shelter of his hut, where he remained until the near-by paramount chief came to his rescue, late that night. My informers advised me to avoid Lake Sonfon; but that would mean a long detour, and I must arrive at Sankan Birua by Christmas. So I decided to take the risk.

At the junction of two main paths, south of Lake Sonfon, I suddenly came across one of the white men whom I had met at Makong the previous Christmas.

"What are you doing up here? Where are you going?" I demanded, as soon as we had completed our surprised and pleased greetings.

"I am on my way to help Riley," he responded. "I'd like to ask you the same questions."

I told him, and we pushed on together toward the lake. When we got to camp, we found that things had quieted down, so we celebrated that night with a game of cricket in front of Riley's cabin. He had made a bat, and was in the habit of having a boy bowl to him for his afternoon's entertainment. It was a real celebration to have two other players to liven things up. We had a merry time, each of us glad to be doing something just for fun once more.

Turning eastward from Lake Sonfon, toward Bintimani, I

reveled in the openness of the grass country, with the "Old Man of the Mountain" (translation of Bintimani) beckoning me forward. The scene reminded me of our West and of the first time I saw Pike's Peak, looming upward from the prairies.

At the base of the mountain the local chief of the foothill village informed me that the ascent could not be made in one day. I must sleep on the mountain. Undaunted, I decided to take six of my best boys, and the absolute essentials for a night out, sending the rest of the boxes and the other boys, with Amadu, around the mountain to meet us on our descent. It was too late to move on then, so we camped in the village.

Wrapped in a heavy blanket of mist, we set out silently the next morning. I smiled to myself as I recalled the trouble we had had in getting a local guide to show us the way. At first, no one would go with me; but finally a native had reluctantly consented to go for five shillings, a prodigious price. They were all afraid of devils on the mountain, the chief said, but why, I could not discover.

Up, up we climbed. The valley had been in orchard bush country, but gradually the mahogany forests grew taller and taller, dark and spooky in the mists. I no longer wondered why the guide thought devils must be about!

As long as the trail was clear, I pushed ahead at a rapid pace. Suddenly I was startled to see enormous circular holes—as much as two feet across—in the path and beside it. I stopped and waited for the guide to catch up and explain them.

"They are elephant tracks," he said, "made after yesterday's rain."

I had known there were elephants in this district of Sierra Leone, but had been told they were of the pygmy type. I wondered if we would get a glimpse of the beasts.

We had long since outstripped the carriers, as we plodded

up and up. At about eleven o'clock, the guide pointed to a place near a brook, where, he explained, we must camp. There would be no better place, for there was no trail beyond, and the boys couldn't take the loads farther. Stationing the watchman here, to await the others, the guide and the boy with my knapsack continued the ascent with me.

Up, up, we climbed. As we moved out of the forest into the orchard bush once more, I could see a precipitous cliff ahead of us. There was our goal.

The grass had gradually become shorter and shorter, until, panting in the ruthless sun, we came to boulders without any growing green things on them. A last long scramble, after pausing for a brief rest in the shadow of a rock, and we had reached the top.

Like many another goal in life, this one was more exciting to strive for than to reach. The harmattan haze, sticky and blue, had settled over the countryside in every direction, completely obliterating my long-hoped-for view.

It must have been three o'clock, or later, judging by the position of the sun, for I had no watch; mine had long since succumbed to the climate.

While I ate a belated lunch, the guide regaled me with tales of the Devil of Bintimani, whose dwelling place this was. He showed me a tin can, which the Devil had left on the summit and in which he had left a note saying that all white visitors were expected to pay ten shillings or incur his wrath. I read the signatures, and decided the Devil could not have become very rich from the fees, for there were only about a dozen names, among them one other woman's. The boys assured me that if I failed to live up to the requirements, bad luck would surely befall me. But I decided, to the guide's obvious disappointment, to cross the Devil, and refrained from dashing him.

After lingering in hopes of catching even a slight view that would repay our effort, we finally started down as fast as the slippery grass would let us. We slid down the steepest places, grabbing great hunks of grass to check our speed. My hobnails had no effect; they were worn smooth, so that they let me skid. I noted with envy how effective were the bare feet of the natives in places like this.

Just as we reached the orchard bush, the guide grunted with alarm. I followed the direction of his upraised chin, and there, below, peacefully grazing, was a whole herd of the dangerous "bush cow," as the native buffalo is called. They hadn't scented us, for we were downwind, so we sat for ten minutes or more, watching them eat. The leader raised his heavily horned head to look around. A snort! We had been seen! Like a flash, the whole herd tore down the mountain and out of sight in the thick forest. We followed, hoping they would not return and charge us.

It was quite dark when we finally reached the little camp site. Then I discovered to my dismay that Amadu—guardian of the precious matches—had gone off with all the matches in his pocket. One of the boys had to be dispatched to a native farm near the foot of the mountain, for a firebrand. After what seemed ages as I waited there in the strange darkness, he returned, holding two smoldering sticks in front of him.

A supper of beans and bananas was hastily consumed, and I crawled into bed. I could see the boys huddled around the fire, for it had suddenly grown cold, the coldest I had known it in Sierra Leone. The wind whistled through the tops of the tall mahogany trees, lulling me to sleep with its delightful coolness.

The next thing I knew, the sun was shining through the

A native reception. The chief, under the umbrella, a mark of distinction, brings me the cow as a dash.

Towering "inselbergs" of granite rising above the orchard bush.

leaves. As I sat up, I was greeted by the chattering of some colobus monkeys, who were watching our camp from a safe perch in the tall trees.

Three of the boys complained of "head-humbug"—the cold had brought on malaria. I gave them each a dose of quinine, for they were obviously ill. It was a sorry-looking troupe that finally reached the small resthouse in the village, where we found Amadu and the other boys.

That evening, five carriers appeared with "belly-palaver," so I got out a small cup and gave each of them three tablespoonfuls of kerosene, with a lump of sugar to help it down, my castor oil having long since been finished.

We remained in camp all the next day, waiting for the boys to recuperate, my pup celebrating by attacking a pet monkey in the village and snapping its back. He had seen too many wild monkeys, chattering at him from the trees, to let this opportunity slip. A shilling was ample recompense, the owner declared.

Turning our backs on Bintimani, we hurried on, averaging at least fifteen to twenty miles a day. It was hard going, for the trails were bad—so bad that the chiefs had to send gangs out ahead of us to clear the trails through the tall elephant grass.

News of my progress had gone ahead of me, for the chiefs came to meet me in each new village. At one village I was greeted by a gaily dressed chief, who appeared with a great umbrella held high over his head, as a symbol of his royalty. When it came to dashing, I was a bit overcome to receive a cow—we were out of the tsetse fly belt now and all the chiefs owned cows. My dash of ten shillings satisfied the chief, but I hoped this would not happen again, for my money was running low. I gave the cow to the boys, for they had worked hard and needed red meat; they celebrated by giving a feast that night, and inviting the villagers.

At another village I was surprised by a terrible din of drums and bean-shakers, to the accompaniment of which the natives danced madly as I approached. The chief came forward on a horse, the first I had seen in the country. When he reached me he got off and offered me a ride, which I refused. Behind the horse trotted a naked youngster, completely covered by a saddle which he carried on his head. Evidently this was the horse's personal boy. Two little black legs, a row of white teeth, and two flashing eyes were all I could make out beneath this strange burden. All the next day, the chief's son followed me on the horse, and always the saddle panted behind on its two little black feet.

Within a day's march of Sankan Birua the chief of Kulia dashed me a large bleating sheep. It would be useful chop for Christmas, so I accepted the present, but asked if I could have a smaller animal. The next morning a boy came toward me, leading a large white lamb, which had been thoroughly scrubbed. When we set out, the lamb refused to budge. Nothing daunted, the boy took the creature by the legs and swung it up around his neck, holding the legs in front. The lamb soon ceased its struggles, and was carried, half-conscious, head hanging limply, the rest of the way to Sankan Birua.

At last we could see Sankan Birua towering high above us. All but the last stage of this forced march was now accomplished. Climbing a narrow, steep path through virgin forests, we reached a spacious plateau, four thousand feet high, about three miles long, and less than a mile wide, from which jagged peaks rose on all sides. By far the most imposing summit was that of Sankan Birua itself. The plateau had been named

"Neremafondia," meaning "short, short grass," which was very appropriate. It was unlike any other country I had seen in Sierra Leone, and quite the most beautiful. Streams had cut steep, wooded ravines, and huge feathery tree ferns filled the smaller gullies.

Lane, the D.C. at Sefadu, had told me that he considered Neremafondia an ideal health resort, where people in Sierra Leone might spend their vacations if facilities were provided. He had built two resthouses, one of grass, the other of mud, both with two rooms and a central open-sided messroom. But he had evidently not visited it during the harmattan season; for, beautiful as it was, it had, at this time of the year, a serious drawback. Every day, from noon to midnight, a gale blew incessantly, and it was bitterly cold. Fortunately, this harmattan died as suddenly as it had come, and the rest of the day was delightful and warm in the sunshine in spite of the altitude. The harmattan also produced a haze which obliterated the view. I was sorry that circumstances had prevented me from visiting Neremafondia at a more auspicious season.

A messenger from Sefadu met me with a note saying that Miss Carey was on her way and would reach the resthouse at the foot of Sankan Birua that night; so I settled down, thankful for the first real rest I had had for weeks.

The next morning I set out to meet Miss Carey. She greeted me with a cheery smile, saying, "Dr. Livingstone, I presume!" There we were, two women, alone except for the boys, on the top of a seldom-visited mountain in West Africa, miles from civilization.

I had wondered how she would manage the climb to the plateau, for she was unused to mountaineering. She arrived in a hammock, and explained that when she got to the steepest places the boys placed the hammock around her waist, and with them pulling on both ends, she climbed, with very little exertion on her part, by merely moving her feet.

We decided to stay in the grass hut, as it was cozier and less exposed than the other one, which was made of mud.

Unfortunately, Miss Carey had caught a cold in the damp mists at Sefadu on the way up, and I was a little worried as we spent a chilly evening in the hut on the plateau, listening to the harmattan raging outside. It was a rather depressing Christmas Eve.

Next morning I was startled out of a sound sleep by loud exclamations. Before me stood Miss Carey, wild-eyed, hair awry, waving a clinical thermometer under my nose.

"Look, Kay!" she cried huskily. "My temperature is 105!"

I scrambled out of bed, thoughts rushing incoherently through my mind. 105! Pneumonia! My course in tropical hygiene had not included pneumonia. Vaguely I remembered that nursing, good nursing, early in the case, was said to help pull a patient through the crisis.

I pushed Miss Carey into bed, at the same time calling for the watchman to build up the fire and bring hot water.

By this time I was thinking more clearly. I decided to take her temperature on my own thermometer, testing it on myself first. I discovered, to our mutual relief, that she was only a point or two above normal; but of course it meant spending Christmas in bed, and she would have to keep out of the wind for a few days.

We were greatly cheered, when, about eleven o'clock that morning, a white man appeared over the edge of the plateau, with his retinue of carriers and loads, including the inevitable sheep and some hens. It was Jim Morris, a young colleague of Miss Carey's, who had likewise chosen to spend his Christmas leave trekking in the north. He had followed my tracks from Bintimani, and, as he had promised to arrive some time during our stay at Neremafondia, had hastened so as to spend Christmas Day with us.

So, while the harmattan howled outside, we enjoyed a snug Christmas within grass walls, eating part of a sheep for dinner. The boys consumed their Christmas dash, which was the remainder of the sheep, and began to feel almost happy, forgetting the cold which they hated, and for which they were ill prepared.

During the days that followed, Jim Morris and I climbed all the peaks on the plateau, including the mighty Sankan Birua, while Miss Carey contented herself with taking her hammock to a sheltered place under the trees, and reading *Kamet Conquered,* preferring to do her hill climbing by proxy.

After a pleasant week, in spite of the bitter wind, we reluctantly left Neremafondia, Jim and I walking on ahead and Miss Carey following in the hammock.

We spent a night in the resthouse at the foot of the plateau, where the chief and his followers entertained us with native dances—mainly Charlestons—and proceeded the next day to Sefadu, to spend the New Year with Brown, who had befriended me three years before at Kenema, and who had been transferred to Sefadu as D.C.

As we stumbled up the hill toward his house, dirty and perspiring after a twenty-mile walk, Brown and his dog came to meet us. Why Brown's dog took a dislike to me I don't know, but he came straight at me and took a big piece out of my khaki shorts, at the same time grazing the skin.

A boy snatched the dog, and I was rushed to the house. Brown treated the wound by rubbing permanganate crystals into the teeth marks. I promised to see a medical officer when

I returned to Freetown. But the story that I heard there about a woman who had been bitten by a cat and who was sent to Paris for Pasteur treatment made me decide to go untreated. For I was on my way to the Gold Coast to join Jock, and a mere dog-bite wasn't going to deflect me.

CHAPTER TWENTY-ONE

AMADU

PAYING OFF the boys was difficult. Some of them felt they belonged to me, having trekked with me for two or three years.

Parting with Amadu was even harder, for he really felt he owned me. Unfortunately, he couldn't be taken to the Gold Coast, because he wouldn't fit in with the Gold Coast natives.

"What would you like to do more than anything else?" I asked him.

"Be proper servant boy," he responded quickly, his eyes shining at the thought of a uniform with brass buttons.

I felt sure he would be taken on as a "proper servant boy," for boys trained by women were in high demand. So I wrote a good letter of recommendation, and said good-by with real regret, for he had been a good and faithful servant.

Life on the Gold Coast was much as I had found it on my previous visit. After finding Jock's camp, we trekked together for a while. Later I went to visit the diamond areas, and to see the gold mines, which were of interest because of the great depth of the mining operations.

When the April rains began, I was ready for something else.

Trekking, and haggling with the natives, and struggling with the heat and humidity no longer held an appeal. So when a letter came from the wife of the Director of the Geological Survey of Nigeria, asking me to visit her there, I decided to do so, for it would be another month before Jock could take his leave. She would be coming out from England on the next boat, and I could join her at Takoradi.

Arriving three days before boat-time, I spent the interim peacefully doing nothing in the spacious resthouse. I reveled in proper meals again, eating a whole pat of butter all by itself at the first meal. I wanted to feel butter, real butter, cool and salty on my tongue. When I was not eating or sleeping, I was sitting in the sun, daydreaming, thinking how blissful it was not to have to walk anywhere. I was like a person emerging from ether —a little vague, not quite sure where I was, not caring what I was doing. It was with great difficulty that I mustered up sufficient energy, the third day, to make the boat.

The two days' sea voyage did me much good, and I watched our vessel thread its way into the lagoon in front of Lagos, the capital of Nigeria, with something of my old interest in life. The shore line with its rows of houses reminded me of San Francisco. It was not like the West Africa I knew; it was all new and modern.

That night we were entertained at dinner in the house of a bank official.

How far this is from a bush camp in Sierra Leone, I thought, glancing about the tastefully appointed room—at the table with its linen and gleaming silver, at the noiseless waiter in his stiffly starched white coat with its rows of shining brass buttons. As I looked at him, a grin spread across his features. Startled, I looked again. There was no mistaking that thin, black, fine-featured face and those alert brown eyes. It was Amadu—his ambition achieved, a "proper" servant boy at last.

A few weeks later, homeward-bound, lounging luxuriously in my deck chair, I gazed at the familiar hills of Freetown as the *Appam* drifted in to its moorings. The Krooboys' shouts as the work of loading went on failed to rouse me this time. Barges, canoes, launches—these belonged to the world of the distant dock, with its specks of human ants milling about the tin sheds. I raised my eyes toward the green summits which cut off the view of the hinterland—a land of unspoiled natives, of thatched huts, of tulip trees whose red petals carpeted the dank ground. I thought of my tent pitched in the quiet of the forest. My mind drifted on, up and down swift-flowing streams, across ridges—gold in a river bed, iron along a divide, molybdenum hidden within a waterfall. No! I would never have to see those jungle secrets ripped open by pick and shovel. The memory of the untouched bush, of my boys, and the forest devils, forever belonged to me.

A harsh grating sound! A clang! The anchor was up! Silently the *Appam* nosed westward. Across the black waters came a rolling echo of thunder—the farewell salute from the Mountains of the Lion.

AN HISTORICAL NOTE ON
SIERRA LEONE

SIERRA LEONE IS the oldest of the British African colonies, the territory in the immediate vicinity of Freetown having been purchased by the British from the native king in the late seventeen hundreds. It became crown colony in the early eighteen hundreds.

Its white population, about a thousand, is concentrated almost entirely in Freetown, which comprises the colony proper; the million and a half natives are scattered through the interior, which is known as the protectorate. Until 1928, when traces of gold were found, the protectorate was comparatively isolated, having been visited only rarely except by government men on duty, or missionaries, most of whom were established near the few roads.

Sierra Leone has had a romantic history. Hanno, the Carthaginian, is assumed to have arrived at what is now Freetown, between 500 and 450 B.C., in command of an expedition of sixty ships sent out by the Senate of Carthage. Whether or not Hanno landed at the present Freetown is not known, but he described a large bay with mountains near it, which he called the Western Horn, and which has been identified as Freetown harbor. At any rate, he departed in haste, alarmed at the number of fires on shore and the sounds of drums and the strange screams of the natives.

The French claim that Norman traders from Rouen and Dieppe visited Sierra Leone and Upper Guinea in 1364–65, but the Portuguese dispute the claim, saying that they were the pioneers in West African trade. Be that as it may, Prince Henry of Portugal, known as the Navigator, sent out an expedition under Pedro da Cintra, who claimed the country in 1462, by right of discovery.

In 1594, Captain Alvares de Almada endeavored to establish a colony in Sierra Leone. Sieur Villault de Bellefond visited the place in 1668, and reported that the king of the country was a convert to Christianity, and that the natives spoke Portuguese and were fearful of strong drink. The natives still use many Portuguese words.

The Portuguese are charged with initiating the practice of exporting West Africans as slaves. In 1562 Sir John Hawkins carried away three hundred natives to sell as slaves to Spaniards on the island of Hispaniola. Other early visitors to the country included Sir Francis Drake and Master Francis Fletcher.

In November, 1618, the Company of Adventurers of London Trading to Africa was formed; and to this company, in 1651, a Council of State granted twenty leagues on each side of the River Cerberro (Sherbro) for its exclusive use. In 1663 Charles II granted a charter to the Company of Royal Adventurers in Africa, which was empowered to supply three thousand Negroes annually to the British West Indies. This was followed by the Royal African Company of England. They are said to have exported more than three hundred thousand slaves between 1713 and 1733. They were followed by the Company of Merchants Trading to Africa. Naturally, Sierra Leone became a noted rendezvous for pirates, and in 1785 the French appeared on the scene, erecting forts on Gambia and Bunce islands in Sierra Leone River. The ruins of the latter remain to this day.

In the meantime, the question of slaves had been arousing much agitation in England. In 1772 Lord Mansfield, Chief Justice of the King's Bench, had ruled that a slave became free the moment he set foot in England. England thus became a goal for slaves, many of whom served in the British Army during the American Revolution and were taken to England and freed as a reward. Thrown upon their own resources, these ex-slaves rapidly became a problem for the authorities, and a society was formed by John Hanway for the relief of these "Black Poor."

About this time, a Dr. Smeathman, a naturalist who had spent some time in Sierra Leone, suggested that a settlement of these freedmen be made there—hence the name Freetown. So on February 22, 1787, three transports, carrying four hundred and eleven settlers—of whom sixty were white women prostitutes who had been shanghaied—set sail from Portsmouth. It was May 9 before they reached Sierra Leone, two and a half months as compared with the ten-day trip on a modern ship. Their hardships were such that by March, 1788, there were only one hundred and thirty of them left.

Various groups of fresh Negroes followed this first one, and in 1792 more than a thousand Negroes, who had been settled in Nova Scotia after being freed by the British as a reward for their services during the American Revolution, were at their own request transferred to Sierra Leone by the British government.

After various vicissitudes, including attack by natives and by the French, Sierra Leone became a crown colony on January 1, 1808.

All the foregoing concerning Sierra Leone has to do with the crown colony, having Freetown as its capital, which comprises a peninsula about 260 square miles in area and, about 70 miles down the coast, the town of Bonthe and a few adjoining districts, making a total of about 2,270 square miles. The rest of the country, about 27,000 square miles in area, was proclaimed a protectorate in 1896 in order to establish a boundary against French encroachment on tribal territory. In size, Sierra Leone compares in area with that of Massachusetts, Vermont, and New Hampshire combined.

The natives of the protectorate are divided into thirteen tribes, the Temne and the Mende being the largest. Their origin is uncertain, but many of them are supposed to be remnants of ancient tribes pushed gradually nearer the coast by Arabs or stronger Negro nations. The inhabitants of the colony are chiefly a mixed community of Negroes of unknown ancestry who are the descendants of freed slaves educated for more than a hundred years by missionaries under the auspices of the British government. Unlike the tribes of the protectorate, who have their own individual languages, the people of the colony possess no indigenous language, but speak a patois or type of pidgin English which is a debased form of English mixed with native and foreign words, locally known as "Creole"; the better educated among them have also a good knowledge of standard English.

In the past there has been comparatively little communication between the coast and the interior. With the gradual spread of education, however, and the opening up of the country through recent mining developments, the natives of the interior will no longer be so isolated, and many changes will necessarily ensue.

BIBLIOGRAPHY

BEATTY, K. L., *Human Leopards,* Hugh Lees, Ltd., London, 1915.

BUTT-THOMPSON, Captain F. W., *Sierra Leone in History and Tradition,* H. F. and G. Witherby, London, 1926.

CANA, FRANK RICHARDSON, F.R.G.S., "Sierra Leone," *Encyclopaedia Britannica,* 14th Ed., vol. 20, 1929, pp. 623–626.

FOWLER-LUNN, KATHARINE, "Hematite Iron Ores of Sierra Leone, West Africa," *Economic Geology,* vol. XXVIII, No. 1, Jan.–Feb., 1933, pp. 59–67.
———, "Molybdenite in Sierra Leone," *The Mining Magazine,* Aug., 1934, pp. 1–3.

GODDARD, T. N., *The Handbook of Sierra Leone,* Grant Richards, Ltd., London, 1925.

LUKE, HARRY C., *A Bibliography of Sierra Leone,* Oxford University Press, Humphrey Milford, London, 1925.

Sierra Leone, Report of the Geological and Mines Department for the Year 1935, printed by the Government Printer, Freetown, 1936.